Approaches to Discourse Analysis

Approaches to Discourse Analysis

Cynthia Gordon, Editor

Georgetown University Press / Washington, DC

The publisher is not responsible for third-party websites or their content. URL links were active at time of publication.

Library of Congress Cataloging-in-Publication Data

   Names: Georgetown University Round Table on Languages and Linguistics (2018:
       Washington, DC), author. | Gordon, Cynthia, 1975– editor.
   Title: Approaches to discourse analysis / Cynthia Gordon, ed.
   Description: Washington, DC : Georgetown University Press, 2021. | Papers presented
       at the 2018 meeting of the Georgetown University Round Table on Languages and
       Linguistics (GURT 2018). | Includes bibliographical references and index.
   Identifiers: LCCN 2020049821 (print) | LCCN 2020049822 (ebook) | ISBN
       9781647121099 (hardcover) | ISBN 9781647121105 (paperback) | ISBN
       9781647121112 (ebook)
   Subjects: LCSH: Discourse analysis—Congresses.
   Classification: LCC P302 .G465 2018 (print) | LCC P302 (ebook) | DDC 401/.41—dc23
   LC record available at https://lccn.loc.gov/2020049821
   LC ebook record available at https://lccn.loc.gov/2020049822

22 21   9 8 7 6 5 4 3 2 First printing

Printed in the United States of America

Cover design by Erin Kirk
Interior design by Thomson Digital

Contents

Illustrations

Figures

Tables

Acknowledgments

THE CHAPTERS IN THIS volume are drawn from the 2018 meeting of the Georgetown University Round Table on Languages and Linguistics (GURT). I am grateful to the contributors to this volume, as well as to all conference participants, for their stimulating work and productive dialogue. GURT 2018 would not have been possible without the dedication and hard work of the doctoral student members of the organizing committee: HoFai (Viggo) Cheng, Felipe Leandro de Jesus, Naomee-Minh Nguyen, Mark Visonà, and Jeremy Wegner. They provided enthusiasm and creativity, attended to tasks big and small with consummate efficiency, and displayed generosity of spirit throughout. I thank them profusely. For her assistance in formatting parts of the manuscript for publication, I thank doctoral student Alexus Wells. Receiving the support, goodwill, and feedback of my colleagues and friends Deborah Tannen and Heidi E. Hamilton has been invaluable. The conference topic, and title of this book, was inspired by Deborah Schiffrin's pioneering work. Her spirit was palpable throughout, from the conference theme's selection to the completion of this manuscript. Her analytic acuity, talent at connecting diverse literatures, dedication to the field and its scholars, and generosity and good humor continue to inspire.

Introduction

CYNTHIA GORDON

THIS VOLUME AROSE FROM the sixty-ninth annual meeting of the Georgetown University Round Table on Languages and Linguistics (GURT 2018). The meeting's theme, "Approaches to Discourse," highlighted the diverse theories and methods, both within the field of linguistics and beyond, to explore language in use, language beyond the sentence, and social interaction. The meeting aimed to acknowledge and explore the richness of the area of inquiry, including not only the contemporary landscape of approaches to discourse, but also the diversity of topics, analytic contexts, and disciplinary foundations.

This theme was inspired, in part, by my own academic path. Prior to my return to the Georgetown University Department of Linguistics as a faculty member in the fall of 2014 (after completing my PhD in the same department 11 years earlier), I had the pleasure of teaching courses in discourse analysis in departments of English (at Wayne State University), Anthropology (at Emory University), and Communication and Rhetorical Studies (at Syracuse University). In the context of these departments, each rooted in a different academic discipline, I learned from colleagues whose academic background and training in discourse differed from my own. I experienced firsthand the recognition expressed by Schiffrin, Tannen, and Hamilton (2015, 5) that "the vastness and diversity of discourse analysis is a strength." Inspired by the rich tradition of Georgetown Linguistics and the vast variety of scholars engaged in analyzing discourse, in conceptualizing GURT 2018, I sought to bring diverse scholars to the table.

The meeting's theme was also inspired by the continuing proliferation of approaches to the analysis of discourse, among them interactional sociolinguistics, linguistic pragmatics, conversation analysis, multimodal discourse analysis, corpus linguistics, cultural discourse analysis, critical discourse analysis, interactional linguistics, and others, including integrated approaches that do not fit neatly under one label. Many journals publish discourse analytic scholarship, including *Language in Society*; *Text & Talk*; *Discourse & Society*; *Discourse Studies*; *Research on Language and Social Interaction*; the *Journal of Sociolinguistics*; the *Journal of Linguistic Anthropology*; *Multilingua*; the *Journal of Pragmatics*; and *Discourse, Context & Media*. As Deborah Tannen observes (in Schiffrin, Tannen, and Hamilton 2015, 3), research in the field has become "so diverse that 'discourse' is almost a synonym for 'language.'" GURT 2018 provided an opportunity to discuss various ways of conceptualizing "discourse," take stock of the various approaches to its study, and put them into dialogue.

Finally, the GURT 2018 theme, along with its name, speaks to the influence of Deborah Schiffrin's (1994) book *Approaches to Discourse*, which, in addition to Schiffrin's many other books and articles, and Schiffrin herself, shaped how I—and many other Georgetown graduate students and faculty members, and countless scholars from around the world—have come to understand and appreciate the richness of the field of discourse analysis. The similarity in this volume's title, *Approaches to Discourse Analysis*, to Schiffrin's book title, is intentional.

The collection includes the papers of the six plenary speakers, as well as five by other scholars that round out a snapshot of "approaches." The approaches are qualitative and quantitative; involve categorizing tokens and turn-by-turn analysis; use a range of transcription conventions; analyze speech, embodied communication, and online texts and images; differently rely on ethnographic and participants' own interpretive insights; and differ in myriad other subtle and not-so-subtle ways. The papers analyze discourse in multiple languages, across multiple contexts, and in multiple modes. Collectively, they highlight the diversity and complexity of the field in terms of methods of data collection, topical foci, and analytic procedures, while emphasizing a unified goal of understanding communication as fundamentally connected to human agency and creativity, as co-constructed, and as embedded in and constitutive of our social and cultural worlds.

Susan U. Philips, in chapter 1, explains "How linguistic anthropologists conceptualize relations among different forms of discourse." Her chapter shows how anthropologists' concern with multiple forms of talk has led to important insights into the interrelatedness of discourse units, the embeddedness of discourse forms in relations of power, and how forms of discourse are socially organized. She also sketches out a historical background of approaches to discourse analysis that have emerged out of linguistic anthropology, and outlines the contributions linguistic anthropologists have made to the study of discourse as it emerged as a field of inquiry in the late 1960s as part of the cross-disciplinary endeavor of sociolinguistics. These include, for example, the use of participant observation and the collection of different forms of discourse as key methods, and the importance of *genre* and *speech event* as concepts. Philips discusses examples drawn from her own research on trial courts in the Kingdom of Tonga (a small south Pacific nation) and in a county court in the city of Tucson, Arizona, in the United States, as well as examples from the studies of other linguistic anthropologists, while outlining notions that have become important not only to linguistic anthropologists in particular, but also discourse analysts in general, such as *intertextuality*, *indexicality*, and *metapragmatics*.

Chapter 2, "'Two different kinds of life': A cultural analysis of Blackfeet discourse," by Donal Carbaugh and Eean Grimshaw, serves as a primer of sorts for cultural discourse analysis, an approach to the study of culturally distinctive discursive practices that grew out of communication studies, with grounding in the ethnography of communication, including use of ethnopoetic transcription practices (e.g., Hymes 1972, 2003). Examining how Blackfeet (Amskapi Piikuni) people (of northern Montana in the United States) speak about Blackfeet people, the authors highlight the discursive construction of identities and meanings regarding feeling, acting, dwelling, and time—all parts of the *cultural discourses*, or participants' taken-for-granted knowledge that shapes language use in, and understandings of, the world, or their *cultural logics*. Carbaugh and Grimshaw highlight, for example, the complex arrangement of time involved in constructing Blackfeet life today as both "contemporary" and "traditional." In so doing, the authors demonstrate how short extracts of talk are connected to larger cultural discourses.

Time is also highlighted in chapter 3, "Gesture, mimesis, and the linguistics of time," by Jürgen Streeck, a scholar with connections to both anthropology and communication studies. He offers a study of embodied action and gesture that draws on conversation analysis, interactional linguistics, and grammaticalization (e.g., Bybee 1998), or the study of the emergence and change of grammar in interaction. He specifically builds on Hopper's (2015) notion of a "linguistics of time," which captures the idea that language constructions are both *emerging* moment by moment in specific interactions and an outcome of, or *emergent* from, such interactions. Examining extracts of video recordings of the everyday work that takes place at an American automobile repair shop where he conducted an in-depth ethnography, Streeck offers a detailed analysis of the trajectory of select hand gestures as they are used, become abstracted, are repeated, and are recontextualized. He shows how, as part of this process, they evolve in form and meaning, thus providing an illustration of the ongoing functioning and evolution of human communication, including both verbal and nonverbal aspects.

In chapter 4, "The ambiguity and polysemy of power and solidarity in professor-student emails and conversations among friends," linguist Deborah Tannen provides a personal and disciplinary retrospective on discourse analysis while tracing the evolution of theories pertaining to power and solidarity, as well as politeness, in interaction. Whereas many existing studies consider students' emails to professors, Tannen examines professors' emails to students, showing that their omission of features that students generally include, such as greetings and opening niceties, are ambiguous: professors tend to see these as reflecting informality and therefore friendliness, but students often see them as rude expressions of power. Professors' omissions of these features are also polysemous insofar as their powerful positions allow them to choose to be informal. Tannen shows a similar pattern with respect to conversations among women friends. For example, a woman who responds to a friend's troubles talk by describing her own troubles could be perceived as matching (connection) or topping (competition) the friend. If "Mine is worse" is perceived as comforting, it could be both. The chapter shows how differences in what Tannen (2005) calls "conversational style" shape everyday encounters and relationships, while also serving as an important reminder for analysts that one way of speaking does not reflect a specific motive or lead to any one effect.

The theme that a single linguistic device or strategy has multiple meanings also surfaces in chapter 5, by Michal Marmorstein, "What do discourse markers mark? Arabic *yaʕni* ('it means') and Hebrew *ya'ani* across modalities and sociolinguistic systems." Marmorstein presents findings regarding uses of the discourse marker *yaʕni* in Egyptian-Arabic conversational interview discourse, in written Egyptian-Arabic as it occurs in casual-personal prose (in blogs), and on Egyptian Wikipedia, and uses of this item as it has transferred into spoken Modern Hebrew (as *ya'ani/ya'anu*). Her chapter, which takes an interactional linguistics perspective, not only highlights the multifunctionality of this discourse marker, but also shows how its meanings systematically vary across sociolinguistic contexts and modalities. For example, in conversational Egyptian-Arabic, the marker serves to facilitate speech production. In written Egyptian-Arabic, it creates textual cohesion while also taking on multiple symbolic meanings (e.g., it indexes a discourse's conversational quality, and thus appears more often in blog discourse than on Wikipedia). In spoken Modern Hebrew, the marker, where it is used infrequently and is seen as Arabic slang, shares some of the functions of its use in Egyptian-Arabic (e.g., facilitating speech production), while also offering an innovation (i.e., it is used to construct ironic stances in conversation). The chapter thus illuminates the use of one marker across modalities and sociolinguistic systems, as well as the regenerative meaning potential of discourse markers in general.

In chapter 6, "Reconsidering the concept of 'total institutions' in light of interactional sociolinguistics: The meaning of the marker 'here,'" Branca Telles Ribeiro and Diana de Souza Pinto examine the construction of situated identities in what Goffman (1961) terms a "total institution"—a forensic psychiatric hospital in Brazil. Specifically, taking an interactional sociolinguistics approach and drawing on Foucault's (e.g., 1975) theorizing on power, the authors analyze small-scale interactions—extracts from a research interview with an inmate/patient and from a focus group conducted with health-care providers in a mental health teaching and research hospital—in light of large-scale sociological and historical systems. Ribeiro and Pinto focus on linguistic deixis—specifically Portuguese *aqui* ("here")—as a resource for positioning the self in multiple contexts. For example, in the interview, the inmate/patient discursively constructs the psychiatric hospital as both a shelter and a prison. Providers also create ambivalent positionings in the focus group; for instance, in discussing the taboo topic of patients' sexual practices, the psychiatric hospital's "public" and "private" spaces are discursively negotiated. The chapter lends insight into the discursive complexity, and co-constructed nature, of identities within institutional life.

Chapter 7, "The expression of authority in US primary care: Offering diagnoses and recommending treatment," by John Heritage, a sociologist, also examines language use in an institutional setting. His conversation analytic study explores the two key actions named in the chapter's title, offering diagnoses and recommending treatment, in a corpus of 225 video-recorded primary care encounters that were gathered in Southern California in the United States. He demonstrates how two forms of authority are verbally expressed: epistemic authority (which relies on physicians' cultural authority and is most clearly manifest in making diagnoses) and deontic authority (which is most evident in recommending treatments, and relies on medicine's cultural authority as well as its social authority based on the perceived powerlessness of patients to improve without medical intervention). His findings, when taken in social and historical context, reveal a decline in the expression of epistemic authority in diagnosis, although patients' responses still demonstrate respect for the profession's epistemic authority. Heritage's analysis also shows how the forms that treatment recommendations take are shaped by a treatment's perceived level of risk and burden. The chapter thus reveals how patterns identified through detailed, turn-by-turn analysis of language in use connect to, and help (re)create, historical and social understandings of particular institutional discourse contexts.

In chapter 8, "Semiotic ideologies and trial discourse: Implications for multi-modal discourse analysis," linguist Susan Ehrlich explores the "meaning potential" of different communicative modes in the context of a rape trial that occurred in the US city of Steubenville, Texas; this trial was notable in that the criminal events were documented, as they unfolded, on social media by the defendants and their friends. Specifically, Ehrlich shows how visual modes of communication (photographs and videos shared on social media) and linguistic modes (text messages, tweets) are oriented to in the trial in terms of their evidentiary capacity. In her analysis, Ehrlich takes an "emic" perspective, departing from much existing work on multimodality, and finds that the lawyers and witnesses ascribed greater truth and evidential value to the visual evidence. She argues that this privileging of visual evidence had a substantial impact on the trial's outcome, and highlights the importance of considering the semiotic ideologies of participants in particular speech events in any examination of how meanings arise in interaction.

Chapter 9, by Najma Al Zidjaly, "Repair as activism on Arabic Twitter," also examines both text and image but in a different linguistic and cultural context: the author analyzes Arabic tweets by activists who have various theological positions but generally share a self-identification as "Ex-Muslim." Integrating Ron Scollon's (2001) theory of mediated discourse analysis and Ron Scollon and Suzie Wong Scollon's (2004) nexus analysis, and building on conversation analytic work on conversational repair (e.g., Schönfeldt and Golato 2003), Al Zidjaly, a linguist, illuminates a phenomenon she terms "multiscale repair," or instances where activist Twitter users incite social reform by making repairs to passages from the Quran and the hadiths (reported sayings by the prophet of Islam), as well as to other "authoritative discourses" (Bakhtin 1981) of Islam. For example, "The nation shall not prosper that turns its affairs to a woman" (a hadith) is "repaired" in a tweet by substituting "to a woman" with "to a man of religion." This replaces lexical items, but also ideas (as the revised message is that it is not women who are bad leaders, but religious men who are). These repairs are multimodally accomplished through features such as symbols and emojis, and occur at the levels of grammar, text, and culture; in making them, these Twitter users take action, display creativity, construct identities, and help incite cultural change.

Chapter 10, by Alla V. Tovares, examines "Online political trolling as Bakhtin's carnival: Putin's 'discrowning' by pro-Ukrainian commenters." It offers a linguistic examination of a type of digital activism, while also demonstrating how Bakhtin's (e.g., 1984) theorizing on "carnival"—a notion developed in the context of the discussion of novelistic discourse and folk culture—applies to the analysis of contemporary online discourse. The concept captures the informal, playful, creative, and subversive nature of the everyday language and laughter of people in the streets or marketplace. Integrating this theorizing and the notion of stance (e.g., Du Bois 2007) and taking an interactional sociolinguistics approach, Tovares explores online comments posted to an article published on the website of a Ukrainian bilingual (Ukrainian-Russian) newspaper. In the playful and rebellious comments to the article—about a limited-edition and extremely expensive version of the iPhone 7 that commemorated Russian president Vladimir Putin's birthday—pro-Ukrainian posters use various linguistic features, such as absurd word combinations and profanities, as well as multimodal strategies, such as an image of Putin wearing a Hitler mustache, to accomplish trolling and thereby "discrown" Putin and his supporters. Analyzing such strategies in the context of a netnography (Nissenbaum and Shifman 2017) she conducted, and in consideration of wider Russian-Ukrainian relations, Tovares highlights how trolling can be understood as a productive, carnivalesque discourse strategy.

Ruth Wodak's "From post-truth to post-shame: Analyzing far-right populist rhetoric" rounds out the volume (chapter 11). Wodak, a linguist, uses critical discourse analysis and the discourse-historical approach (Wodak 2015) to uncover the "micro-politics" of far-right political parties such as Jörg Haider's *Austrian Freedom Party* and Silvio Berlusconi's *Forza Italia*, and of far-right politicians such as former US president Donald Trump and Hungarian Prime Minister Victor Orbán. She demonstrates how these groups and politicians (re)produce their ideologies in the media, on posters, and in speeches and slogans. Considering context as multi-layered (e.g., the historical context and the textual context), Wodak highlights the construction of "us versus them" (e.g., *the people* versus *the élites*), the degradation of productive dialogue, and the "shameless normalization" (Wodak 2018) of non-compliance with internationally agreed-upon rights and conventions. She explores strategies such as uses of metaphor (e.g., Trump's use of *migrants as floods* to separate "us" from "them" and to demonize "them") and euphemism (e.g., Austrian minister of Interior Affairs Herbert Kickl's proposal to rename "reception centers" [*Aufnahmezentrumi*] for asylum seekers as "departure centers" [*Ausreisezentrum*—a term that insinuates the concept of *Abschiebezentrum*, or "deportation center"]). While illuminating the contours of populist rhetoric, the chapter also calls attention to the power of discourse analysis to unpack how ideologies are constructed, how they are dispersed, and how they can be changed.

Collectively, these chapters lend insights into micro-linguistic strategies, multimodality, meaning-making, relationship and identity negotiation, ideological constructions, cultural practices, and our social worlds. They demonstrate the importance of the diverse perspectives that various approaches to discourse bring to bear on human communication, while also providing readers a window onto the branches of our discipline, and how they diverge, intertwine, and blossom.

References

Bakhtin, Mikhail. 1981. *The dialogic imagination*. Austin: University of Texas Press.
———. 1984. *Rabelais and his world*. Bloomington: Indiana University Press.
Bybee, Joan L. 1998. Cognitive processes in grammaticalization. In Michael Tomasello (ed.), *The new psychology of language* (vol. II). Mahwah, NJ: Lawrence Erlbaum. 145–168.
Du Bois, John. 2007. The stance triangle. In Robert Englebretson (ed.), *Stancetaking in discourse: Subjectivity, evaluation, interaction*. Amsterdam: John Benjamins. 139–182.

Foucault, Michel. 1975. *Discipline and punish: The birth of the prison.* Alan Sheridan (trans.). London: Penguin.

Goffman, Erving. 1961. *Asylums.* New York: Anchor Books.

Hopper, Paul J. 2015. Hermann Paul's emergent grammar. In Peter Auer and Robert W. Murray (eds.), *Hermann Paul's "Principles of Language History" revisited.* Berlin: de Gruyter. 237–256.

Hymes, Dell. 1972. Models of the interaction of language and social life. In John J. Gumperz and Dell Hymes (eds.), *Directions in sociolinguistics: The ethnography of communication.* New York: Holt, Rinehart, & Winston. 35–71.

———. 2003. *Now I know only so far: Essays in ethnopoetics.* Lincoln: University of Nebraska Press.

Nissenbaum, Asaf and Limor Shifman. 2017. Internet memes as contested cultural capital: The case of 4chan's/b/board. *New Media & Society* 19 (4): 483–501.

Schiffrin, Deborah. 1994. *Approaches to discourse.* Oxford and Cambridge: Blackwell.

Schiffrin, Deborah, Deborah Tannen and Heidi E. Hamilton. 2015. Introduction to the first edition. In Deborah Tannen, Heidi E. Hamilton, and Deborah Schiffrin (eds.), *Handbook of discourse analysis* (2nd edition). Chichester, UK: John Wiley & Sons. 1–7.

Schönfeldt, Juliane and Andrea Golato. 2003. Repair in chats: A conversation analytic approach. *Research on Language and Social Interaction* 36 (3): 241–284.

Scollon, Ron. 2001. *Mediated discourse: The nexus of practice.* London: Routledge.

Scollon, Ron and Suzie Wong Scollon. 2004. *Nexus analysis: Discourse and the emerging internet.* London: Routledge.

Tannen, Deborah. 2005. *Conversational style: Analyzing talk among friends, New edition with new introduction.* Oxford University Press. (First edition, Norwood, NJ: Ablex, 1984.)

Wodak, Ruth. 2015. *The politics of fear: What right-wing populist discourses mean.* London: Sage.

———. 2018. Vom Rand in die Mitte—"Schamlose Normalisierung." *Politische Vierteljahres Zeitschrift* 75. doi: 10.1007/s11615-018-0079-7.

1

How Linguistic Anthropologists Conceptualize Relations among Different Forms of Discourse

SUSAN U. PHILIPS

ALTHOUGH THE VARIOUS ACADEMIC disciplines that contribute to discourse analysis have a great deal in common, we also each have some typical features that distinguish us. In sociology and linguistics it is more common to focus analytically on one single form of discourse at a time. Conversation, interview, and narrative are the three forms of talk that have received the greatest methodological attention. In anthropology it is common for scholars to examine more than one kind of discourse from the same research context and to analyze the nature of relations among those forms of discourse. Anthropological contributions to discourse analysis have often focused on such relationships. In this chapter I describe how this focus on relations among forms of discourse came about theoretically and methodologically and show how some of those relations work in language use. Ultimately it is a human characteristic of language that we deliberately vary the way we organize discourse to accomplish different social ends.

I first discuss some of the commonalities in approaches to discourse that were part of sociolinguistics as it emerged as a cross-disciplinary endeavor in the late 1960s. We still share these commonalities across linguistics, anthropology, and sociology. Then I describe some features characteristic of approaches to discourse in linguistic anthropology, focusing on the rationale for examination of multiple forms of discourse.

The following three sections focus on how the anthropological concern with multiple forms of talk includes ideas about how forms of discourse are related to one another. I draw on my own past research projects as well as those of others to consider three key developments in anthropological discussions of how forms of discourse are related to each other:

First, there is an enduring tradition of thinking of forms of discourse as *socially organized*, as operating within a discourse system that is also a sociocultural system. Second, linguistic anthropologists have put forth a set of *interpretive concepts* concerned with how people make sense of discourse by relating units of discourse to one another. Here I discuss metapragmatic concepts of discourse relatedness that show us how very much control people have over the way they think about and organize discourse. Finally, I consider how forms of discourse are embedded in *power relations*, another common anthropological theme.

Intellectual History

Discourse analysis as we know it today emerged within the context of the development of sociolinguistics in the 1960s. Sociolinguistics was a cross-disciplinary endeavor primarily involving linguistics, sociology, and anthropology, but also psychology and philosophy. It brought together kinds of discourse for analysis not really considered together before, such as written and spoken language, and casual and formal language. New kinds of empirical analysis depended on the development of easily portable recording equipment. The disciplines involved all gave attention in one way or another to the identification of units of interaction. For any comparison of multiple instances of an activity, or comparison of different activities, such identification was methodologically necessary.

Erving Goffman's (1963) conceptualization of the "encounter" as a bounded interactional entity characterized by a shared focus of talk was probably the most important stimulus to the identification of units, followed by conversation analysts' description of the sequential organization of openings and closings that bounded conversations (Sacks and Schegloff 1973; Schegloff 1972). Different disciplines used different terms to talk about basic units of interaction. Philosophers and their followers spoke of "speech acts." Goffman himself later proposed the phrase "forms of talk" (Goffman 1981).

Ethnographers of communication in anthropology were influenced by Dell Hymes and John Gumperz (Gumperz and Hymes 1964) to think in terms of larger units of interaction that encompassed smaller units of interaction through their introduction of the concepts of speech situation (following Goffman 1964), speech event, and speech act. And while this three-way distinction was given attention by linguists writing about discourse analysis in anthropology, including Muriel Saville-Troike (1982) and Deborah Schiffrin (1994), the concept of genre was in many ways more central for anthropologists studying talk.

Genre was and is an inherently comparative and relative concept. It tends to evoke or bring to mind relatively planned and clearly bounded forms of talk that are individually performed in public, such as the common examples of prayer, lecture, song, and story. This anthropological focus on genre was in part due to how, in Hymes's teaching (1966–1968), he focused a great deal on his own analysis of Native American myths as units of interaction. He used Chinookan myths to illustrate how a given genre would be characterized by and even constrained to have particular linguistic features. For example, both Hymes in his teaching and Moore (2015, 25) argue that these myths were identifiable as myths, rather than as history or legend, by tense marking that conveyed the events as occurring in a mythic past. Hymes also used characteristic myth beginnings and endings to illustrate the boundedness of genres that justified sometimes pulling them out of context for examination. He similarly analyzed the predictable internal sequential structure of myths to illustrate sequentiality in discourse (e.g., Hymes 1981). In these ways he encouraged his students to think in terms of clearly bounded units of interaction. Hymes himself focused primarily on myth in his own research, and, as Kroskrity and Webster (2015) have argued, he influenced generations of students in the ethnopoetic analysis of narratives to focus on text-internal properties of discourse. Both Blommaert (2009) and Moore (2015) describe how a more situated and interactive concept of narrative discourse in some ethnopoetic analysis was in turn influenced by Hymes's beautifully elaborated concept of ethnographic studies of language as the key to understanding situated meaning, itself a necessary component of a theory of meaning.

Many linguistic anthropologists influenced by Hymes have made a point of recording more than one kind of discourse, and of considering how the forms they record are positioned within the larger speech economy of a community. This methodological commitment did not grow directly out of Hymes's own practices, which were focused on informant elicitation of myths. Instead, this commitment to multiple forms of discourse stemmed from his and John Gumperz's programmatic vision of the nature of language. From their point of view, the linguistic structure of a language should be viewed as a set of resources to be drawn upon selectively in the accomplishment of activities conceived by local speakers and observers as obviously different cultural activities. This means that in some but not necessarily all ways, actual linguistic structure will not be the same in all situations. *Crucially the discourse genre or form of talk organizes the diversity of language forms* to create culturally meaningful social activity.

For example, consider how we understand the statistical frequency of statements relative to questions differently in different forms of talk. In some interactions one speaker produces mostly questions and the other speaker produces mostly statements, now to be understood as answers to the questions. That is what a lot of my data looks like, with teachers asking students questions and judges asking criminal defendants questions. In other interactions, both questions and statements are being produced by both parties to an interaction. A conversation could conceivably look like that. The ways that linguistic structures are *ordered* in different forms of discourse thus play a role in the accomplishment of different cultural activities. To think in terms of different cultural activities in turn requires conceptualizing forms of discourse as bounded in some way. The term "speech genre" is used to refer to such forms in anthropology, as in folklore and literature.

Following the influential collaborative work between Gumperz and Hymes at the University of California, Berkeley, Hymes moved to the University of Pennsylvania. The first generation of Hymes's students at the University of Pennsylvania carried out ethnographic research projects that involved recording multiple forms of talk, and not just the highly redundant publicly performed genres studied by earlier generations, but also more open-ended and varied conversations. This recording of multiple forms of discourse took place within what were conceptualized as ethnographic research projects. In anthropology, ethnography canonically means working in another culture where people speak a language other than English and spending at least a year immersed in the culture, preferably living with the people one is working with. Participant observation is a key source of data. Participant observation refers to the dual goals of engaging in activities with the people one is learning about, while paying attention through focused observation of what is going on. Audio and visual recording are understood to be an extension of participant observation. The speech recorded is, if possible, socially occurring speech. This means one records activities that are part of the fabric of the society in which the research takes place, rather than activities staged by the researcher. The researcher is typically present, but not a very active participant, and intends not to alter how things would go if he or she were not present. That does not mean that more interventionist activities, such as interviews and experiments, do not take place. Interviews provide information that can't be obtained otherwise and often the interviews take the form of debriefings in which knowledgeable people help the researcher understand the social occurring activities that are the focus of the research.

Joel Sherzer's (1974) early ethnographic research with the Kuna Indians of Panama illustrates this approach as it was conceptualized within the ethnography of speaking. Sherzer described the range of speech events and speech genres in Kuna communities. He showed how a set of forms of talk, including chanting in political meetings, in curing rituals, and in female puberty ceremonies, shared certain linguistic properties that set them apart from everyday speech. These properties included the phonological quality of less vowel elision, nominal and verbal affixes, and kernel-like sentences with much repetition of information normally deleted after initial introduction in more everyday speech. There was, therefore, a public speaking style that was highly valued and performed only by men.

This illustrates the linguistic anthropological commitment to thinking in terms of multiple forms of talk and how they are systematically differentiated linguistically and yet related to one another at the same time. These features of anthropological work on discourse have persisted through time.

As I indicated at the beginning, I will now consider three different kinds of relationships among different forms of discourse to which anthropologists have given attention. First, attention has focused enduringly on the *social organization* of forms of discourse—on how different units of discourse are systematically organized in such a way as to constitute the social structure of a speech community. Second, several concepts in linguistic anthropology have focused on the *interpretive process* through which parties to an interaction make sense of ongoing speech in a particular genre by relating it to other speech, sometimes to speech in other forms of talk. These include the concepts of intertextuality, indexicality, interdiscursivity, and metapragmatics. I will be focusing on how forms of talk are related in metapragmatic activity. Third, I will consider how different forms of discourse can enter into *relations of power.*

The Social Organization of Forms of Discourse

In the early days of sociolinguistics, linguistic anthropologists gave considerable attention to the social organization of speech by identifying whole domains of discourse that were shown to be linguistically distinct from one another yet bound up in a single social system. Written and spoken speech were linguistically different. Planned and unplanned speech were held to be different in ways related to the written-spoken dichotomy (Ochs and Bennett-Kastor 1977). Formal and informal speech had linguistic characteristics that differentiated them. The public-private dichotomy was another such domain distinction. Political economic research showed whole language codes to be socially organized into different economically determined social domains. Charles Ferguson's (1964) concept of diglossia, in which two varieties of language were used in different social contexts, was an influential example of a linguistically constituted domain difference. Actual forms of discourse underlie such domain distinctions, and different forms of discourse are related to each other partly through similarities and differences in their ordering of linguistic forms.

Relations among forms of discourse can, for example, play a role in constituting different levels of institutional organization. In my own research in the Kingdom of Tonga, a small South Pacific nation, I observed that there are two levels of trial courts (Philips 2016). The lower-level Magistrate's Court hears misdemeanor criminal cases and minor civil cases. The higher-level Supreme Court hears criminal felony cases and more expensive civil cases. Both courts process defendants through a sequence of bounded units of interaction. Both courts have the same legal role identities, such as lawyer, judge, defendant, and witness. In both courts, talk consists primarily of legal personnel asking questions that are answered by witnesses. The cases in the higher-level Tongan Supreme Court are, however, considered more "serious," and those cases take much more time. This greater amount of time results from interactional expansions of the same kind of discourse units one encounters in the lower court. The higher-court cases involve more lawyers eliciting testimony from a given witness. More witnesses are questioned by each lawyer, and each witness is asked more questions. In other words, the same interactional units we find in the lower-level court are both expanded and multiplied. There are more testimonies and more question-answer pairs to each testimony in the higher-level court. This expansion of discourse units constitutes and displays the greater seriousness of the attention given to the cases. In these ways the two courts are related by all they have in common in their discourse units, but also differentiated in that relationship by, among other things, the expansions available in the higher-level court.

Other scholars similarly compare forms of talk located in different structural positions within a social system. For example, Briggs and Mantini-Briggs (2003), examining discourse about a cholera epidemic in Venezuela, compare interviews with individuals located in different positions within the public health system. They conceptualize the people involved in addressing the epidemic as located in a political economic system that ranges from residents of an indigenous village with no health care to global organizations like the World Health Organization. In between are health-care professionals located in communities of increasing size and political and economic complexity, such as a doctor in a small-town clinic, a regional epidemiologist, and the director of a hospital. The authors show how the explanations and characterizations of the cholera epidemic in those speakers' discourse representations vary. Those in the intermediate positions within the Venezuelan political economic system blamed the Warao indigenous people, who first got the disease, for the epidemic. They were blamed for failing to be modern in their health practices, even as such practices were denied them by the state. The medical professionals shared their views with radio and newspaper media and these views spread throughout the country. The Warao view, which blamed contact with fishermen on their coastline, did not circulate in the same way. Only later did quite distinctive global epidemiological research discourse forms indicate that the epidemic began in Peru and spread from there through the region. Clearly multiple processes were at play in the spread of the epidemic, but what concerned the Briggses was both the racist blaming of the Warao, and more centrally the way speakers' political economic positions were determining what discourses came to be treated as truth, as reality.

The general point here, then, is that anthropologists record and compare discourse produced in different parts of a social system and show from the similarities and differences how discourse organizes and relates multiple interpretive perspectives. In the next section I discuss how people create relations between forms of talk in the ways they think, and the ways they talk about those forms of talk.

Metapragmatic Treatment of Relations between Forms of Discourse

A second area of anthropological discourse analysis that considers relations between forms of discourse concerns how humans make sense of discourse in part by thinking and talking about how the talk they are involved in is related to other instances of talk. This is, then, an interpretive issue, and an issue of meaning-making. Several closely related concepts have addressed this issue, including the concepts of intertextuality, indexicality, and interdiscursivity. The term "metapragmatics" (Silverstein 1993) refers to talk about language use. Such talk about language use can be experienced as ad hoc and fleeting comment in response to an immediately preceding turn, as in expressions such as "What did you just say?" and "I agree." Metapragmatics can also be conventionalized and widespread, as for example when children are told, "Say thank you." Metapragmatic talk can be oriented toward what has been said in the past. It can be linked to what is going on in the immediate present. It can also be about the possible imagined talk of the future.

In the institutional discourses I have studied, talk about units of discourse and their relations is quite widespread and varied. The main research project where I systematically elicited the views of my subjects on their speech that I had recorded was my study of judges on the Pima County Superior Court bench in Tucson, Arizona (Philips 1998). In that study, I met with the individual judges in their chambers after every recording session to give them an opportunity to comment on the proceedings they had just presided over. My focus was on how the judges took Guilty Pleas. My questions were open ended: "Why did you do the procedure as you did?," "Was there anything unusual about this particular just-recorded session?," and "I notice [this or that] about the way you do the plea compared with some other judges. Is there any particular reason?"

It turned out the judges were aware of what they and other judges did in the procedure, and they shared ways of thinking and talking about it. Judges in one group said that they tried to do the procedure exactly the same way each time to adhere to the written law. Those in the other group said they tried to tailor each plea to the individual defendants in front of them. From the judges' point of view, this difference in their metapragmatics affected every unit of discourse in the internal sequential structure of the plea and was a constant that tied the parts of the procedure together and gave it coherence.

In addition, not all of the discourse units within the guilty plea were included by all of the judges, and this too was deliberate. For example, the judges who had a standardized unit called Social Background Questions early in the procedure used the information they elicited from the defendants to try to tailor their pleas to individuals. The judges who standardized their pleas thought the questions were unnecessary. Moreover, all of the judges also saw meaning in the sequential order of the units internal to the guilty plea, and not all of them had the same order of units. For example, some judges asked the defendants to explicitly plead guilty before getting them to agree to a Factual Basis, i.e., to agree to a statement of what they did that constituted a crime. These judges thought it was easier to get the defendants to agree to the Factual Basis if they had already essentially confessed. Other judges reversed the order. They wanted the defendants to provide a Factual Basis before the actual formal plea of "guilty" to make sure the defendants really understood what they were pleading guilty to.

These differences correlated with a judge's political orientation of conservative or liberal. The liberal judges saw their duty as watching over the defendants to make sure their pleas were valid, and these were the judges who intended to tailor the plea to the individual, included the discourse unit of Social Background Questions, and only asked for a plea after hearing the Factual Basis. The conservative judges saw the defendants as not needing any more protection from the state and as having been well briefed by their lawyers and by numerous written warnings about the right to a trial they were giving up. They did not feel the onus was on them alone to make sure a plea was valid, did not feel the need to ask Social Background Questions because they intended to standardize the Plea and not tailor it to the individual, and they took the Plea of guilty before eliciting an abbreviated confession or Factual Basis to make sure the defendant would not refuse to admit to the facts of the case.

These judges, then, enacted metapragmatic interpretations of the written law governing the Guilty Plea that were personal, yet also shared with other judges, through how they took admissions of guilt from criminal defendants. They did this through how much they varied the things they said from one defendant to the next, through conscious manipulation of the order of the units within the plea, and through the inclusion versus exclusion of particular units.

The kind of explicit orienting talk I have described here shows how salient judges' awareness is of bounded units of discourse, of the relations among the units, of the sequential ordering of units, and of the local meanings that can be attributed to those relations.

Another example of metapragmatic talk about talk comes from E. Summerson Carr's (2011) study of a drug treatment program for homeless women who were cocaine addicted, a program that Carr calls Fresh Beginnings. Carr describes how the individual and group therapy that constituted the program required the women to access their own individual inner feelings and talk about them. The counselors for the program were dedicated to the idea that if the women could change the way they talked in very specific ways, they would no longer need to be addicted to cocaine. Women could not advance through the program without taking on this particular way of talking about inner feelings. Carr marshals a set of discourse artifacts (printed materials available in the therapy building) that instruct clients on how to talk and how not to talk in order to get well. These sources sort out kinds of talk that will get you nowhere from kinds of talk that will keep you in the program and maintain your access to housing and child care. Carr also describes the voices of the clients and their views on this therapy using several sources, including her interviews with individuals in the program, her hanging out with them on the front porch of the therapy building, and her participation with them in the development of a client advisory committee. She also witnessed client representative participation in advisory board meetings. At the board meetings, representatives from various homeless service organizations that provided clients to the Fresh Beginnings therapy discussed policy and administration.

Many clients explicitly complained about the pressure in group therapy to open up about painful and embarrassing life experiences as was demanded by the focus on inner states. This focus apparently meant a focus on one's own personal life problems in the Fresh Beginnings therapeutic concept. Some clients approached the therapeutic ideology cynically, mouthing the words but not believing in the treatment idea or efficacy. Others left. Still others embraced the approach sincerely.

From different kinds of discourse in and around the therapy program, located in different kinds of activities available to Carr, she is able to tie specific metapragmatic positions to specific activities and social identities and show how they are part of a larger social system. Metapragmatic activity is indexically connected to the talk that it is about—the speech of now is linked to forms of talk experienced in the past and imagined for the future.

Power and Relations among Forms of Discourse

Since its inception, sociolinguistics has been concerned with how language is implicated in relations of power, or relations of domination and subordination. Linguistic anthropology shares the view with other disciplines focused on discourse that social realities are constituted through communication in face-to-face interaction. This reality-creating itself is one key form of power.

Forms of discourse and their relations have been part of this articulation of the reality-creating role of language. In linguistic anthropology, cultural theory has greatly influenced how this basic idea has played out. Generally, forms of discourse are seen as socially organized in ways that give some people greater power than others in the process of reality constitution. Probably the best-known example of such organization is the view in feminist cultural and linguistic anthropology that cross-culturally, men control public forms of discourse, which are widely shared, while women are limited to less influential private forms of discourse. This gives men greater power in producing sociocultural realities through talk. In the Briggs and Mantini-Briggs (2003) analysis of the cholera epidemic, the authors make it clear that medical control of forms of discourse related to health meant that medical personnel in contact with media controlled the reality that blamed the Warao for the epidemic and erased the Warao's view of the reality of the situation.

In my own work I have seen that teachers (Philips 1983) and judges (Philips 1998) have far more institutionally determined control over the constitution of legal and educational realities than the students and litigants with whom they interact. This holds true across forms of talk that take place in classrooms and courtrooms. Judges and teachers control the turns at talk of others and further constrain what others can say through the nature of the questions they ask. Legal and educational complexes are related by virtue of being arms of states that develop common strategies for controlling people across cultural domains and institutions. Carr's (2011) discussion of the Fresh Beginnings drug therapy program similarly shows how counselors have far greater control over forms of discourse in and around the therapy than the clients do.

A second kind of power given attention in anthropological discourse analysis is the power exercised by European colonizers of societies in the New World, Africa, and the Pacific. When two of my research projects and sites are compared, one can see how European legal and educational institutions have been applied to the non-European contexts of Warm Springs classrooms (Philips 1983) and Tongan courtrooms (Philips 2016). From the seventeenth through the twentieth century the three institutional complexes of religion, education, and law were widely introduced by the British to parts of the world outside of Europe through the imposition of colonial power. This exercise of power involved the replacement and transformation of whole areas of life. These institutions have in turn been transformed by the participation of colonized people in the activities of the institutions. Critics of this imposition of institutions have directed attention to the psychological harm and loss of power experienced by people colonized by Europeans. At the same time these same institutions link non-European nation states to transnational and even global educational, legal, and religious processes.

The ways in which British law has been replicated in British colonies can easily be illustrated by comparison of my findings in US courts (Philips 1998) and Tongan courts (Philips 2004), bearing in mind that both the United States and Tonga were once British colonies. The same legal elements in the same legal order were present in criminal cases in both the Pima County Superior Court in Tucson, Arizona, and the Magistrate's Courts in Tonga. In Tucson, three separate procedures on three separate occasions were held to find a defendant guilty of a crime. The Nature of the Charge was provided in an Initial Appearance procedure. The Factual Basis for the charge was given in the Guilty Plea. The actual sentence naming the punishment was given in the Sentencing. In Tonga, the same three forms of discourse (i.e., the Nature of the Charge, the Factual Basis for the charge, and the Sentencing) were brought together in a single procedure in the same sequential order, yet each remained distinct as a unit of discourse within the larger guilty plea.

This example shows how very close the replication of discourse sequencing and content is in two legal systems whose law derives from English common law. This is the case even though the courts are thousands of miles apart and carrying out the procedures in different languages. US and Tongan law thus have a great deal in common and these commonalities make it easier for transnational legal cases to be prosecuted. In this way the forms of discourse in the court systems continue to be related to each other in a global social organization of law.

Western European Christian religious denominations have similarly introduced and imposed religious forms of discourse on colonized populations that are very close in form and content to the original sources. Hanks (2010) has described in great detail how such specific genres of written discourse were used by Catholic missionaries colonizing Maya indigenous people as part of their conversion. The development of the genres of Mayan-Spanish dictionaries and Spanish grammars of Mayan is a basic foundational step in the wholesale transfer of Catholic religious discourse forms from Spanish missionaries to Maya indigenous people. These basic genres of translingual alignment of Mayan with Spanish include many Catholic or religion-specific examples of Mayan usage. The examples make it clear that Mayan word meanings are being altered in their semantic range through the recognizably religious sentences used as examples in dictionaries and grammars.

From here the process of conversion moves to the translation from Spanish into Mayan of specifically religious genres, such as prayer and sermons. An additional step for Hanks is the movement of forms of religious discourse into colonial political and legal processes so that, for example, petitions to colonial political authorities have many of the qualities of prayers.

So far I have considered two kinds of power involving relations among forms of discourse. The first concerns the reality-creating power of language, which is culturally central to all interactions. We see that in institutional discourses, representatives of the bureaucracies typically control the production of forms of discourse through which clients, patients, and students are processed, so they have far greater power in this respect in the reality-creating process.

The second kind of power concerns colonial imposition of the institutional complexes of law, education, and religion (and later medicine) by Western Europeans and their strategies for exercising control over colonized populations. In my two examples, whole packages of legal and religious discourse with their attendant framings of reality are translated. People are made to participate in the interactional formats of courts and churches. Activity in such institutions replaces activities that existed before European contact.

My last example of how forms of discourse are related in anthropological discussions of language and power focuses on the idea that forms of discourse are ranked relative to each other in prestige, persuasiveness, and authority (Meek 2020). Recall that higher- and lower-level trial courts in Tonga have similar kinds of discourse units and participant identities, but the higher court gives much more time and attention to each case through repetitions of every level of discourse organization: each witness is asked more questions; there are more witnesses called by each lawyer so there are more testimonies for each side; and sometimes there are more lawyers for each side, which also multiplies the number of witness testimonies and questions within each testimony.

The expansion of the number of repetitions of the types of units of discourse at each level of organization in the higher-court cases, as I have already noted, is a way of responding to the idea that the higher-level cases are more serious, and in this sense more important (Philips 2016). The two court levels are not only organizationally related, but they are also in a hierarchical relationship in terms of prestige and authority. The forms of talk in the two courts are ranked relative to each other. Greater amounts of cultural energy are given to each case in the higher trial court than is true of each case at the lower-court level. The higher court can also overturn decisions of the lower court. The higher court is seen as more powerful, and in some cases to be feared, with a greater capacity to shape the lived experience of Tongans. All this, by the way, could also be said of American court levels. This discourse relatedness is an inheritance of British colonial rule and continues to be influenced by Anglo-American law. Similarly, in the Venezuelan cholera epidemic, some forms of discourse and sources of discourse clearly were ranked higher than others and were more widely disseminated to take on the aura of truth.

The examples of colonial ways that relations between forms of discourse embody power dynamics are analytically tied here to the closeness of linguistic anthropology to the colonial experience. This closeness comes through direct experiences of the legacies of colonialism, the almost inescapable residues of colonialism in anthropologists' field experiences, and through the theorization of colonialism and nation state formation in cultural anthropology. There are other models of power relationships within anthropology that could also be applied to relations among forms of discourse, the most enduring being a political economic model of social inequality (Philips 2003).

Conclusion

I suggested at the beginning that when we consider the various approaches to discourse analysis, linguistic anthropologists characteristically think of relations between different forms of discourse as part of the nature of human discourse more than scholars in other traditions. Discourse is inherently multiple in nature, not only in linguistic properties but in the boundedness of interactional units, their turn economies, their internal sequencing, and the capacity of interactional units for expansion and contraction.

This anthropological disposition to focus on the multiplicity of forms of discourse stems from the heritage of Hymes and Gumperz's concept of the ethnography of communication, in which language is conceptualized as a set of resources to be drawn upon selectively to achieve different social ends through different forms of discourse.

Forms of discourse are understood to be socially organized and in a relationship that is expressed in part through both their commonalities and their differences. Forms of discourse are also related through culturally shared metapragmatics. We have great conscious control over how we include or fail to include units of discourse and in how and why we order them, and some of that gets articulated verbally. Finally, forms of discourse enter into power-laden relationships. Forms of discourse are ranked in various ways, and some higher-ranked forms have a greater influence over the creation of shared realities than others.

No discourse form ever exists in isolation, and the ways forms of discourse are related in the process of human communication is part of the nature of language itself.

Acknowledgments

This chapter is dedicated to the memory of Debby Schiffrin. She encouraged us to think comparatively about different approaches to discourse and laid foundations for "discourse" as an enduring conceptual phenomenon in linguistics. I thank Cynthia Gordon and the student organizers of the 2018 Georgetown University Round Table for the opportunity to offer my views on anthropological discourse analysis. A special thanks to Perry Gilmore and Deborah Tannen for their comments.

References

Blommaert, Jan. 2009. Ethnography and democracy: Hymes's political theory of language. *Text and Talk* 29: 257–76.

Briggs, Charles and Clara Mantini-Briggs. 2003. *Stories in the time of cholera: Racial profiling during a medical nightmare.* Berkeley: University of California Press.

Carr, E. Summerson. 2011. *Scripting addiction: The politics of therapeutic talk and American sobriety.* Princeton: Princeton University Press.

Ferguson, Charles. 1964. Diglossia. In D. Hymes (ed.), *Language in culture and society.* New York: Harper and Row. 429–39.

Goffman, Erving. 1963. *Behavior in public places: Notes on the social organization of gatherings.* New York: Free Press.

———. 1964. The neglected situation. *American Anthropologist* 66: 133–36.

———. 1981. *Forms of talk.* Philadelphia: University of Pennsylvania Press.

Gumperz, John J. and Dell Hymes (eds.). 1964. The ethnography of communication. *American Anthropologist*, Special Publication, Part 2, 66: v–186.

Hanks, William. 2010. *Converting words: Maya in the age of the cross.* Berkeley: University of California Press.

Hymes, Dell. 1981. The 'wife' who 'goes out' like a man: Reinterpretation of a Clackamas Chinook myth. In *"In vain I tried to tell you": Essays in Native American ethnopoetics.* Philadelphia: University of Pennsylvania Press. 274–308.

Kroskrity, Paul and Anthony K. Webster (eds.). 2015. *The legacy of Dell Hymes: Ethnopoetics, narrative inequality, and voice.* Bloomington: Indiana University Press.

Meek, Barbra A. 2020. Racing Indian language, language-ing an Indian race: Linguistic racisms and representations of indigeneity. In H. Samy Alim, Angela Reyes and Paul Kroskrity (eds.), *Oxford Handbook of Language and Race.* Oxford: Oxford University Press. 369–91.

Moore, Robert. 2015. Reinventing ethnopoetics. In Paul V. Kroskrity and Anthony K. Webster (eds.), *The legacy of Dell Hymes: Ethnopoetics, narrative inequality, and voices.* Bloomington: Indiana University Press. 11–36.

Ochs, Elinor and Tina Bennett-Kastor (eds.). 1977. *Discourse across time and space.* Southern California Occasional Papers in Linguistics (SCOPIL), Number 5. Los Angeles: University of Southern California, Department of Linguistics.

Philips, Susan. 1983. *The invisible culture: Communication in classroom and community on the Warm Springs Reservation.* New York: Longman. Reprinted by Waveland Press, Prospect Heights, IL (1993).

———. 1998. *Ideology in the language of judges: How judges practice law, politics, and courtroom control.* New York: Oxford University Press.

———. 2003. Language and social inequality. In Alessandro Duranti (ed.), *A companion to linguistic anthropology.* Oxford: Blackwell Publishing. 474–95.

———. 2004. The organization of ideological diversity in discourse: Modern and neotraditional visions of the Tongan state. *American Ethnologist* 31: 231–50.

———. 2016. Balancing the scales of justice in Tonga. In E. Summerson Carr and Michael Lempert (eds.), *Scale: Discourse and dimensions of social life*. Berkeley: University of California Press. 112–32.

Sacks, Harvey and Emanuel A. Schegloff. 1973. Opening up closings. *Semiotica* 8: 289–327.

Saville-Troike, Muriel. 1982. *The ethnography of communication: An introduction*. Oxford: Basil Blackwell.

Schegloff, Emanuel A. 1972. Sequencing in conversational openings. In John J. Gumperz and Dell Hymes (eds.), *Directions in sociolinguistics: The ethnography of communication*. New York: Holt, Rinehart & Winston. 346–80.

Schiffrin, Deborah. 1994. *Approaches to discourse*. Oxford: Blackwell.

Sherzer, Joel. (1974) 1989. Namakke, sunmakke, kormakke: Three types of Cuna speech events. In Richard Bauman and Joel Sherzer (eds.), *Explorations in the ethnography of speaking*. New York: Cambridge University Press. 263–82.

Silverstein, Michael. 1993. Metapragmatic discourse and metapragmatic function. In John A. Lucy (ed.), *Reflexive language: Reported speech and metapragmatics*. New York: Cambridge University Press. 33–58.

2

"Two Different Kinds of Life": A Cultural Analysis of Blackfeet Discourse

DONAL CARBAUGH AND EEAN GRIMSHAW

OUR PURPOSE IN THIS chapter is twofold: we analyze a discursive practice used by Blackfeet people to say something about themselves, and in the process we offer a sort of primer in cultural discourse analysis. The materials for the former are drawn from Blackfeet (Amskapi Piikuni) people of northern Montana in the United States. As we examine these materials we will make explicit some of the concepts and procedures we use for cultural discourse analyses. By the end, we hope to contribute an understanding about a Blackfeet practice of communication as well as to introduce a perspective on discourse analysis, especially one based in cultural concepts, principles, and premises.

Introduction: By Way of Speaking

A leader of the Blackfeet (Amskapi Piikuni) nation, Chief Earl Old Person, who served as a Blackfeet Tribal Council Member for more than fifty years, was asked by an interviewer from Montana TV about his people, an indigenous group whose traditional homeland is in northern Montana in the United States. He measured his words carefully, as he wanted both his tribal members and non-tribal listeners to understand something important to him and his people. In a reflective voice, he said:[1]

```
1 Within the people today,
2    they uh, it's something that
3    they feel good about, to identify themselves as the Blackfeet.
4         This is our uh identity
5         and it goes way back.
```

As Chief Old Person discussed ways of living among Blackfeet people, he deemed it important to say a bit more about the point on line 3 about identity, specifically by mentioning what it involves today as an "Indian" way:

```
46 We have two different kinds of life.
47    We have our traditional way, our Indian way of life,
48    and then we enter into the, life today, modern way.
```

In brief, he reports that "the people today" "feel good" about being "Blackfeet": he points out that this "identity" as Blackfeet people "goes way back." About our "people today" he says that there are "two different kinds of life"; one is "our traditional way, our Indian way of life"; another is a "modern way," one which "we enter into." Chief Old Person's discourse invites a listener to understand Blackfeet people today accordingly, as those whose identity arises from a deep historical root and as those who have different ways of living, traditional Indian and modern ways.

Mr. Old Person is not alone in this sort of description of the Blackfeet today. Another prominent member of the Blackfeet tribe, Rising Wolf, was asked by an interviewer what people should know about Blackfeet people and culture. Without hesitation, his comments assumed a similar form. He began by saying this:

```
1 There's two different ways probably, you can go at it
2    One would be traditional, because I was raised by a traditional culture and language...
3    The other would be the more contemporary way, the assimilation, Christianity part of it...
```

Like Chief Earl Old Person, Rising Wolf points verbally to "two different ways...you can go at it," one he calls "traditional," the other, "contemporary."

We begin hearing in these comments from these speakers a Blackfeet way of speaking about Blackfeet people. We will find that this way runs deep in its meanings about Blackfeet traditions and lives today. We will find also that these brief snippets of discourse are inextricably tied to a larger cultural discourse as well as to counter discourses. This discourse is being structured to address a universal dilemma: How do we change current circumstances for the better while also preserving the best of our tradition(s)? We call our way of exploring deeply meaningful language like this, such as the brief comments being made here and the larger discourses of which they are inextricably a part, cultural discourse analysis.

Cultural Discourse Analysis

Cultural discourse analysis is a complex investigative procedure that is designed to address these sorts of questions: What culturally distinctive practices of discourse do people use? How are these practices being produced, patterned, or structured in social scenes? What participants' meanings are being presumed, actively created, and/or resisted through these discursive practices?

Responses to these questions are created through several specific modes, or procedures, of analysis, with each mode being designed to make a specific type of claim.

Above, we have fixed on the page some real examples of language as it is used, in this case by Blackfeet speakers. An important first step, then, is a *descriptive mode of analysis*. This is a set of procedures designed to make claims of this form: X discourse actually occurred in this social situation in this way, or X language was actually used in this situated way. The descriptive phase of analysis is typically completed first and involves both a process of discovery, of some focal communication practice, followed by its careful documentation.

The discovery process draws to the analyst's attention some type of discourse that is indeed happening—as opposed to hypothetical examples—and typically involves a sense that this bit of discourse is culturally rich. For example, above we find comments like those being made by Chief Old Person and Rising Wolf; each is an actually occurring comment, with each being repeated, and each, we eventually find, dense in participants' meanings. In other words, we have discovered a discursive device; we find that it recurs or is patterned with each use being similar in some ways to the others and thus provides with the others evidence of a pattern. We add, also, a sense that the discourse is deemed significant and important to its users. We emphasize to begin, then, that the descriptive mode involves, first, discovering such a pattern and describing its social use, as well as transcribing it in an exacting way.

As for transcribing or documenting the social use of the pattern, analysts of cultural discourse often use specific components to offer a systematic description, drawing attention to the setting, participants, acts in sequence, key or tone, and instruments used in producing the discursive practice (Hymes 1972). This theory of description provides an invaluable aid in documenting the details of the social situations in which the language was used.

The transcription offered above is a version of ethnopoetic transcription as previously introduced and used by many others (see recently Cerulli 2017; Hymes 2003; Webster and Kroskrity 2013). This sort of transcription draws attention to several features in the discourse, such as parallel structures of language, propositional content, rhetorical devices, and dynamics of verse/stanza, as well as other stylized means for structuring content.

Returning to the instances of discourse above, we can characterize the transcription as a way of "reporting culture" (see Carbaugh and Berry 2017). We note in this Blackfeet case that the pattern involves at least these elements:

- A two-part, linguistic structure that symbolically juxtaposes two classes or cultural types of features;
- One class involves modern-life: "life today"; "modern way"; "contemporary way"; "Christianity";
- A second involves traditional-life: an "Indian way"; "traditional culture and language"; "it goes way back";
- This symbolic contrast activates cyclical conceptions of life and time (which we develop further below).

Regarding the latter, the two contrasting features of the cultural pattern activate indigenous conceptions of time along three interrelated cultural dimensions. At one end is the idea that our "traditional Indian way" goes "way back," indeed to the beginning. This point on the continuum anchors, in one sense, a historical report about the way things were in the past (in the beginning, at time-1), linking "our Indian way of life" to an earlier time, deep into an ancestral past. However, the report is not simply a report about this earlier period of time, although it is partly that. A second dimension of time makes explicit that this past is active in historically based ways of living today; this sort of practice is ongoing and a crucially important part of Blackfeet identity today. In fact, it can be actively used, as Old Person puts it, as "we enter into the, life today." For example, in subsequent instances below we find traditional ways being practiced in order to "raise" at least some young people and children today (with time-1 knowledge into time-2 living). We will find also, as we explore this aspect of the discourse, below, that this "traditional Indian way" (from time-1) is further not only threatened today (at time-2), but too often lost. Yet there is also a bright light into the future (linking times 1 and 3). We will return to these important aspects of temporality below.

This way of reporting Blackfeet culture, then, involves agonistic discourse, or a layering of cultural terms, about two ways of life, traditional and modern ways; the report activates temporal dimensions of time, some of which are deeply rooted in traditional ways, some as ambiguously related to today's practices, with some linked to a future where traditional ways will also continue Blackfeet ways (yet others may not). The pattern of discourse, therefore, exists in a symbolic juxtaposition of traditional and modern ways, along Blackfeet temporal dimensions that are deep and complex in their cultural meanings.

We have already introduced some findings from our second mode of analysis, which consists of various *interpretive* procedures. These procedures are designed to create claims of this sort: X discourse activates these sorts of meanings to participants. In other words, when discourse is structured this way by participants, it has cultural meanings that can be known and explicated systematically by analysts.

One form of interpretive explication involves formulating what we call *cultural propositions*. These keep the analyst very close to the data by placing participants' terms, in quotes, into statements of belief, and/or value, which capture meanings that are significant and important to participants. To reiterate, the above corpus of data provides evidence of cultural propositions like the following: (1) Our "people today" "feel good" about "identify[ing] themselves as the Blackfeet"; (2) Being Blackfeet is an "identity" that "goes way back"; (3) Blackfeet people have "two different kinds of life," "our traditional...Indian way" and a "modern" or "contemporary way."

This way of treating discursive data is a beginning phase of interpretive analysis, laying bases for further analyses that capture the semantic features that are active in the discourse of concern. A next interpretive phase can involve formulating statements of meaning at a higher level of abstraction. We call these statements *cultural premises*. For the sake of illustration, relative to this data, we could formulate these cultural premises: reports of Blackfeet identity involve symbolic contrasts between traditional and modern ways; these ways involve cyclical conceptions of time. In order to analyze precisely these additional meanings, in terms of our theory, we identify when a *discursive hub* is active, like Blackfeet identity here, then give special attention to *radiants of meaning* that may help in grasping the deeper cultural meanings about identity in the discourse. The concepts of hub and meaning draw attention, respectively, to actual bits of discourse (i.e., a discursive hub) and the implicit cultural meanings members hear activated in that hub of discourse (i.e., the radiants of meanings). The radiants around a hub of identity like "Blackfeet identity," according to the theory, might involve meanings about action (what people can and should do, as such), feeling (what people can and should feel), and dwelling (what people understand to be the nature of things), with this symbolic identity also activating cultural conceptions of time (when—at what time—is the concern of the people and practice).[2]

Our point is this: further interpretive analyses are needed to understand especially the cultural meanings in the discourse. We do so by formulating cultural propositions and premises being activated in the discourse, here through the symbolic contrasting terms, with this contrast being on the surface hub of identity but also involving radiants of meanings about acting, feeling, dwelling, and time. We analyze and illustrate these in more detail by introducing some additional data.

The agonistic contrasts and temporal dimensions occur in a discourse pattern we can conceptualize further as a mini-maxi form, that is, it is a minimal agonistic form, as it occurs in a few words, but we also hear in this form maximal semantic power. In short, the form is a "mini-maxing phenomenon," a minimal linguistic form with maximal semantic power (see Basso 1988, 123).

Consider the following comment made in 2015 (p. 201) by Mr. Smokey Rides at the Door during an interview with a researcher. He had been asked about Blackfeet spiritual life, ways it is active today, and how these ways involve people in the Blackfeet-Glacier country today. Partly, he referenced the importance of calling upon as well as hearing ancestors when addressing the challenges of living today. He used the following formulation when he was reporting this feature of his Blackfeet ways:

```
10 When you talk about speaking to spirits…
11    You call upon people who went before you…
12 In contemporary society
13    You just don't know where that help will come from.
```

Mr. Rides at the Door refers to a traditional way of "speaking to spirits" (lines 10–11); this way brings traditional knowledge to one's current situation in ways that inform who one is (Blackfeet), what one should do ("speak to spirits"), how one feels about one's immediate challenge (action should be guided by wisdom), and what is best as a way of dwelling in the world today. As one listens to the "people who went before you," you can become better connected, aligned with and attuned to the spiritual-material world in which one lives, every day. The spiritual messages help renew this sense of being connected to our earth, while also reminding us of our ethic to care deeply for all of creation. These few words tap into a deep historical root through its form of expression, an anchoring of Blackfeet ways deeply that can, and should, inform traditional Blackfeet practices today.[3]

This way of life is contrasted by Smokey Rides at the Door with "contemporary society," in which "you just don't know where that help will come from" (lines 12–13). By juxtaposing the traditional with this contemporary way, we can hear the risk of not

tending one's historical roots of Blackfeet identity and action, as symbolic and material creation itself can become threatened from little cultivation and care. Further, if
one forgets the aid of the "people who went before you," one struggles to find where
to go for "help" and what to do. This of course results in a loss of one's way, but with a
possible renewal being found in learning and practicing one's traditional ways.

The agonistic contrast is elaborated further by Mr. Rides at the Door:

```
41 Western civilization is beginning to realize that by taking and taking and taking
42   our diminishment of the earth is drawing near.
43   Our glaciers are drying up...
...
52 We can continue to learn from our traditions, acting from them.
53 We will see the regeneration of Mother Earth and the people that are living on it.
54   That's why Indian people are so important.
55 We haven't ventured very far from that understanding of our connection to Mother Earth.
```

Rides at the Door's terms of the contrast contain evidence for the following cultural propositions: "Western civilization" is characterized by "taking and taking and
taking," which results in "diminishment"; "Acting" upon our Blackfeet "traditions," "our
connection to Mother Earth," can result in "regeneration"; "That's why Indian people
are so important." In short, traditional ways help reconnect and attune people to their
world; this can serve as a corrective to contemporary acts such as taking too much,
environmental degradation, feeling at a loss, being uncertain about where to turn, or
what to do, yielding to a bland assimilation, further religious persecution, and the like.

Enlarging the Discourse

The analysis of cultural discourse is built on the view that each discursive practice,
like the Blackfeet one that reports culture, is intimately tied to others. How each is tied
to others is part of what the analyst can explore and needs to discover in each case.
A result of this process of discovery can lead to enlarging the discourse of concern
and in the process one can gain a better idea of the nature and cultural meaning of a
specific device, like that of reporting one's culture.

When exploring the above Blackfeet practice, we found larger discourses in
which the practice was embedded and being used. One is the video produced about
Blackfeet people by Montana TV in 2015. Chief Earl Old Person appears in this video,
where he speaks the instances above. What we notice also in this video is the way his
verbal reports about Blackfeet people provide the orienting framing of this larger
video document about Blackfeet people. Notice how his remarks both open and close
the video (most of the video is presented and transcribed here in ethnopoetic form):

```
Chief Earl Old Person [EOP, Blackfeet]:
1 Within the people today,
2   they uh, it's something that
```

3   they feel good about, to identify themselves as the Blackfeet.
4   This is our uh identity
5   and it goes way back.
6 Jim Higgins [Blackfeet]:
7 The Blackfeet were, uh, very eh interesting people uh
8   We were explorers.
9   We uh traveled from the Saskatchewan River in Canada
10   all the way down to ole Mexico.
11   We traveled the backbone of the world which
12   We call the Rockies.
13 Lea Whitford [Blackfeet]:
14 I think it's important to share with our families and our children, the values, our histories
15   because that helps them ground themselves in their identity
16   and that's going to be WAY more important than anything materialistic
17   that they could pick up and have.
18 My favorite thing is just being able to roam all over Blackfoot territory
19   look at the landscape from uh native perspectives that can ok
20   my ancestors were here
21   like to see what the landscape has as far as stories
22   and what it can tell us as people today.
23 EOP: Our land base is something that
24   we want to retain, to keep,
25   because our land base is the backbone of our reservation.
...
39 JH: Come to Blackfeet and visit us.
40   Talk to our elders.
41   We have a lot to offer.
42   We have historical sites uh
43   We have a museum
44   We have uh senior citizens
45   They're always willing to talk to people and share
46 EOP: We have two different kinds of life.
47   We have our traditional way, our Indian way of life,
48   and then we enter into the, life today, modern way.
49 Lea Whitford: We're real fortunate that we have tribal leaders
50   that envision for the people, uh a positive future.
51 Earl Old Person: Our life is good,
52   and it can be good,
53   it's up to us.
[End of video]

We can begin by noticing the specific discursive practice we are examining in lines 1–5, and then again in lines 46–53. The final lines provide the by now familiar juxtaposition of the "two different kinds of life" that are not only "good," but "can be good, it's up to us."

Looking at the discourse in this video text, we find evidence of several cultural propositions. We formulate them here and identify [in brackets] some of the elemental *discursive hubs* that are being used to elaborate the main hub of Blackfeet identity:

1. "The **people today**" have "something **they** *feel good* about" [hubs of **identity**, *feeling*] (lines 1–3, 41, 49–50, 51–52);
2. This is "their **identity as the Blackfeet**"; this "goes way back" [**identity**, time 1↔2] (lines 3–5, 14–15, 42, 47);
3. Blackfeet identity is connected to a "landscape" and our "**ancestors**" [dwelling, **identity**] (lines 9–12, 18–22, 23–25, 42);
4. "Blackfoot territory" is a "favorite thing," a "landscape" that can be felt or seen and acted upon, as when we "roam" and "look" in a "**native** perspective" [dwelling, action, identity, time 1↔2] (lines 18–19);
5. The land has "stories" it can "tell"; it speaks a sacred voice [dwelling, time 1↔2, action] (lines 21–22);
6. "Our land" must be [kept and retained], it is our "**backbone**" [dwelling, **identity**] (lines 24–25);
7. Blackfeet have "**a lot to offer**," our elders are "always willing to talk to people and share" [**identity**, action] (lines 39–45);
8. The moral: A "positive future" is "up to **us**" [time 1→2→3, **identity**] (lines 50, 53).

This larger strip of audiovisual discourse and its propositional claims extend our understanding of this agonistic play in several ways. First, as the discourse makes a claim about a Blackfeet identity, it also elaborates that claim, in this case, through terms of feeling, time, dwelling, and action. This is noted above in propositions 1 through 8. In cultural discourse theory, we conceptualize the linguistic terms that are instances of each—feeling, time, dwelling, and action, respectively—as noted above, as *discursive hubs,* by which we mean explicit terms that are active in a discourse, thereby saying something about feeling (proposition 1), time (propositions 2, 4, 5, 8), dwelling (propositions 3–6), and action (propositions 4, 5, 7). This sort of noticing is guided by the theory, which invites further investigation, when productive, of the discursive hubs of identity, action, feeling, relating, and dwelling (see Carbaugh and Cerulli 2017; Carbaugh and Sotirova 2015; see also Scollo and Milburn 2019). By exploring the additional hubs, we enhance our understanding by enlarging the discourse of concern systematically to other linguistic items that are attached to the focal discourse pattern of concern.

Also, in the above transcript, we note on lines 39–45 a kind of invitation from Blackfeet member Jim Higgins to "visit us" and "talk to our elders." While this has a generic hearing, perhaps something like a Chamber of Commerce message, we find in this case a special exigence for the invitation. Our field notes are replete with comments made by non-native people who live off of the reservation and have limited to no contact with native peoples. A full analysis of those is not possible here, but we can summarize the following stereotypical claims made about native identity and places included in them: (1) the reservations are places that are extremely poor and economically deprived; (2) Indian people and the reservations are hostile and violent places; (3) the violence is fueled by alcohol and drugs; (4) reservation Indians are lawless and not under state and federal law; therefore, you should not go there but if you must, be extremely careful. The last point is a familiar one on Montana's airways, as it stems partly from a longtime, popular radio personality Paul Harvey, who said in an oft-repeated line, "If you want to get away with murder, go to the Blackfeet Reservation" (quoting Paul Harvey, 2009). One of us has been repeatedly advised to carry a weapon if going to the Blackfeet reservation.

The above, then, enlarges the discourse of concern in multiple ways. With the video, we are taken deeper into the meanings of "Blackfeet identity" from participants' views, including the messages we have explicated about feeling (proposition 1), time (propositions 2, 4–5, 8), dwelling (propositions 3–6), and action (proposition 7). Consideration of the video also takes us more broadly into an exigence for the video itself, redressing as it does a negative view of native people as untoward and reservations as inhospitable. Relative to this stereotypical set of claims, a countermessage is being sent: Blackfeet have a lot to feel good about, including their reservation lands and landscape, its sacred qualities, important stories, and yes, a positive future. The video, then, offers a counter discourse to the non-native one, which portrays native people and places otherwise.

These concerns in the counter discourse and counter-voices also deepen our capacity to interpret meanings, for example in Chief Earl Old Person's utterance:

```
46 We have two different kinds of life.
47    We have our traditional way, our Indian way of life,
48    and then we enter into the, life today, modern way.
```

What is meant here by "life today, modern way"? We find, now, equivocal symbolic meanings at play. In one direction are modern or contemporary sorts of practice that involve "help" from or that are informed by "the ancestors"—as mentioned also as "help" by Smokey Rides at the Door. These routine ways today are being guided by elder wisdom and function, as Lea Whitford suggests, as a proper education of Blackfeet children, a way for Blackfeet people to "ground themselves in their identity" (line 15). This involves active knowledge about traditional ways that is being taught to children and further applied to various contemporary circumstances (time 1→2). Blackfeet scholar Rosalyn LaPier (2017, xxvii) has reserved the word "traditional" similarly, to apply to "individuals with a strong sense of their own individual identity that is grounded in their significant understanding of Native language, religious belief systems, tribal ecological knowledge, and community history." The communal knowledge afforded by the language, local landscape, and community is crucial for traditional living.

There is risk in moving away from traditional ways, but also remedy available if needed. When talking with Blackfeet cultural coordinator Two Bears, he said this as we were visiting a special place on the reservation: "This is an ideal place for those of our people having trouble with drugs or alcohol. They could come out here and think about things. It's ideal for that" (quoted in Carbaugh 2005, 105). The point Two Bears is making here, in this place, is that "our people" can have such trouble today. This meaning is active at times when the phrase "contemporary way" is being used. Here, the meaning is that some troubling activities such as these are unmoored from earlier traditional practices because these activities were nonexistent in the earlier time-1; the disconnection is amplified when people today are uninformed about the traditional ways that can equip them for a better life. In these cases, the contemporary world has overshadowed traditional ways, with time-2 becoming unconnected from time-1.

In these meanings of the "contemporary way," there is not only disconnection possible but also the need for a kind of remedial voice, a reconnecting of the relationship between time-1 and time-2. Smokey Rides at the Door (2015, 200) expresses both options explicitly:

```
1 When you take your contemporary teachings and mold it with your tradition
2     You'll find that there are more ways of approaching a situation…
3          Each person in their deliberations to get the answers to their questions
4               has to go through a series of motions, emotions,
5 and when you go through the series
6    you feel complete.
7 It's a different way of knowing than the one taught in school.
```

Note the first point, when time-2 practices are informed by time-1, "when you take your contemporary teachings and mold it with your tradition," a "complete" form of action and personage is possible. But there is another way that is "taught in school." This other voice was expressed by Blackfeet member Joseph Stone, who explained how the loss of traditional ways leads to sickness and mental health issues.[4] When this happens, time-2 practice is being systematically severed from time-1, leaving participants unmoored from the deep wisdom that guides traditional Blackfeet ways. The inequitable circumstances of one's life, Mr. Stone explains, can be stacked against integrating traditional ways into the modern world. This can be extremely frustrating. Another Blackfeet, Gordon Belcourt, discussed as examples how the police were called when an extended Blackfeet family gathered together beside a loved one in a hospital room to comfort them. Belcourt also recounted a diagnosis of delirium attributed to a native man who was simply calling for water in his native Blackfoot language. In both social situations, traditional ways were deemed suspect by the officers who enforced other, nontraditional policies, and thus subverted traditional ways.

The verbal portrait being drawn here between today's world and traditional ways is complex and complicated. Blackfeet people can lose touch with traditional ways, and Blackfeet people can try to practice traditional ways in a modern world, such as comforting a loved one or using one's native language, but the schism between time-1 and time-2 can be so great that the efforts are unjustly thwarted and inequitably subjugated, and thus rendered ineffectual. Blackfeet leader Leon Rattler, among others, has deeply lamented this loss. A continuous rekindling of this important link through efforts such as these, and education of others in the importance of efforts like these, is crucial for a "positive future" to be effectively realized as envisioned by Earl Old Person, Joseph Stone, Gordon Belcourt, Leon Rattler, us, and many, many others. Our very modest efforts at noticing and understanding this discourse is one such contribution.

The above analyses include a *comparative mode* of analysis in multiple ways, dramatically between deprived and endowed peoples/practices. These analyses are

designed to make claims about discursive usages, within and across cases. The agonistic discourse of concern to us here not only contrasts Blackfeet and non-Blackfeet
ways generally, as when non-native discourse negatively stereotypes and disempowers
indigenous people, but moreover conceives of "two ways" within Blackfeet life today
as "contemporary" and "traditional." This symbolic juxtaposition makes deep messages about different versions of social life explicit with these involving differences in
the matters of lifestyle (traditional-modern), language (Blackfoot-English), religion
(spiritual and non-spiritual living), education (Westernized public-school practices
at the expense of traditional elder-based education), and health (Indian-other ways).

These matters are juxtaposed and played within a complex arrangement of time.
There are time-1 practices, which were conducted by ancestors in the traditional way.
These involve use of traditional Blackfoot language, communication among all agents
in the universe, rituals of regeneration, and sacred stories attached to a landscape, all
supporting Blackfeet action and personhood.[5] These meanings of traditional-life are
contrasted in a most pronounced way with a "contemporary" world that ignores, is
uninformed about, deliberately denigrates, and/or is unaware of these dimensions of
life. We have understood these to be time-2 (without time-1) practices. These offer
at times nearly insurmountable constraints to traditional living. The point is made
that we, Blackfeet, in turn, do not feel good about the barriers to our traditional ways
that actively run counter to those ways; with these barriers being encountered in and
sometimes "taught in school," confronted in health care, and exacerbated for some
who experience difficulties with alcohol and drugs. In more formal terms, these barriers can be established by others, as in acts of genocide or banning spiritual ceremonies, as active ways of separating time-1 from times 2 and 3.

Counter to the above are traditional practices that are continuing today—time-1
into time-2 practices—which are taught to Blackfeet children, practiced in sacred ceremonies, and activated through a traditional form of Blackfeet "listening" and "speaking to spirits," cultural forms that can bring Blackfeet "ancestors" into our life and in
the process invigorate our people today. Through these practices, traditional ways can
address, enliven, and energize circumstances of everyday, contemporary living, as
time-1 knowledge overcomes difficulties one encounters in time-2. The meanings of
acts such as these are informed by time-1 considerations and thus consult those (time
2→1), but also are practiced in the contemporary world in light of those consultations
(time 1→2). We summarize this cyclical aspect of time as time 1↔2.

This, then, brings us to the lament expressed by Leon Rattler (and many others
about the cultural loss and obstruction of traditional ways), thereby bringing "good
feeling" about a "positive future" into being (a vision for time-3). After all, this good
life for our people (from time 1↔2 to time-3) is "up to us," to *all of us*.

Discussion

When I (DC) was attending the inauguration of Blackfeet Tribal Council members
on July 11 of 1996, one inductee said, "It's important that we listen to each other and
stay current on things but also that we rely on the traditional ways of our elders." A
second member who was being reinducted said: "Whatever I have done has been

done on the basis of our elders' teachings.... We must continue to listen to our traditional ways." Both activated the juxtaposition of contemporary and traditional ways; both expressed the significance and importance of traditional ways as a means of addressing contemporary issues or problems. In short, both utilized in this inauguration the discourse of concern to us in this chapter. We emphasize that the discourse of concern to us here is a robust one, as it has recurring significance and importance in our data over at least a thirty-year period; we know it runs over a much, much longer period of time than this.

Blackfeet historian and environmental scientist Rosalyn LaPier, in the preface to her recent book, writes specifically about Blackfeet conceptions of time. In her words (2017, p. xxi), "time in Blackfeet society is a complex concept and different from the Western concept of time." Her essays show how Blackfeet have recounted earlier times, in earlier times, and today, while living in traditional ways. In a similar spirit, Howard Harrod (1992, 20) has studied the ritual actions and symbolic forms of Plains peoples, discovering in them the experience of traditional ways, a living practice of deep, symbolic power. He concludes his studies of Plains Indian—including Blackfeet—religion and morality: "We do not need to know with certainty the age or the evolutionary trajectory of the traditions which we confront in the mid-nineteenth century in order to appreciate their depth and symbolic power. Indeed, we will come to see…specific instances of what is primordial and pervasive in human experience." As traditional ways are acknowledged, recalled, and practiced today, as LaPier indicates, Blackfeet time assumes a complex, cyclical, and deep form.

In Native American discourse, the cultural category of "traditional ways" is linked to acting in ways that are mindful of "seven generations," a discursive thread that is woven prominently throughout Native America. As Professor David Wilkins (Lumbee) has written about this: "There isn't a day that goes by in Indian Country that we don't hear something about the Seven Generations.... Much can be learned from [Indian] nations that respect their ancestors, themselves, and those to come. Such nations exemplify the true meaning of the Seven Generations by maintaining their integrity as peoples. [Oglala Sioux author] Vine Deloria, Jr. spoke of the Seven Generations in very practical terms. In his cantankerous way, he would express extreme annoyance at the romanticism of the concept as it was popularly used. Because, as explained to him, the generations we are sworn to protect and revere are the seven we are most immediately connected to. Think about it for a moment. It is possible that many of us have known or will know our great-grandparents, grandparents, parents, our children, grandchildren, and great-grandchildren. Even if we aren't fortunate enough to have been in the physical presence of those who came before us, we usually have stories, songs, and photos that have been shared so that we feel a connection. We also want to make sure our kids and grandkids are healthy, safe and aware of where they come from. So, counting our own generation—ourselves, siblings, and cousins— we are accountable to those seven generations, not some imagined futuristic peoples two hundred years down the road" (2015; see Deloria 1999, 179ff.). This is part of the backbone of traditional ways, acting in ways that go backward into time while also seeing forward into future spaces.

Our attention has been piqued by this kind of discourse as it is produced by Blackfeet people when they verbally present their culture to others and to themselves. We have also tried to demonstrate ways of analyzing this discourse that identifies its deep cultural shapes and meanings.

Our efforts have occurred first by discovering that there is such a discourse to study. Brief discursive snippets can go by quickly; indeed, finding there is such depth and value in a few words can take time and attention. Through descriptive analyses, we have provided ethnopoetic transcriptions designed to identify this sort of discourse and to draw attention to its symbolic contrasts, parallel structures, and propositional meanings. Eventually we were able to state the more abstract elements of the agonistic pattern, identifying its linguistic and cultural features. Through our interpretive analyses, we were able to explicate specific meanings in the form of cultural propositions, cultural premises, and semantic contrasts. Our comparative analyses brought to the foreground complex contrastive meanings between indigenous and other ways, as well as between the past and future, between traditional native and contemporary ways, to practices that disempower wise traditional ways (see Little Bear, 2000).

Across these modes of our analyses, we paid attention to several discursive hubs that are active in this cultural discourse, focusing on the hub of identity, but also considering hubs of time, action, feeling, and dwelling. The cultural discourse, then, we find, includes participants' taken-for-granted knowledge, respectively, about when things occur (time), who they are and will become (identity), what people are doing (action), the emotions being activated (feeling), and how this is attached to the nature of things (dwelling). Together, the system of discursive hubs, symbolic contrasts, cultural propositions, and premises supply a deep *cultural logic* at use in the discourse.

As for the main cultural logic in the discourse, we find it to be complex and summarize it as follows: "contemporary life" identifies ways of living that are mostly nontraditional; this can involve Westernized (nontraditional) forms of education and religion, obstacles to traditional ways from others in various social contexts like hospitals, separation from Mother Earth, and attendant problems with mental and physical health. "Traditional ways" identify historically based practices of living, honoring the ways of ancestors, Indian forms of education and religion, proper connections to one's place in the world, and attendant good feelings that result from these ways. While the two ways contrast, starkly, the Blackfeet capacity to manage both—typically navigating the contemporary world with the benefit of traditional ways—is expressed at least by Smokey Rides at the Door and Rising Wolf.

In the course of our analyses, we have taken up an additional theoretical consideration, the discursive hub of time in particular. We are building here with the benefit of earlier work where Katriel and Livio (2019, 69–70) found the following "four aspects of temporality came to the fore in our analyses, as the temporality associated with discourses of social change was grounded in: (1) a linear (rather than cyclical) view of time; (2) a future (rather than past or present) orientation, whether it is infused by a sense of hope as in the first case or by a sense of threat as in the second; (3) a concern with timing; and (4) a sense of urgency." Taking each in turn, in light of our findings, and using our notational scheme, we propose elaborating the temporal hub with the following conceptions of time: (1) that are possibly linear (time 1→2→3) and/or cyclical (time 1↔2↔3); (2) that focus in various ways (at times 1, 2, or 3; or at time 1→2; and so on); (3) that can become an explicitly elaborated matter of concern in, and about, a discourse; and (4) that has immediacy or practical efficacy taking precedence with regard to a communicative practice. In this way, with Katriel and Livio (2019), we have systematically extended considerations in cultural discourses by inviting future explorations of these features of temporality in its metacultural commentary.

Our notation of the three dimensions of time risks a simplified misunderstanding. The temporal process at play here is not exactly synonymous with the concepts of past, present, and future. Our point, introduced here and developed below, is that the time-1 feature can be a reference to a way things were done in the past, but that it can also be the grounding of a present practice into a deeply important historical past. These ideas of time are not only linear from time 1 to time 2; they are also cyclical, time 2 to time 1 and back. Time is being treated, then, as both a practice in the past (time-1) AND as a present practice with explicitly understood roots in the past (time 1↔2). This indicates an important cultural point: there are a set of Blackfeet practices today that are based in an ancient wisdom, like that of the Seven Generations, which has survived various tests and threats of time. Time-2, then, is at its simplest a way of referencing a present-day task, like raising children, with this task possibly involving earlier time-1 practices (time 1→2). Time 2 practices can also involve other contemporary practices that are not as deeply rooted in the past as traditional practices are, or those that are independent of any knowledge of those practices (simply Time-2). Time-2 can also involve difficulties, as we will see, which can be addressed by looking back and consulting ancestral wisdom (time 2↔1) while also looking forward. Time-3 involves forward-looking projections, some like the wisdom of Seven Generations, which are based in Time-1 practices (Time 1↔3), some that are active in specific practices today (Time 1→2→3), or, some perhaps not anchored clearly in traditional ways as such but also explicitly forward looking (Time 2→3). There is also the possibility of actions projected into future times that deliberately remove people from their traditional ways—thus, simply Time-3. The temporal dimension, then, is based in cyclical Blackfeet conceptions of time, each being possibly connected to others, as such.

While our final comments highlight this cultural discourse and the ways it can be studied, there is much further work to do. This Blackfeet discourse includes a deep critical feature, evident when Smokey Rides at the Door mentions being schooled in ways counter to traditional ways, when Gordon Belcourt described how police were called to a traditional gathering for healing, and when a man speaking Blackfoot was diagnosed as delirious. This critical discourse is currently under more detailed investigation, as it has also been in earlier papers. We also find exciting and creative ways of understanding the Blackfoot language and its teaching when done in traditional ways. These among many other tentacles of this rich cultural discourse offer much for future study. There is much we need to know as we visit our contemporary worlds through the wisdom of traditional ways, as many wise ones have been doing, long before us.

Acknowledgments

We acknowledge several who have provided inspiration and aid to us as we worked on this essay. Particularly notable during our time in Blackfeet Country during the summer of 2018 are Jack Gladstone, Robert Hall, Darnell Rides at the Door, and Smokey Rides at the Door.

Notes

1 The transcription method used here is discussed below and is based in ethnopoetics (see Hymes 2003).
2 The preceding paragraph includes several concepts that have been explicated in detail elsewhere (Carbaugh 2007a), including the development of the theory (Scollo 2011) and the concepts of discursive hub and radiant of meaning (e.g., Carbaugh and Cerulli 2017). The hubs of identity and metacommunicative action are introduced in Carbaugh (1988), with detailed development of the hub of identity in Carbaugh (1996) and the hub of meta-pragmatic action in Carbaugh (2017). The hub of dwelling is explicated fully and demonstrated (Carbaugh 2007b; Carbaugh and Cerulli 2013; Cerulli 2017; Milstein 2011) as is the hub of feeling (Carbaugh 1990, 2017). A recent volume discusses and utilizes the theory in great detail through studies in multiple languages and societies; the volume is nicely organized around each hub/radiant (Scollo and Milburn 2018). This note is simply illustrative with a large and growing literature behind it.
3 The form of expression used here has been analyzed in greater detail in an earlier paper (Carbaugh 2002).
4 The following is drawn from "Leader laments loss of Indian traditions," an article by Diane Cochran in the *Billings Gazette* (November 19, 2009). See also the works by Joseph P. Gone and team (e.g., Gone 2008).
5 The wording in this sentence reflects, respectively, prior detailed studies of Blackfeet communication and culture (Carbaugh 2005, chapters 6 and 7; Carbaugh 2001, 2002, 2018) as well as the central themes of an in-progress monograph.

References

Basso, Keith. 1988. Speaking with names: Language and landscape among the western Apache. *Cultural Anthropology* 3: 99–130.

Carbaugh, Donal. 1988. *Talking American: Cultural discourses on DONAHUE.* Norwood, NJ: Ablex.

_____. 1990. Toward a perspective on cultural communication and intercultural contact. *Semiotica* 80: 15–35.

_____. 1996. *Situating selves: The communication of social identities in American scenes.* Albany: SUNY Press.

_____. 2001. "The people will come to you": Blackfeet narrative as a resource for contemporary living. In Jens Brockmeier and Donal Carbaugh (eds.), *Narrative and identity.* Amsterdam: John Benjamins. 103–27.

_____. 2002. "I speak the language of the universe": A universally particularizing form of Native American discourse. In David Li (ed.), *Discourses in search of members: In honor of Ron Scollon.* New York and Oxford: University Press of America. 319–34.

_____. 2005. *Cultures in Conversation.* London and New York: Lawrence Erlbaum Associates.

_____. 2007a. Cultural Discourse Analysis: The investigation of communication practices with special attention to intercultural encounters. *Journal of Intercultural Communication Research* 36: 167–82.

_____. 2007b. Quoting "the environment": Touchstones on earth. *Environmental Communication: The Journal of Nature and Culture* 1: 63–73.

_____. 2017. Cultural discourses of emotion at the death of bin Laden. Keynote at the Ethnography of Communication conference. Mount Saint Vincent College, June.

_____. 2018. Two different ways of knowing the Glacier area. In Jessica Thompson and Ana Houseal (eds.), *America's largest classroom: What we learn from our national parks*. Berkeley: University of California Press. 34–49.

Carbaugh, Donal and Michael Berry. 2017. *Reporting cultures on 60 Minutes: Missing the Finnish line in an American broadcast*. New York and London: Routledge.

Carbaugh, Donal and Tovar Cerulli. 2013. Cultural discourses of dwelling: Investigating environmental communication as a place-based practice. *Environmental Communication: The Journal of Nature and Culture* 7 (1): 4–23.

_____. 2017. Cultural discourse analysis. In Young Yun Kim (gen. ed.) and Kelly McKay-Semmler (assoc. ed.), *The international encyclopedia of intercultural communication*. Hoboken, NJ: John Wiley & Sons. 1–9. doi: 10.1002/9781118783665.ieicc0117.

Carbaugh, Donal and Nadezhda Sotirova. 2015. Language use and culture. In Janet M. Bennett (ed.), *The Sage encyclopedia of intercultural competence*. Thousand Oaks, CA: Sage. 581–585. http://dx.doi. org/10.4135/9781483346267.n189.

Cerulli, Tovar. 2017. "Ma'iingan is our brother": Ojibwe and non-Ojibwe ways of speaking about wolves. In Donal Carbaugh (ed.), *The handbook of communication in cross-cultural perspective*. New York and London: Routledge. 247–60.

Cochran, Diane. 2009. Leader laments loss of Indian traditions. *Billings Gazette*, November 19, 2009.

Deloria, Vine. 1999. *For this land: Writings on religion in America*. New York and London: Routledge.

Gone, Joseph P. 2008. "So I can be like a whiteman": The cultural psychology of space and place in American Indian mental health. *Culture & Psychology* 14: 369–400.

Harrod, Howard. 1992. *Renewing the world: Plains Indian religion and morality*. Tucson and London: University of Arizona Press.

Harvey, Paul. 2009. Quoted in Brenda Austin, Murder in Montana, *Indian Country Today*, September 15.

Hymes, Dell. 1972. Models of the interaction of language and social life. In John J. Gumperz and Dell Hymes (eds.), *Directions in sociolinguistics: The ethnography of communication*. New York: Holt, Rinehart & Winston. 35–71.

_____. 2003. *Now I know only so far: Essays in ethnopoetics*. Lincoln: University of Nebraska Press.

Katriel, Tamar and Oren Livio. 2019. When discourse matters: Temporality in discursive action. In Michelle Scollo and Trudy Milburn (eds.), *Engaging and transforming global communication through cultural discourse analysis: A tribute to Donal Carbaugh*. Lanham and London: Fairleigh Dickinson University Press.

LaPier, Rosalyn. 2017. *Invisible reality: Storytellers, storytakers, and the supernatural world of the Blackfeet*. Lincoln: University of Nebraska Press and the American Philosophical Society.

Little Bear, Leroy. 2000. World views colliding. In M. Battiste (ed.), *Reclaiming indigenous voice and vision* (no page numbers). Vancouver: University of British Columbia.

Milstein, Tema. 2011. Nature identification: The power of pointing and naming. *Environmental Communication* 5 (1): 3–24.

Rides at the Door, Smokey. 2015. Quote. In S. Thompson (ed.), *People before the Park: The Kootenai and Blackfeet before Glacier National Park*. Helena: Montana Historical Society Press. 202–3.

Scollo, Michelle. 2011. Cultural approaches to discourse analysis: A theoretical and methodological conversation with special focus on Donal Carbaugh's Cultural Discourse Theory. *Journal of Multicultural Discourses* 6 (1): 1–32.

Scollo, Michelle and Trudy Milburn (eds.). 2018. *Engaging and transforming global communication through Cultural Discourse Analysis: A tribute to Donal Carbaugh*. Lanham and London: Fairleigh Dickinson University Press.

Webster, Anthony and Paul Kroskrity. 2013. Introducing ethnopoetics: Hymes's legacy. *Journal of Folklore Research* 50 (1–3): 1–11. doi:10.2979/jfolkrese.50.1–3.1.

Wilkins, David. 2015. How to honor the seven generations. *Indian Country Today*, June 18, https://indiancountrymedianetwork.com/news/opinions/how-to-honor-the-seven-generations/.

3

Gesture, Mimesis, and the Linguistics of Time

JÜRGEN STREECK

WE ARE PRESENTLY WITNESSING the emergence of a "linguistics of time" (Hopper 2015), in which language forms and constructions are understood to be both *emerging*—in (and responsive to) moment-by-moment interaction—and *emergent*, that is, a transitory outcome of ongoing speaking practice, not its stable foundation. This chapter makes the case for the place of the study of embodied action and gesture within a linguistics of time: observing how humans work and interact across real-life contexts, among the processes we can observe is gestural forms being abstracted from physical, "hands-on" actions, sedimented through repetition, and taken to other contexts as devices for displaced reference and depiction. We also observe gestures that are in common use and not related to personal bodily experience, but whose forms nevertheless retain a relation to a material world available to the hands and reveal their origin in real-world action. The data I analyze—short video segments of interactions at an auto shop (see Streeck 2017)—suggests that, as gestures emerge and become sedimented in a community, their changing semiotic features let Peirce's sign types—indexical, iconic, symbolic—appear as stages in an ongoing evolution. In this chapter, I examine and discuss the trajectory of a few hand gestures from invention to sedimentation, from indexical to displaced and abstract reference, and from indexical meaning-making to iconic representation and symbolization, in an attempt to demonstrate the continuity in the sedimentation of gestures and languages and to show that the very practices and mechanisms that made the beginnings of human language possible are continuing apace.

It has been fascinating to observe in recent years how a growing number of linguists have been recasting language structure, once considered a timeless—synchronic—phenomenon, as something that in each and every respect constitutes an unfolding in time. They have revoked the abstraction of writing, which presents utterances so that, differently from "real life," they can be apprehended at once, at a glance, like pictures, creating the illusion that bursts of talk enter the world at once, fully formed, instantaneously understood. Writing conceals the temporality—the "unfoldingness"—of language behind the instantaneousness of vision, replacing succession in time by spatial co-presence.

Temporality is characteristic of spoken language in at least three respects (Auer 2009): first, a language unit—an utterance—is *transitory*, "rapidly fading." Language vanishes at the very moment that it appears. "The 'present' of spoken language is limited to the time span within which the speaker and the hearer can retain it in [short-term, J.S.] memory" (Auer 2009, 2). Language units in their original, spoken form thus have the ontological status of events, not things. Second, (spoken) language is also *irreversible*; the arrow of time only flies in one direction: whatever has been uttered cannot be taken back; and when the right context to make a point or get something done passes, it may not come back (Schegloff, Jefferson and Sacks 1977). Third, Auer argues, the temporality of spoken language also includes the synchronization of speaker's and listener's consciousness: listeners process talk at the time that it is being produced in increments, and speakers respond to their responses. Listeners do not process incoming speech as a series of units that are "always already complete," but that are unfolding, shifting back and forth between an understanding of what is being said now in relation to what was said before (retrospection) and an anticipation of how the unit might continue and end (prospective orientation; Schutz 1967).

The temporality of language has been given attention especially in two fields: conversation analysis and interactional linguistics on one hand, and grammaticalization (Bybee 1998; Heine, Claudi and Hünnemeyer 1991; Hopper and Traugott 1993), the study of the emergence and change of grammar in the practice of speaking, on the other. The two approaches deal with language on altogether different timescales: conversation analysis and interactional linguistics capture the moment-by-moment emergence of language units in social interaction and investigate how utterance design, including syntax, is implicated in the moment-by-moment unfolding of social interaction. "Grammaticalization," in contrast, refers to processes of language change that take place on historical timescales. As Hopper puts it, conversation analysts are interested in the *emerging* of grammatical units in interaction; linguists working within the grammaticalization paradigm treat grammar as *emergent* (Hopper 2011, 26), that is, as always evolving, never "complete." These fields have, with some notable exceptions (e.g., Auer 1996; Ford, Fox and Thompson 1998), evolved in almost complete isolation from one another, but now their convergence, expectable for some time, seems to have begun (Auer and Pfänder 2011; Hopper 2015; see also Laury, Etelämaki and Couper-Kuhlen 2014).

Conversation Analysis

Conversation analysts, a long time ago (Schegloff 1979), pointed out that many linguists treated units such as sentences, clauses, and phrases "with hindsight," as units whose final shapes correspond to the "intention" that the speaker had from the beginning and that are structured in some kind of hierarchical arrangement of constituents—sentences that "might as well be written." But the actual production of any such unit, from the syllable up, is a linear process in time, an unfolding.

A listener cannot hear an utterance at once like readers can see a sentence "at a glance," and whatever units and relations can be specified in a grammar must be specified as units and relations in time. Listeners also *anticipate* certain developing features of an emerging unit, such as, when is it likely to end? What phrase, word, or syllable will be the last one? Listeners' protentive abilities are supported by the *projective* features of linguistic structures (Streeck 1995; Streeck and Jordan 2009). But the temporality of spoken language also includes *retention*, or "latency" (Auer 2015): utterances and their structures, as long as they reverberate in short-term memory, remain available to be used in subsequent talk by the speaker and others. In talk in interaction, we rarely build our utterances "from scratch"; it is much more likely that we incrementally add on to, and thereby transform, the material provided by others (see also Tannen 2006). Charles Goodwin has called this process "co-operative transformation": "New action is built by decomposing, and reusing with transformation, the resources made available by the earlier actions of others.... Building action by accumulatively incorporating resources provided by others creates a distinctive form of sociality: it is one of the ways in which we inhabit each other's actions" (Goodwin 2018, 1, 31). Schegloff (1996) has proposed that we reconceive grammar as "positionally sensitive." Not what constructions are possible and what they mean matters, but which constructions accomplish what at specific positions within turns and sequences of talk.

Grammaticalization

Research on *grammaticalization*—the large and growing field of study of how grammatical structures evolve from words and their recurrent adjacent positioning in discourse—has approached language from the outset as a temporal affair: it studies grammar as incessant grammaticalization.

Grammaticalization (or "grammaticization," see Bybee 1998; Givón and Malle 2002; Heine, Claudi and Hünnemeyer 1991; Hopper and Traugott, 1993) "is...the process by which a lexical item or a sequence of items becomes a grammatical morpheme" (Bybee 1998, 146). This process, too, is "positionally sensitive," in that only words that habitually occur next to certain other words can undergo loss of structure as is characteristic of the emergence of purely grammatical forms (such as the purely temporal "gonna" that has emerged from the habitual next-positioning of "going" and "to" in complement constructions: "going to do X"). "Structure, or regularity, comes out of discourse and is shaped by discourse as much as it shapes discourse in an ongoing process" (Hopper 1998, 142).

Prototypical examples of grammaticalization such as the rise of the English tense marker "go" emerge from situations in which an intended activity indeed requires "going to" (i.e., a movement to the location where it can be carried out) and thus involves the passing of time (though not too much time). This meaning component (it takes a moment of time to get where one is going) is recruited to figuratively and routinely encode a sense of "near future," as the temporal usage is generalized step by step to contexts where movement is no longer involved at all ("It's going to surprise you.") Natural language grammar is an ongoing product of such processes, and accordingly "the central project of linguistics would be the study not of 'grammar' but of 'grammaticalization'—the ways in which some collectively possessed inventory of forms available for the construction of discourse become 'sedimented' through repeated use, and eventually are recognized as being to a greater or lesser degree 'grammatical'" (Hopper 1992, 366f).

By turning our attention to the ongoing emergence of grammar, researchers in this field have given us another view of language as dynamic, alive, and constantly emerging and changing. The synchronic state of a language—for example, the co-existence of different senses of "go" in contemporary English—reflects the different stages of grammaticalization that the word has reached; it is an imprint and expression of a succession of stages of grammaticalization. Seemingly unrelated meanings represent different, ordered stages of the grammaticalization histories of words, each new usage typically representing an extension of the contexts in which the word/form was used.

Thus, while both conversation analysts and grammaticalization researchers investigate languages as they unfold in time, the timescales of these unfoldings are far apart and seem unconnected: how bursts of language structure and are structured in interaction does not seem to have much to do with processes like the evolution of the "gonna" construction and how, springing from an inventive solution to a conceptualization problem, it gradually became generalized and took root in the community of speakers of English as a grammaticized tense-marker. And yet, the sphere where language change takes place consists of just such moments of "online," real-time (face-to-face or mediated) conversation, and social interaction therefore is the eye of the needle through which all (situationally) emerging and (historically) emergent constructions must pass. There simply are no two distinct realities, as Hopper (2015) points out.

Studying language means studying *sedimentation*, and sedimentation begins when an utterance is repeated. Sedimentation begins as a mere possibility when in some particular situation a form or construction or metaphor appears that responds to specific *local* sense-making needs, but whose existence as a shared form may not transcend the current situation. It is a form *on the way to sedimentation*, sedimented for a moment as a component of an activity shared by a few people, and then abandoned; Ford and Fox (2015) call such phenomena "ephemeral grammar." We should study language under the auspices of its "temporal movement toward sedimentation" (Ford and Fox 2015, 96): "The fact that language is always sedimenting…means that understanding by language cannot be dependent on *sedimented* forms. Forms need not be fully sedimented. By this interpretation of emergence, sedimentation of form can be understood as a continuum, with highly ephemeral at one end and relatively stably-sedimented at the other. We take emergence to be endemic to language use, always operating but not inevitably leading to stable forms beyond the moment of interaction.… Language form can be created on the fly and just for a bounded moment of interaction. (Ford and Fox 2015, 97–98).

Hopper (2015, 252) proclaims that the new linguistics "that will trace a new road away from the dead end of Saussurean structuralism" will be a "Linguistics of Time, in which linear progression along the time line…will constitute a starting assumption."

Gestures: Emerging and Emergent

Temporal features of spoken language have also been studied in relation to the temporalities of the broader activities in which it is embedded (Mondada 2012; Streeck, Goodwin and LeBaron 2011) and the bodily communication modalities that accompany it (Deppermann and Streeck 2018), including posture, gesture, and gaze. The enormous temporal elasticity of spoken language has been appraised in contexts such as surgery (Mondada 2011) and dance instruction (Keevallik 2015), where precision timing and synchronization of component acts are of paramount importance. A bodily communication modality whose temporal features and coordination with spoken language are exceptionally well understood are hand gestures. Gestures are transitory in much the same way as spoken words are, and yet, even though gestures can be "frozen" and held in ways language sounds cannot, they appear to be even more ephemeral than words, and certainly more elusive. This is so because hand gestures rarely receive conscious attention in the way words do, neither by viewers nor makers, and therefore, unless we retrain our attention, we cannot normally say what gestures we have just seen or made. Moreover, hand gestures, although they are visual phenomena, do not lend themselves to graphic abstraction in the way phonemes do. Finally and ironically, even though writing systems are made up of habitualized gestures, gestures cannot be written. Gestures do not leave traces on our minds the way words do, and yet "latency" phenomena are very common in gesture, as we will see below.

Like spoken language, gesture is a communication modality characterized by great temporal elasticity, and its temporal features and temporal coordination with pragmatic, semantic, syntactic, and prosodic units of speech are well understood, thanks in large part to the studies of Adam Kendon (Kendon 1972, 1980, 2004). One remarkable feature is that hand gestures often precede their spoken affiliates and thus *project* them, show that they are "in play" (Schegloff 1984). For example, depictive gestures tend to be performed before the descriptive noun phrases with which they co-refer are uttered, and a gesture that displays the nature of a speech act is often found at the beginning of or just prior to that speech act, "pre-viewing" it (Streeck and Hartge 1992). Coordination, thus, does not necessarily mean synchrony in the emerging of gesture and speech.

But here I want to focus on gestures not only as emerging, but also as sedimenting and thus as *emergent* phenomena, in the sense in which Hopper has defined the term: as communicative actions that are "on the way" to attaining system-like, transcendent properties by becoming independent of specific, concrete situations and environments and capable of giving structure to classes of situations or environments. In the case of gesture, this process resembles lexicalization more than grammaticalization. In the following, I examine and discuss the trajectory of hand gestures from invention to sedimentation, from indexical to displaced and abstract reference, and from indexical meaning-making to iconic representation and symbolization. Gesture researchers cannot draw on the kind of evidence that historical linguists can: whereas the comparative methods of historical linguists produce reliable reconstructions of earlier historical stages of a language and thus of paths of derivation and descent, we have no evidence of "earlier stages" of any "gestural system"—and do not even know what the term "system" could possibly mean with respect to gesture, given that we cannot exclude any hand movement from the domain of gesture as we can decide that a string of words is not a sentence in a given language.

Hand gestures have so far been studied as spontaneous productions of individuals, revealing their thought processes at the time (e.g., Goldin-Meadow 2003; McNeill 2005); as recurrent cultural forms, examined for their functions in varying interactional contexts (e.g., Kendon 1995; Müller 2003); and as situated, locally organized indexical practices by which objects and environments are annotated (Goodwin 2007; LeBaron and Streeck 2000). Much of my own research on gesture, however, has developed from a corpus of the gestures that a single person made during the course of one (work) day (approximately five thousand). That person is the very busy owner of an auto repair shop, and he copes with an incessant onslaught of problems that are cognitively complex yet "hands on" and often require extensive and precise communication (with employees, customers, and suppliers). Hand gestures in varying capacities are indispensable components of this person's communicative equipment, and the data enables us to see how he invents and reuses them and then takes them to new communicative situations. In other words, we see some of this person's communicative equipment *as it evolves*; we can track its trajectory from invention to sedimentation. I analyze this trajectory as a sequence of three abstractions: from action or sensation to gesture; from indexical to displaced reference; and from literal to metaphorical significance.

First Abstraction: From Action to Gesture

In the first data extract (extract 1), the shop owner, Mr. C., is trying to figure out why a customer's car does not start. The customer, Ms. N., is standing by, watching him. He removes the air filter from the carburetor and promptly diagnoses a misplaced bracket as the likely problem source: it keeps the choke closed so that the engine is burning too much gas without gaining any power.[1] He takes the bracket between his fingers and repositions it, experimenting with the fit. When he finds it and realizes that the bracket needs to be repositioned by reorienting it 90 degrees, he abstracts from the action the moment when it fails—the bracket gets pushed down instead of staying in place—and repeats it several times, demonstrating to the customer how the bracket can and apparently has been misplaced (see figure 3.1). Then he reinserts the bracket in its right position and promises that he will "do something to make it stick here." (Dots in the transcript identify the moments when the screen shots were taken.)

```
1      Mr. C. This ( - - ) I just pick up this • like this
              ( - - - - )
2             It should go here like th•is.
              (1.0)
3             You see?
              (1.0)
4             By accident.
```

```
5              That's why it make no power,
6              it's closed on the choke here.
7              It's close the choke like this, you see?
               (- - -)
10             By accident somebody did this.
               (- - - -)
11             Like th•is.
               (- - - -)
12             Like this.
13             You push ga:s it won't accelerate good.
14             But I wanna do something to make it stick here now.
```

The "gesture" here is simply the simulating repetition of the action of misplacing the bracket. The gesture is not a form, but an operation: an instrumental (and in this case faulty) act is repeated for communicative purposes; the actor discloses a state of affairs by demonstratively repeating his own failure. This is a basic mimetic practice. Understanding what is being communicated does not require much beyond understanding the instrumental act itself and seeing that it does not end in success. This primary understanding is grounded in our human ability to make sense of the bodily acts of others by recognizing how they relate to their *Umwelt* (Uexküll 1957)

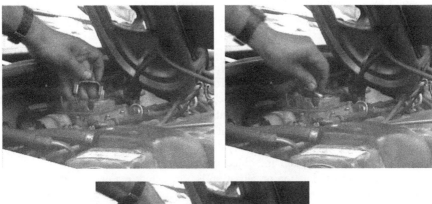

Figure 3.1. Action performed and repeated

or ecological niche; it is not mediated by signs.[2] This point is important. If we want to explain in a noncircular fashion how bodily signs emerge—and have originally emerged—in the midst of human activity, we cannot assume a preestablished order of sign-mediated understanding. Rather, understanding bodily signs such as the indexical operations in extract 1 presupposes the *direct* understanding of the actions upon which they are performed and whose relevant features they extract.

Mimesis is the deliberate reproduction of an action for communication (or rehearsal; Kirsh 2010). Donald writes: "Mimesis rests on the ability to produce conscious, self-initiated, representational acts that are...not linguistic.... Mimesis is fundamentally different from imitation...in that it involves the *invention* of intentional representations.... Mimetic representation involves the ability to 'parse' one's own motor actions into components and then recombine these components in various ways, to reproduce the essential features of an event.... Mimetic skill results in the sharing of knowledge" (Donald 1991, 168–73).

Observing Mr. C. in extract 1, we do not recognize and make sense of a specific gesture but rather understand the *operation* that extracts meaning from a recent instrumental act. The operation is a basic practice of mimetic communication. Of course, it is an indexical mode of communication: the communicative act derives meaning from its contiguity with the instrumental act. The gestured version abstracts and sediments the essential feature of the situation, the misplacement of the bracket.

The abstraction exemplified in extract 1 in which a state of affairs is made transparent by a gestural repetition of an object-related act is only one of several ways in which instrumental acts disclose and display meaning when they become transformed into gestures. The auto shop is also home to frequent *exploratory* actions of the hands, actions geared toward extracting properties—qualia—from objects. Modes of "active touch" (Gibson 1962), too, can be amplified and modified to communicative ends, broadcasting properties and states of objects to which only the hand has direct access. What matters in such cases are the *transmodal* capacities of the human hand (cf., the fact that it can gather information [sensations] in one sensory modality [through touch] but display it in another [visually]). The perceived "light" quality of someone's touch can convey the soft texture of an object's surface, the brevity of contact between palm and object can convey that it is hot.

When a situated action or sensation is abstracted in a gesture, it is being *sedimented* at the same time. It is recorded in a form, and that form can then be reenacted or performed to evoke the original experience and analyze it or analyze some other situation or experience by analogy to it.[3]

Second Abstraction: Displaced Reference

After repairing the car—he uses a wire to secure the bracket in its proper place—we can see Mr. C. take the gesture that he formed during the inspection to another context, a postmortem with the author. He explains to him what the problem was and in the process performs a schematic and modified version of the action with which he demonstrated the bracket's misplacement to his customer. Once an indexical gesture has been sedimented and its meaning "fixed" in the presence of the object with which it is coupled, it can be taken to another context to evoke the original event. The gesture is now used for displaced reference. Originating "where hands meet things" (LeBaron and Streeck 2000, 120), it is "pulled off of" the object (abstracted—"pulled off from," the root meaning of Latin *abs-trahere*) and brought into an environment where it serves as an image, a representation of the original "involvement whole" (Dreyfus 1991) of hand and thing. Applying Peirce's terminology, we would call this an iconic gesture. Mr. C. performs a schematic "reposition bracket" action with his right hand as he holds his left hand supine, using it as a ground on which the depictive gesture—and figuratively the object to which it refers—is placed.

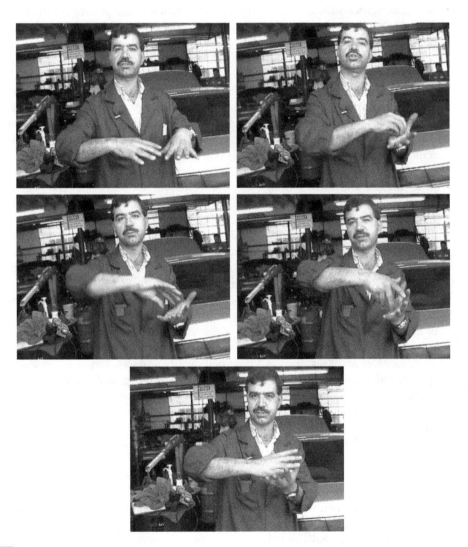

Figure 3.2. Actions reenacted, depicted, generalized, and conceptualized

```
1  Mr. C.    And accidentally she pulled that,
2            and it's missing the safety lock.
3            And when she put it b•ack together
4            she don't know how it should g•o.
5  J         Right.
6  Mr. C.    And she put it d•ifferent way,
7            she fl•ip it,
8            and she make the choke cl•ose.
```

Comparing the two gestures (see figures 3.2A and 3.2C–D), we see that they are quite different, the first being much closer to the original action (see the similarity of hand shapes in figures 3.1A and 3.2C). The second iteration of the gesture is further removed not only in time, but also in shape from the original; the hand's prehensile posture corresponds to the whole of the bracket, not the rod by which it was in reality held (visible in figures 3.1B and 3.2D). The hand's posture is thus abstracted further from the object it once held. When he says "she make the choke close," Mr. C.'s "making close(d)" gesture is even more removed from any action on his part, because his hand now simulates the action of the choke itself, a round disk that he had pointed out to his customer when he began to inspect the carburetor of her car. The gestural depictions in the series in extract 2 are increasingly abstract, i.e., removed from the setting that the gesturing hands had previously explored and experienced.

Compared to actions in the material world during which hands physically couple with concrete and specific things, gestural depictions are schematic[4] and generic. Often, motion pattern and hand shape are altered, simplified, or amplified, in line with the communicative task at hand. But it is the same procedural knowledge, knowing *how to perform* the generic manual act, that governs both instrumental action and gesture. In other words, the gesture, as it is performed away from the world, retains the sense and the "muscle," or "motor memory" (Kirsh 2010; Krakauer and Shadmehr 2006), of real actions in the material world.

Action gestures—gestures abstracted from material, object-related actions—are versatile depictive devices, as they implicitly always refer to objects as well, either in the role of undergoer or instrument of the action. Understanding iconic gestures requires that we are familiar with the world that the gestures evoke (a world of tangible, movable objects, masses and their malleability, surfaces, and so on, as well as specific, culturally meaningful artifacts), which can be recognized in motions of the hand. Researchers who are studying emerging home and village sign systems in small communities with a handful of deaf members report that such schematized actions are the first depictive signs that develop and that they are enacted not only to refer to actions but also to objects on which or with which they are routinely performed (Haviland 2013; Tkachman and Sandler 2013).

Thus, while the primary gestural abstraction is the derivation of an enactive manual schema from a specific practical action in the world at hand, a second abstraction occurs when the gesture is taken out of its original habitat and becomes a device for displaced reference—i.e., for reference from within one context to another, spatiotemporally distant one—or cross-contextual representation and depiction, designed and able to evoke actions, objects, or scenes in their absence. This marks the transition from *indexical* to *iconic* communication. It corresponds to the turn from "side-by-side" communication with a joint focus on the *Umwelt*, or an object at hand, to face-to-face communication about an *absent* world. Leroi-Gourhan (1993) has argued that in human history, displaced reference is the result of an expansion of the operating chains of material reproduction, from the face-to-face society of consociates to distant yet reachable communities and their habitats, and thus the beginning of trade and the making of *polyliths* (Goodwin 2018; Reynolds 1994), i.e., artifacts made from heterogeneous parts that originate in different places. When that happened, human groups began to transcend mimetic culture and enter the stage that Donald (1991, ch. 7) calls "mythic culture," characterized by the ability to describe and explain the world in stories and language. But even in our own "theoretic culture" (1991, ch. 8), characterized not only by symbolic language but also by "external memory storage" in the form of writing and other representational artifacts, mimetic culture has not disappeared but continues to enable and underwrite the conduct of face-to-face interaction and symbolic communication, and broadly the transmission and acquisition of corporeal skills, including the speaking of language (Goodwin 2018). Mimesis continues to feed the emergence of new gestural signs in contemporary interactions, some of them becoming sedimented in some group's shared habitus, others disappearing after the activity in which they originate ends.

Third Abstraction: Metaphor

The auto-shop owner ended his account of the problem with a three-part summary— "all the car smoke, wasting gas, no power"—each part of which he accompanied with a hand-over gesture, a forward rotation of the hand that ended in a presentation posture, the palm facing up, the first two one-handed, the third and final one bilateral. The nondominant hand is held open and facing up like a receptacle during the first two gestures, a residue of a prior, two-handed depiction.

```
1   All the car smoke,
2   wasting gas
3   no power.
```

Figuratively, Mr. C. is handing over facts, and the progression from one-handed to bimanual action appears to mark the third one as a result of the first two and the statement as a conclusion. The gesture is an operation on the discourse itself, selecting parts of it as if they were things that can be held in hand and handed over to someone else. The hands speak the language of object transfer. Of course, gestures are often fuzzier in form than action verbs like "present" and "give" and "hand over" suggest, and minimal variations in the trajectory or effort of movement or in hand shape can suggest redescriptions. For example, a terminal "freezing" or hold of a "hand-over" gesture makes it appear as a presenting rather than a giving motion, but when the hand then stays in this position, depending on the listener's reaction, it can transform into a solicitation, an empty receptacle waiting to be filled by the listener's response. While our descriptive verbs sometimes appear overdetermined and overly specific, it

Figure 3.3. Conclusions handed over: "All the car smoke, wasting gas, no power"

is not possible to render the sense that the hand gestures convey by describing them in strictly etic terms. Humans do not perceive motion, but action, in the movement of other human bodies, and usually viewers agree on the sense that they take away from familiar gestures such as those of the hand-over kind.[5] Viewers also seem to feel that these gestures are "transitive" actions in the sense that they imply an intentional object: they are schematic versions of actions that do something *to* something, and that something must be inferred.[6] Given that there is nothing that is *literally* handed over, this kind, like many other gestures that speakers make when they gesture without depicting any referential object, action, and so on, is a kind of metaphorical gesture.[7]

How do these *symbolic* hand-over gestures relate to the concrete, indexical, and iconic bracket-repositioning gestures in extracts 1 and 2? The hand-over gestures neither have a recent situated origin and history, nor have they transparently been abstracted from actions that involve some *specific* physical object. We can only speculate about their history, their trajectory from invention to sedimentation as a commonly enacted gestural metaphor, but we can do so in two different ways. On the one hand, following the suggestion inherent in the concept of metaphor itself, we can construe the trajectory as an imaginative projection, from one domain of experience, a concrete one, onto another, abstract one (cf. Lakoff and Johnson 1980). There is assumed to be a direct mapping from source-domain to target-domain. Alternatively, we can conceive the developmental trajectory as a stepwise generalization, comparable to the "clines" that characterize the sedimentation of grammatical morphemes in spoken languages, in which acts of presenting, giving, and soliciting were gradually generalized to an ever-widening range of contexts, along with—or perhaps in the aftermath of—other gestural acts that have migrated from physical to social and discursive contexts, such as gestures of rejection, exclusion, removal, and demotion. "Conduit gestures" (McNeill 1992), which figure the conversational process as a transaction with objects or as a conduit through which things can travel, have been interpreted by cognitive psycholinguists as vehicles—bodily expressions—of a more encompassing underlying (mental) "conceptual metaphor," the so-called "conduit metaphor" (Reddy 1979), that is, a culturally shared thought formation.

    Given the frequency of hand-over gestures not only in this corpus, but everywhere we look, it is evident that, even though Mr. C.'s hand-over gestures are among his personal habits, they are not an idiosyncratic habit. Rather, they are enactments of cultural forms, routines that are sedimented "in society" and incorporated by mimesis, by incessant observations of others in conversation. Note that I am suggesting that some gestures emerge via abstraction from concrete personal action and experience; others, which presumably have come into existence in a similar fashion, have become common symbolic currency and are thus acquired as "prefabricated" forms/practices. Given, furthermore, the transcultural ubiquity of conduit gestures, instead of regarding them as expressions of a widespread, if not universal, cognitive model of discourse, one can regard them as an expression of the distinct cognitive style and *being-in-the-world* of the human life-form, which both center around a pair of hands (Sheets-Johnstone 2012; Streeck 2017).

Discussion

Observing one person's hand gestures as he copes with the routine yet complex communicative tasks of a day, we see that at times he "invents" gestures by abstracting a schematic (object-less) motor-action schema from his own manual actions in the world. But the term "invention"—Donald (1991) writes of "symbolic inventions"—is perhaps not quite appropriate here, as the gesture's emergence is rather a simple, mindless, quasi-automatic operation: the hand simply retracts from its counterpart, the object, but continues what it is doing. The ingenuity of our ancestral inhabitants and makers of mimetic culture was to recognize the communicative—and later the symbolic—potential of that little abstraction. It is the beginning of simulation, and it begins to feed a cumulative culture when simulations are reiterated and sedimented as habits. However, while Donald (1991, 168) suggests that "mimesis rests on the ability to produce conscious, self-initiated, representational acts," I do not think that these quasi-automatic representational versions of actions require prior conscious intent. Rather, as G. H. Mead (1934) has proposed, human consciousness has arisen from the organism's "ex post facto" recognition of the communicative intent driving its own actions by way of the responses of others. Consciousness is an epiphenomenon of communication, not a precondition for it.

    At other times we see this person depict the actions he has recently taken and what his hands have detected, relying on his "muscle memory" as he transports the motor patterns of these actions into other situations, at a later time, perhaps not unlike the ancient hunter-gatherer or proto-trader returning home and having relevant experiences to share. This constitutes a step forward from indexical to iconic signs. When we think of it as an achievement of our ancestral mimetic culture, we can see in it an example of one way in which embodied knowledge, acquired by single bodies, was being shared in part by simulative re-performances. This transition also marks the beginnings of "conversation," of face-to-face communication *about* the world in its absence, of *displaced reference*. Leroi-Gourhan (1993) posited that displaced reference and ultimately language presuppose a spatial expansion of the *operating chains* of hominine. Only displaced reference requires iconic communication; face-to-face societies living in the here and now can get by on purely indexical means (Tomlinson 2015). When gestures are invented and then "reused" in the manner described in this chapter (from exploratory action to gestural narration), the process replicates or re-instantiates that broad shift from indexical, "hands-on," "jointly focused," world-*disclosing* communication to detached, "uncoupled," mutually focused, world-*representing* communication. In sum, as we observe Mr. C. abstract iconic gestures from his recent actions we see a prehistoric turn reenacted. Mimesis continues to feed the emergence of new gestures, which may be reiterated and sedimented for just a while or escape their original context and begin to circulate within some community.

Finally, we saw Mr. C. make motions whose forms were indistinguishable from iconic or depictive gestures but which were transparently not about the world "out there," but about the present communicative act itself. Mr. C. represented his reportings of facts as acts of handing over things. He represented the communicative act as a specific physical act, in an act of manual conceptualization or symbolization. However, we noted that Mr. C.'s gestures here, in contrast to the ones in extracts 1 and 2, were not really "his" gestures, grounded in his own body's experience, but "the culture's," shared by everyone and kept in circulation by unbroken chains of mimesis and repetition. We cannot observe nor reconstruct the genesis of these gestures that everyone makes, even though the imagery they provide makes sense to us.

Conversation analysis has taught us a great deal about the sociotemporal nature of spoken language as our prime medium of social interaction and about the need to think of language units in terms of their emerging over time. Grammaticalization research discloses the temporality of language by revealing that the seemingly fixed, "prefabricated" schematic constructions and categories that make up the grammars of human languages are in fact unstable, interim products of the *activity* of speaking. Grammar, writes Bybee,

> is *automatization* or "chunking" of motor actions.... Grammatical constructions of all types are automated, generalized motor routines and subroutines that can be strung together or embedded in one another to produce fluent speech.... The changes in form that occur in the grammaticalization process closely resemble changes that occur as nonlinguistic skills are practiced and become automatized. With repetition, sequences or units that were previously independent come to be processed as a single unit or chunk.... The whole chunk begins to reduce in form.... These basic principles of automatization apply to all kinds of motor activities: playing a musical instrument, playing a sport, stirring pancake batter (Bybee 1998, 153).

The processes of grammaticalization that are being studied all take place within connected discourse or conversation, a mode of interaction that I have described as being "turned away from," not physically engaged with, the world. Grammaticalization processes such as the rise of spatial prepositions, conjunctions, and many other forms can only take place within connected discourse. As if to spite their own name, conversation analysts instead have turned more and more to—and have become deeply immersed in the study of—interaction within and with the material world, in settings in which talk and gesture are "environmentally coupled" (Goodwin 2007) and working toward a broader understanding of the multimodality of human interaction and communication. What we do not have is any developed understanding of ways in which "early" indexical means of linguistic communication evolve that function only in combination with bodily acts and that are grounded in mimetic, preconceptual, intercorporeal understandings. Keevallik, who has studied grammatical forms and the coordination of body movement and syntax in the context of such activities as dance instruction (2015) and cleaning out a sheep staple (2018a), has recently raised the question "What does embodied interaction tell us about grammar?" and proposed to seek to explain certain grammatical constructions in terms of their functioning within specific contexts of embodied interaction (Keevallik 2018b).

I hope to have illustrated here that, looking at the right kind of data, we can witness how symbolic action evolves from nonsymbolic motor action and how meaning is literally taken by hands from the things with which they engage and sedimented as form by repetition, and, at times, incorporation by others. Not so much parts of any grammar, these gestures constitute a transitory, ephemeral manual lexicon and coexist in everyday discourse with "historically evolved," seemingly timeless forms, gestures premade, as it were, by the "invisible hand" (Keller 1994) and inherited by every new member of the culture. As we observe the abstractions involved in the emergence and sedimentation of gestures, we witness a process that is arguably "older" than grammaticalization, enabled by preconceptual modes of mimetic understanding (Müller 2016), tied initially to the here and now but then available for reference and depiction across space and time. We observe how intersubjectivity mediated by signs emerges quasi-automatically from intercorporeality, from our socialized bodies' understanding of what, in this shared world, the other body is up to in this scene at this moment, moving in the way that it does.

What makes the present moment in time so exciting for our field is that we are now able to observe and track the full range of embodied social and cognitive processes that constitute the ongoing origin and evolution of language and mind, and to study them in ways that are adequate to their temporal features as living, unfolding, and embodied phenomena.

Notes

1 These scenes are analyzed in greater detail in Streeck 2017, chs. 4 and 5. The video recordings can be viewed on the author's website: http://jurgenstreeck.net.
2 See Hutchins and Johnson (2009) and Andrén (2017) for analogous arguments and examples.

3   The meanings abstracted from objects and the environment by the gesturalization of exploratory or instrumental actions can also be inscribed upon the objects themselves. Thus, once handled and bespoken in a certain kind of way, an object can "embody" and "retain" these specific senses that the actions have taken from or impressed upon it (Streeck 1996).

4   Note that the Greek word "schema" originally denoted a wrestler's hold; schematization in the context of gesture often involves characteristic "prehensile postures," which define classes of objects that can be held in the manner depicted.

5   Adam Kendon has given a comprehensive account of what he calls the "o"-family, a family of open-handed gestures (Kendon 2004, ch. 13; Müller 2003).

6   The gestures are intentional by being about an object, not in the sense that they are made with any specific intention (goal). For a more detailed account of this and other metaphorical gestures, see Streeck (2008; 2009, ch. 7; 2017, ch. 5.8). Andrén (2017) has studied in detail how in the communication of young children the successive stages of object transfer give rise to gestures.

7   About gestures as metaphors, see Cienki and Müller (2009); Müller (2007).

References

Andrén, Mats. 2017. Children's expressive handling of objects in a shared world. In Christian Meyer, Jürgen Streeck and J. Scott Jordan (eds.), *Intercorporeality: Emerging socialities in interaction*. Oxford: Oxford University Press. 105–42.

Auer, Peter. 1996. The pre-front field in spoken German and its relevance as a grammaticalization position. *Pragmatics* 6 (3): 295–322.

———. 2009. On-line syntax: Thoughts on the temporality of spoken language. *Language Sciences* 31: 1–13.

———. 2015. Reflections on Hermann Paul as a usage-based grammarian. In Peter Auer and Robert W. Murray (eds.), *Hermann Paul's "Principles of Language History" revisited*. Berlin: de Gruyter. 177–207.

Auer, Peter and Stefan Pfänder (eds.). 2011. *Constructions. Emerging and emergent*. Berlin: de Gruyter.

Bybee, Joan L. 1998. Cognitive processes in grammaticalization. In Michael Tomasello (ed.), *The new psychology of language* (vol. II). Mahwah, NJ: Lawrence Erlbaum. 145–68.

Cienki, Alan and Cornelia Müller (eds.). 2009. *Metaphor and gesture*. Amsterdam: John Benjamins.

Deppermann, Arnulf and Jürgen Streeck (eds.). 2018. *Time in embodied interaction*. Amsterdam: John Benjamins.

Donald, Merlin. 1991. *Origins of the modern mind*. Cambridge, MA: Harvard University Press.

Dreyfus, Hubert L. 1991. *Being-in-the-world: A commentary on Heidegger's* Being and Time, *division I*. Cambridge, MA: MIT Press.

Ford, Cecilia E. and Barbara A. Fox. 2015. Ephemeral grammar: At the far end of emergence. In Arnulf Deppermann and Susanne Günthner (eds.), *Temporality in interaction*. Amsterdam: John Benjamins. 95–122.

Ford, Cecilia E., Barbara A. Fox and Sandra A. Thompson. 1998. Social interaction and grammar. In Michael Tomasello (ed.), *The new psychology of language* (vol. II). Mahwah, NJ: Lawrence Erlbaum. 119–44.

Gibson, James J. 1962. Observations on active touch. *Psychological Review* 69 (6): 477–91.

Givón, Talmy and Bertram F. Malle. 2002. *The evolution of language out of pre-language*. Amsterdam: John Benjamins.

Goldin-Meadow, Susan. 2003. *Hearing gesture: How our hands help us think*. Cambridge, MA: Belknap Press of Harvard University Press.

Goodwin, Charles. 2007. Environmentally coupled gestures. In Susan D. Duncan, Justine Cassell and Elena T. Levy (eds.), *Gesture and the dynamic dimension of language: Essays in honor of David McNeill*. Amsterdam: John Benjamins. 195–212.

———. 2018. *Co-operative action*. Cambridge: Cambridge University Press.

Haviland, John B. 2013. The emerging grammar of nouns in a first generation sign language: Specification, iconicity, and syntax. *Gesture* 13 (3): 309–53.

Heine, Bernd, Ulrike Claudi and Friederike Hünnemeyer. 1991. *Grammaticalization. A conceptual framework.* Chicago: University of Chicago Press.

Hopper, Paul J. 1992. Emergence of grammar. In William Bright (ed.), *International encyclopedia of linguistics* (vol. I). Oxford: Oxford University Press. 364–67.

——. 1998. Emergent grammar. In Michael Tomasello (ed.), *The new psychology of language: Cognitive and functional approaches to language structure* (vol. I). Mahwah, NJ: Lawrence Erlbaum. 155–76.

——. 2011. Emergent grammar and temporality in interactional linguistics. In Peter Auer and Stefan Pfänder (eds.), *Constructions: Emerging and emergent.* Berlin: de Gruyter. 22–44.

——. 2015. Hermann Paul's emergent grammar. In Peter Auer and Robert W. Murray (eds.), *Hermann Paul's 'Principles of Language History' revisited.* Berlin: de Gruyter. 237–56.

Hopper, Paul J. and Elizabeth Closs Traugott. 1993. *Grammaticalization.* Cambridge: Cambridge University Press.

Hutchins, Edwin and Christine M. Johnson. 2009. Modeling the emergence of language as an embodied collective cognitive activity. *Topics in Cognitive Science* 1 (3): 523–46.

Keevallik, Leelo. 2015. Coordinating the temporalities of talk and dance. In Arnulf Deppermann and Susanne Günthner (eds.), *Temporality in interaction.* Amsterdam: John Benjamins. 309–35.

——. 2018a. The temporal organization of conversation while mucking out a sheep stable. In Arnulf Deppermann and Jürgen Streeck (eds.), *Time in embodied interaction.* Amsterdam: John Benjamins. 97–122.

——. 2018b. What does embodied interaction tell us about grammar? *Research on Language & Social Interaction* 51 (1): 1–21.

Keller, Rudi. 1994. *On language change: The invisible hand in language.* London: Routledge.

Kendon, Adam. 1972. Some relationships between body motion and speech. In Aron Wolfe Seigman and Benjamin Pope (eds.), *Studies in dyadic communication.* Elmsford, NY: Pergamon Press. 177–210.

——. 1980. Gesticulation and speech: Two aspects of the process of utterance. In M. R. Kay (ed.), *The relationship between verbal and nonverbal behavior.* The Hague: Mouton. 207–77.

——. 1995. Gestures as illocutionary and discourse structure markers in Southern Italian conversation. *Journal of Pragmatics* 23 (3): 247–79.

——. 2004. *Gesture: Visible action as utterance.* Cambridge: Cambridge University Press.

Kirsh, David. 2010. Thinking with the body. In Stellan Ohlsson and Richard Catrambone (eds.), *Proceedings of the 32nd Annual Conference of the Cognitive Science Society.* Austin, TX: Cognitive Science Society. 2864–69.

Krakauer, John W. and Reza Shadmehr. 2006. Consolidation of motor memory. *Trends in Neurosciences* 29: 58–64.

Lakoff, George and Mark Johnson. 1980. *Metaphors we live by.* Chicago: University of Chicago Press.

Laury, Ritva, Marja Etelämäki and Elizabeth Couper-Kuhlen. 2014. Introduction (to special issue: "Approaches to grammar for interactional linguistics"). *Pragmatics* 24 (3): 435–52.

LeBaron, Curtis D. and Jürgen Streeck. 2000. Gestures, knowledge, and the world. In David McNeill (ed.), *Language and gesture.* Cambridge: Cambridge University Press. 118–38.

Leroi-Gourhan, André. (1964) 1993. *Gesture and speech* (trans: Anna Bostock Berger). Cambridge, MA: MIT Press.

McNeill, David. 1992. *Hand and mind. What gestures reveal about thought.* Chicago: University of Chicago Press.

——. 2005. *Gesture and thought.* Chicago: University of Chicago Press.

Mead, George Herbert. 1934. *Mind, self and society.* Chicago: University of Chicago Press.

Mondada, Lorenza. 2011. The organization of concurrent courses of action in surgical demonstrations. In Jürgen Streeck, Charles Goodwin and Curtis LeBaron (eds.), *Embodied interaction: Language and body in the material world.* New York: Cambridge University Press. 207–26.

——. 2012. Talking and driving: Multiactivity in the car. *Semiotica* 191: 233–56.

Müller, Cornelia. 2003. Forms and uses of the palm up open hand. In Cornelia Müller and Roland Posner (eds.), *The semantics and pragmatics of everyday gestures: Proceedings of the Berlin conference 1988.* Berlin: Weidler. 234–56.

———. 2007. A dynamic view of metaphor, gesture, and thought. In Susan D. Duncan, Justine Cassell and Elena T. Levy (eds.), *Gesture and the dynamic dimension of language: Essays in honor of David McNeill*. Amsterdam: John Benjamins. 109–16.

———. 2016. From mimesis to meaning: A systematics of gestural mimesis for concrete and abstract referential gestures. In Jordan Zlatev, Göran Sonesson and Piotr Konderak (eds.), *Meaning, mind and communication: Explorations in cognitive semiotics*. Frankfurt am Main: Peter Lang. 211–26.

Reddy, Michael J. 1979. The conduit metaphor: A case of frame conflict in our language about language. In Andrew Ortony (ed.), *Metaphor and thought*. Cambridge: Cambridge University Press. 284–324.

Reynolds, Peter C. 1994. The complementary theory of language and tool use. In Kathleen R. Gibson and Tim Ingold (eds.), *Tools, language and cognition in human evolution*. Cambridge: Cambridge University Press. 407–28.

Schegloff, E. A. 1979. On the relevance of repair to syntax-for-conversation. In Talmy Givón (ed.), *Discourse and syntax* (vol. 12). New York: Academic Press. 261–88.

———. 1984. On some gestures' relation to talk. In J. Maxwell Atkinson and John Heritage (eds.), *Structures of social action*. Cambridge: Cambridge University Press. 266–95.

———. 1996. Turn organization: One intersection of grammar and interaction. In Elinor Ochs, Emanuel A. Schegloff and Sandra Thompson (eds.), *Grammar and interaction*. Cambridge: Cambridge University Press. 52–133.

Schegloff, Emanuel A., Gail Jefferson and Harvey Sacks. 1977. The preference for self-correction in the organization of repair in conversation. *Language* 53 (2): 361–82.

Schutz, Alfred. (1932) 1967. *The phenomenology of the social world*. Evanston, IL: Northwestern University Press.

Sheets-Johnstone, Maxine. 2012. *The primacy of movement* (2nd ed.). Amsterdam: John Benjamins.

Streeck, Jürgen. 1995. On projection. In Esther N. Goody (ed.), *Social intelligence and interaction*. Cambridge: Cambridge University Press. 87–110.

———. 1996. How to do things with things: Objets trouvés and symbolization. *Human Studies* 19: 365–84.

———. 2008. Metaphor and gesture: A view from the microanalysis of interaction. In Alan Cienki and Cornelia Müller (eds.), *Metaphor and gesture*. Amsterdam: John Benjamins. 259–264.

———. 2009. *Gesturecraft. The manu-facture of meaning*. Amsterdam: John Benjamins.

———. 2017. *Self-making man: A day of action, life, and language*. New York: Cambridge University Press.

Streeck, Jürgen, Charles Goodwin and Curtis LeBaron (eds.). 2011. *Embodied interaction: Language and body in the material world*. New York: Cambridge University Press.

Streeck, Jürgen and Ulrike Hartge. 1992. Previews: Gestures at the transition place. In Peter Auer and Aldo di Luzio (eds.), *The contextualization of language*. Amsterdam: John Benjamins. 138–58.

Streeck, Jürgen and J. Scott Jordan (eds.). 2009. Anticipation and projection in embodied interaction. Special double issue. *Discourse Processes* 46: 2–3.

Tannen, Deborah. 2006. Intertextuality in interaction: Reframing family arguments in public and private. *Text & Talk* (Special issue: Family discourse, framing family) 26(4/5): 597–617. Guest editors, Deborah Tannen and Marjorie Harness Goodwin.

Tkachman, Oksana and Wendy Sandler. 2013. The noun-verb distinction in two young sign languages. *Gesture* 13 (3): 253–86.

Tomlinson, Gary. 2015. *A million years of music. The emergence of human modernity*. New York: Zone Books.

Uexküll, Jakob von. 1957. A stroll through the worlds of animals and men: A picture book of invisible worlds. In Claire H. Schiller (ed. and trans.), *Instinctive behavior: The development of a modern concept*. New York: International Universities Press. 5–80.

4

The Ambiguity and Polysemy of Power and Solidarity in Professor-Student Emails and Conversations among Friends

DEBORAH TANNEN

FINDING MYSELF HERE, ON the last day of the 2018 Georgetown University Round Table, I'm reminded of the Round Table I organized in 1981, "Analyzing Discourse: Text and Talk." Looking back from '18 to '81 calls to mind the evolution of the field as well as of my own theoretical perspectives over those thirty-seven years: nearly four decades of analyzing discourse. My remarks today will be a kind of personal as well as disciplinary retrospective. I will go back to Robin Lakoff's (1973) groundbreaking introduction of politeness theory (which is part of what inspired me to pursue the study of linguistics) and to Brown and Gilman's (1960) foundational notion of power and solidarity in order to explain what I refer to in my own work as the ambiguity and polysemy of power and solidarity, as well as the necessity of taking this dynamic into account in order to understand conversational interaction. I will illustrate these concepts in examples from two quite different domains: first, emails exchanged between professors and students, and second, conversations among women friends, the subject of my book *You're the Only One I Can Tell* (Tannen 2017).

Professor-Student Email Exchanges

I first began thinking about emails sent by professors to students as reflecting, and illuminating, the ambiguity and polysemy of power and solidarity when I read an assignment submitted to me by an undergraduate student. Among the requirements of the class in which this student was enrolled are what I call "field notes," in each of which students recount an interaction they participated in, then analyze it by applying theories and methods we covered in class. This student wrote a field note in which he presented and commented on an email exchange he had with a professor. Because he did not wish to identify the professor, and I therefore could not seek permission to quote the professor's emails, I will give an idea of the exchange, and of the student's comments on it, by presenting hypothetical emails that I wrote myself, patterned on the real ones that the student presented and analyzed but including no information or wording that could identify either the professor or the student.[1]

The exchange begins with a query posited by the student:

> Dear Professor Smith,
>
> I am in the process of registering for courses for next term and would like to make sure that a course I'm planning to take will fulfill a requirement for my degree. I have decided to take "Introduction to Understanding" and "Problems of International Negotiations." I know that the course "Problems of International Negotiations" can fulfill requirements for many other programs as well. Therefore, while I am sure "Introduction to Understanding" fulfills a requirement for my program, I just wanted to confirm that "Problems of International Negotiations" would also do so.
>
> Thank you for your attention.
>
> Yours truly,
>
> John Feffer

Here is the professor's response:

> Both courses will count for your program. However, Introduction to Understanding fulfills a specific requirement for your program while International Negotiations would count as an elective.

I didn't notice anything remarkable about this professor's reply. In my view, the student should have been satisfied, as the professor answered the question clearly and fully. But the student was not pleased. In his field note, he observed:

> No salutation, no signature! And since there is also a course titled "Approaches to International Negotiations," I needed to make sure the professor actually meant "Problems of International Negotiations." So I wrote again:

> Dear Professor,
>
> I appreciate your reply to my query. I just wanted to make sure that "Problems of International Negotiations" would be counted the same as "Approaches to International Negotiations." So I am writing to confirm that "Problems of International Negotiations" (which is what I would like to take) counts for my program.
>
> I am grateful for your clarification.
>
> With all best wishes, and with many thanks,
>
> John

The professor replied:

> Yes!

This reply also sounded unremarkable to me. It, too, answered John's question clearly. Moreover, the exclamation point evinced good will. What I found remarkable was John's comment on it:

"Yes!," that was it!

…

Again, the email included no salutation or proper closing. The monosyllabic reply made me feel that I was bothering the professor with my questions. It could even lead to misunderstandings, as it was so cryptic.

John went on to say that this professor's email style was not anomalous. Many professors, he complained, wrote similar emails, failing to observe proper email etiquette. In addition to resenting the omission of formal elements, John also complained that many professors' emails end with an automatic signature, another indication of disregard.

When I read this field note, I was stunned, not only because the professor's emails seemed perfectly acceptable to me but also—especially—because they closely resemble emails I myself had sent to students. It never occurred to me that they could be perceived as offensive. In order to learn whether John's reaction to this professor's, and other professors', emails was idiosyncratic, I read his field note to the class, which erupted in a chorus of agreement. The other students, too, said they regularly receive such emails from professors, and most also said that they too find them rude. I have gotten similar reactions from many classes since: every student is able to bring in similar examples—and they often do, for their own field notes, in which they explain why they find their professors' truncated email styles offensive.

My consciousness raised, I began to notice that most students' emails to me—especially those initiating a request or query—follow this pattern:

A salutation (usually in the form of Dear Professor Tannen)

An opening greeting (often the now-routinized hope that I'm well, or about the weather)

A full explanation of a request, in grammatical sentences with proper capitalization and punctuation

Closing well wishes and/or thanks

"Sincerely" (or the like)

Name (usually first name but sometimes full name)

I also began to notice that my responses tended to omit some or all of these elements, leaving only a substantive reply to the query, often in truncated form and devoid of the requirements of formal writing, like punctuation and capitalization.

Here is just one of many similar exchanges I was chagrined to find archived on my own server. A student sent the following request:

Hi Professor!

I hope your summer is going well! I'm starting to apply to internships for the fall, and I wanted to ask if you'd be willing to be included in my academic references? I don't believe I need any letters of recommendation, but I would like to provide the contact information of professors who know my work. Could you let me know if it's alright if I list you, and if so what contact information would be best? (which email address and/or office phone etc.).

Thanks so much!

Kate Thompson

It was all there: the salutation, including a respectful form of direct address (not my name, but "Professor"), the friendly opening greeting ("I hope your summer is going well!"), a full explanation of the request in grammatical, properly punctuated sentences, softened with circumlocutions ("I wanted to ask if...," "Could you let me know if..."), the friendly and appreciative closing ("Thanks so much!") and a signature ("Kate Thompson").

Here is how I responded. (Gwynne was my assistant at the time):

yes of course

best to use my official email address and phone: tannend@georgetown.edu 202/687-5910

that way Gwynne will be alerted and make sure I meet deadlines, etc.

Rereading this, I could hear John's—or any student's—potential complaint: "No greeting! No friendly beginning! No kind regards! No signature! No capitalization to start sentences or periods to end them!"

Faced with this incriminating evidence, I had to ask myself how I could justify such disregard, and why I had been oblivious to the negative impression my email style could, and in at least some cases would, make on recipients. The answer was obvious: the ambiguity of power and solidarity. Though I didn't think it through at the time, I am certain that I thought I was being casual and therefore friendly. In contrast, John (and, I now know, some and probably most other students) would interpret my informality as rude. In other words, the markers of informality were ambiguous: they could mean friendliness (solidarity) or disrespect (a reflection of my professorial power).

Though I am now keenly aware of this ambiguity, I continue to be surprised by the differing responses to email practices of which my students make me aware. Just recently, in a field note analyzing her own email exchange with a professor, a student complained that the professor "does not even take the time or effort to delete the 'Sent from my iPhone.'" Again, I was caught off guard to see my own practice disapproved—and, from my point of view, misinterpreted. When I use my iPhone to send emails, I leave that automatic warning so recipients will know that any infelicities in my message, including its brevity, are due to that mechanical limitation. How unfair—how ambiguous!—that the student gets the precise impression that I am trying to preclude: lack of care both for the message and for her.

This is just one of many assumptions I had taken for granted that I have learned are the opposite of students'. Another comment in a recent field note made me realize that the meaning of "casual" is itself ambiguous: the student used that very word to describe why she found a professor's email reply to a query rude: "he responded in a very blunt and casual manner." In explaining her reaction, she referred to the professor's use of the markers of informality I just illustrated in my own, and also to his signing off with his first name—something I'm willing to bet the professor thought would be appreciated. In her discussion, the student wrote that although she realizes the professor was probably trying to express solidarity, she "still found (and still finds) the bluntness and level of casualness in his email to be rude and condescending."

The term—the concept—"condescending" sheds light on the ambiguity of power and solidarity. Another of this student's comments explains this beautifully: "As a student who wrote a formal and much longer email, I expected at least a somewhat formal email back, and when I received the opposite, I interpreted the email as rude." What she went on to say is key: "It is generally understood that it would be rude for me, the student, to email him, the professor, in the fashion he emailed me, so to me, regardless of what his intent was, sending an email like this to me was not a sign of solidarity but rather one of power, and came across poorly." In other words, a professor's use of solidarity markers signals power because only professors have the option of using them in this context. Thus, professors' casualness in emails is not only ambiguous but also polysemous. That is, it can *both* be friendly *and* express power: I was indeed being friendly, but because only I had the privilege of choosing to be casual as a sign of friendliness, I was also expressing my power. Therein lies the polysemy of power and solidarity in professor-student emails.

This polysemy is pervasive in professor-student relationships, and therefore in our email exchanges. The student I'm calling John was offended that his professor did not address him by name, whereas he addressed the professor by name. But the name he used for his professor was title last name, whereas he would have liked his professor to address him by his first name. Had the professor done so, his salutation would have been polysemous: reflecting solidarity by matching John's use of a salutation, but reflecting the power differential by using first name whereas the student used title last name.

This power relationship is reflected, moreover, in the fact that the overwhelming majority of prior research examines students' and not professors' emails (Bella and Sifianou 2012; Biesenbach-Lucas 2007; Bolkan and Holmgren 2012; Boshrabadi and Sarabi 2016; Chejnová 2014; Chen 2015; Deveci and Hmida 2017; Economidou-Kogetsidis 2011; Ewald 2016; Hartford and Bardovi-Harlig 1996; Jones et al. 2016; Kim et al. 2016; Knupsky and Nagy-Bell 2011; Merrison et al. 2012; Mohamadi 2014; Nikleva 2018; Salazar Campillo 2018; Savić 2018, Stephens, Houser and Cowan 2009; Thomas-Tate, Daugherty and Bartkoski 2015; Zhu 2017). Those that examine professors' emails, or both, are far fewer (for example, Costello 2011; Dickinson 2017; Lam 2014, 2016).

The ubiquity of the contrast between professors' and students' emails, and the significance of the contrast, is reflected in this cartoon from a webcomic about the life of graduate students (see figure 4.1).[2] It is not by chance, furthermore, that this cartoon appears on a website for students. That I had paid no attention to the differences between my way of emailing students and their ways of emailing me in itself reflects the power difference between us. Paying no attention is a privilege enjoyed by professors, because offending students—as we often do, I was chagrined to learn—has few or no negative consequences for us, whereas there are many potential negative consequences for students if they offend professors.

AVERAGE TIME SPENT COMPOSING ONE E-MAIL

WWW.PHDCOMICS.COM

Figure 4.1. Cartoon showing contrast between a professor's and a grad student's emails, from the student's perspective (*Piled Higher and Deeper* by Jorge Cham, www.phdcomics.com)

Politeness Theory and Being Polite

The differences in email practices of professors and students take us into the territory not only of power and solidarity but also of politeness theory. I say this not only because students who object to the cryptic emails they receive from professors almost always say they found them "rude." Rather, I say it because the theoretical framework of power and solidarity is inextricably intertwined with that of politeness theory. That's why this technical sense of politeness is frequently confused with the common parlance notion of being polite. To unpack that claim, I'll begin with my own theoretical beginnings in the phenomenon I call conversational style and its relation to professor-student emails.

From the perspective of the nontechnical sense of politeness, my realization that students find emails like those I send rude is similar to the realization that inspired my dissertation and the theory of conversational style that I first developed there and have expanded and elaborated since: the shock I experienced as a (very polite) native of New York City finding myself considered rude in California. Among the sources of that unsettling result were discovering that questions intended to show interest were perceived as intrusive; that talking along to show enthusiastic listenership (what I later dubbed "cooperative overlap") was mistaken for interruption; and that respectful directness could come across as offensive bluntness. I attributed these and other misjudgments to differences in conversational style based on regional and ethnic influences. But how could the same ways of speaking be considered polite in one place and rude in another? I found a partial answer in Robin Lakoff's (1973) "rules of politeness," which inspired Brown and Levinson's ([1978] 1987) framework, which in turn inspired the now vast and ever-expanding literature on politeness theory (and its recent offshoot, impoliteness theory).

Lakoff devised her rules of politeness in response to Grice's (1967) rules of conversation, which she renamed "rules of clarity," pointing out that Grice's rules make sense only if clarity is the sole goal of an interaction—which, she also points out, it never is when humans are interacting. Her rules of politeness are

1. Don't impose
2. Give options
3. Make the other feel good; be friendly

Lakoff associates each rule with a communicative style: distance, deference, and camaraderie, respectively. I frequently illustrate these styles with reference to a hypothetical question, "Would you like something to drink?" A distant style, following rule 1, Don't impose, would lead to the reply "No thank you," whether or not the speaker is thirsty. A deferent style, following rule 2, Give options, might yield "I'll have whatever you're having." And camaraderie style, following rule 3, Be friendly, might result in "Yes, please, that would be lovely." A stronger form of camaraderie might lead to "I'd love a coke." Even stronger yet, a very close friend or family member might not wait to be offered but ask, "Have you got anything to drink?"—or go right to the refrigerator and help themselves. These varying ways of applying rule 3, Be friendly, are a reminder that an individual's style can reflect Lakoff's rules in different ways, to different degrees, and in different combinations.

Though Lakoff called her rules "politeness," her theory was not about being polite in the sense of polite vs. rude—what my student John referred to as "etiquette"—but rather in the sense of rules of politeness vs. rules of clarity. That is, she was suggesting that in order to understand the language of everyday conversation, linguists need a theory that takes into account the requirements of social interaction. That doesn't mean, however, that there is no relationship between her rules of politeness and the nontechnical notion of being polite. On the contrary, her rules provide a theoretical framework that accounts for what people assume to be polite or rude—and for cross-cultural differences in those assumptions.

Lakoff's rules of politeness did not derive from it, but I saw a connection to Brown and Gilman's 1960 article "The Pronouns of Power and Solidarity," which examines the choice of formal or informal second-person pronouns in languages that have such a pronominal distinction, such as French (*vous* and *tu*) and Spanish (*usted* and *tu*). A parallel in English is use of first name vs. title last name. Just as my student noted that a professor who writes noticeably casual emails is condescending, for Brown and Gilman it isn't the use of the pronoun *tu* (or of first name) that creates solidarity; rather, it is symmetry. Solidarity prevails when friends address each other by first name, but also when coworkers address each other by title last name. In contrast, power prevails not when the pronoun *vous* or title last name is used, but when the use of pronouns or forms of names is asymmetrical. In other words, if one party uses the informal pronoun or first name and the other must use the formal pronoun or title last name, they are in a relationship of unequal power. This is the norm when professors and students interact.

That scholars often lose sight of the ambiguity of power and solidarity became obvious to me when I encountered papers in the field—and there were many—that identified particular ways of speaking as serving power. (Scholars, for some reason, have been far more interested in identifying "power maneuvers" in discourse than in what I call "connection maneuvers.") I would immediately think of situations in which the same way of speaking could signal solidarity—and might, indeed, be intended to signal it in the very discourse under analysis. For example, it is common for scholars to refer to as "interruption" any instance in which a speaker begins speaking before another has finished. But I knew that such instances could be "cooperative overlap." That is, a speaker might begin speaking while another has the floor (hence "overlap") not in order to wrest the floor but to show enthusiastic listenership (hence, "coopera- tive"). In that case, the one who begins to speak assumes that the one speaking will not yield the floor unless they want to. This assumption is shared in a conversational ecosystem in which it is agreed that a really good conversation should have no per- ceptible silences, and a way to avoid such silences is to keep speaking (albeit in ways that signal you're running out of steam) until someone else begins. Thus, beginning to speak while another is speaking is ambiguous because it could be an interruption (an attempt to take the floor before the other is ready to relinquish it)—that is, a power play—or cooperative overlap (a way to show enthusiastic listenership and make sure there are no uncomfortable silences)—you might say, a connection play. Now imag- ine a conversation among a number of speakers who agree that exuberant use of not only cooperative overlap but also interruption makes for a really good conversation: everyone feels free to interrupt, so no one feels stymied or intruded upon if others try to take the floor while they're speaking. Everyone trusts that others who really don't want to yield the floor will just keep talking or return later to complete their thoughts. In this scenario, speaking along is polysemous, because it is both an attempt to take the floor while another has rights to it and a way of showing enthusiastic listenership. (For a fuller discussion of the ambiguity and polysemy of power and solidarity as seen in a range of linguistic strategies, see Tannen 1994.)

Conversations among Women Friends

Lakoff's rules of politeness, as well as the ambiguity and polysemy of power and solidarity, became pivotal again when I undertook a study of conversations among women friends (Tannen 2017). For example, two friends were taking a walk around a lake; one was telling the other about a personal problem. The listener occasionally interrupted her friend's account by pointing out something in their environment: a particularly beautiful flower or a duck followed by ducklings gliding in a line behind her across the surface of the lake. Suddenly, the speaker stopped walking and protest- ed, "You haven't listened to a word I've said." This exchange was reported to me by the listener, who told me she was hurt by her friend's accusation, and also baffled by it. Of course she'd been listening. She called her friend's attention to sights she believed her friend would appreciate not because she wasn't listening but because sharing enjoy- ment of their environment was another form of connection, analogous to and (in her view) reinforcing the connection created by troubles talk. It was ambiguous, because her friend interpreted her cooperative overlap, intended as a show of connection, as an interruption indicating she wasn't interested in her friend's talk.

Such potential ambiguity is ubiquitous in friendship, as in all relationships. A woman told me she was hurt because she had told a friend that her mother was in the hospital and the friend never asked how her mother was doing. When confront-ed, the friend said she had learned from her own family that one shouldn't ask about anything as sensitive as illness; if someone wants you to know, they will tell you. A similar ambiguity explains differing styles with respect to asking personal ques-tions: Is it a show of interest or nosy and intrusive? When a personal question, like a conversational move such as overlap, is meant as solidarity but taken as intrusive, it comes across as rude. And when solidarity is expected but not offered, that too can come across as rude. I was explaining to a friend who has what I have described as a "high-involvement style" about Robin Lakoff's rules of politeness. I pointed out that some speakers tend to apply Lakoff's rule Maintain camaraderie, while others tend to apply her rule Don't impose. My friend interjected, "But the not imposing is so offensive!"

In writing about everyday conversations, I sometimes refer not to power and solidarity but to the related concepts: competition and connection. For the study that led to my book about women friends, I held focused conversations with eighty girls and women between the ages of seven and ninety-seven. I call them "focused conversations" rather than "interviews" because I did not follow a preset protocol or ask a predetermined list of questions. Instead, I began by saying something like, "Tell me about your friendships with women." Sometimes I added options: "You can start with who your friends are now, or you can go back to your friends from childhood, or to who were the most important friends over your life." Sometimes I asked, later on, questions related to topics I knew I'd be interested in, like "Have you ever cut off a friend or been cut off?" (The example of friends walking around a lake emerged from one such focused conversation.) In these conversations, and in examples I encountered everywhere once I began thinking in these terms, it became clear that competition and connection are ambiguous and polysemous in women's friendships. An example emerged in an incident that occurred at the 2016 Olympics.

Anna and Lisa Hahner, identical twins representing Germany, came in eighty-first and eighty-second in the women's marathon. When a photo of the twins crossing the finish line holding hands was widely disseminated, they were criticized by German track and field officials for having been insufficiently competitive. In the words of the sports director of the German Athletics Federation, "Every athlete should be moti-vated to demonstrate his or her best performance and aim for the best possible result." He and his colleagues apparently felt that one or both runners had compromised their time in order to stay together—and to engineer their photo-op finish. But Anna explained that they hadn't planned to join hands. Unable to keep up with her sister's pace she had fallen behind, but: "After forty kilometers there was a turning point, and I knew, 'Okay Anna, two kilometers to go to close the gap to Lisa. I invested all I had and three hundred meters before the finish line, I was next to Lisa. It was a magical moment that we could finish this marathon together." It was the magic of that mo-ment that inspired them to spontaneously reach for each other's hands as they ap-proached the finish line.[3]

Was Anna Hahner driven by connection or competition? Did seeing her sister ahead of her trigger competition—she didn't want to be beaten by her sister—or connection—wanting to catch up to her sister, so they could finish together? It is ambiguous: it could have been either. It is also polysemous: the competitive urge not to let her sister beat her may have been indistinguishable from the lure of finishing together.

The connection-competition ambiguity seen in this example is inseparable from a dynamic particular to women's friendships, as to other relationships among women as well: the valorizing of being the same. Sameness was part of Brown and Gilman's (1960) definition of solidarity, which they described as a "set of relations which are symmetrical; for example, attended the same school, have the same parents, practice the same profession..." As far back as the research I conducted for my book *You Just Don't Understand: Women and Men in Conversation* (Tannen 1990), I encountered evidence that girls and women, more than boys and men, tend to speak in ways that emphasize sameness. This is seen in the iconic rejoinders, "I feel the same way"; "I do that, too"; and "The same thing happened to me." In our focused conversations, women often referred to sameness as a basis for friendship. For example, one woman said of a friend, "We have the same sense of humor. We are both complete dorks." Another said of her best friend, "We're both writers, both Japanese, and don't have children so we don't have to feign interest as we do in other friends' children." This speaker also said, "At first I thought we couldn't be friends because she's too beautiful and too high-strung," but as their talk turned to their cats, she began to feel a connection. This last example is significant not only because it references sameness as the basis for connection, but also because it assumes that competition is a barrier. The notion that a woman who is "too beautiful" could not be a friend is one of many comments I heard that indicated an assumption that a friend should not be better than you. In the conversations I conducted, and again, in many other contexts, I encountered examples of girls and women being rejected by friends because they excelled.

In her memoir *The Lost Landscape*, Joyce Carol Oates (2015, 123–24) tells how, when she was in seventh grade, she became a Methodist in order to get close to her friend Jean. A reverend in their church encouraged both girls to enter a competition to memorize a hundred verses of the Gospel according to St. John. Joyce excelled at this task, and she won the competition. But she lost her friend, who accused, "You think you're so smart!"—and ended the friendship. Accusations like "You think you're so smart!" were recalled by many women who told me of hurtful—even traumatic—endings of friendships when they were girls. When women told me about such hurtful experiences and recounted the accusations hurled by the rejecting friends, the vast majority were versions of "She's snobby," "She's stuck up," or "She thinks she's something." In other words, she thinks she's better.

Among the most striking such examples was told to me by a woman who said she still feels guilty because when she was in high school, her friend group turned on and ejected a girl who had been her good friend in junior high—and she didn't stand up for her, but instead went along with the group. "It's true," the woman said of the friend, "she was really good at sports and cute. And she had made friends with some older girls. But she didn't deserve what we did to her." This explanation took my breath away: being physically attractive and excelling at sports are characteristics that are often described as reasons that boys gain status in their groups. But here they were referred to as offenses. Though the woman who told me this did not say so explicitly, I heard unspoken in the background the accusation "She thought she was better than us."

If "I'm the same" reinforces connection, then "I'm different" can be heard as "I'm better," suggesting competition. And this tendency to not only value but demand sameness, in order to avoid implications of competition, was mentioned by several women I spoke to as reasons they find friendships with women to be challenging. One woman said she finds friendship with women "difficult terrain to navigate," and that consequently she prefers men as friends. To explain, she said that she finds men seem to expect difference, whereas her women friends can't abide it. If she expresses opinions different from theirs, they accuse her of being judgmental. Another woman expressed a similar sentiment: "My women friends don't let you be different. If a friend says she has a problem and I say, 'That's not a problem for me,' she complains, 'Don't put me down.'"

Even responses like "I'm the same" and "The same thing happened to me," which express—and help establish—connection can also express competition. When a friend responds to a troubles talk account by telling a matching story, it can be heard as a reassuring, "I'm the same." But it can also be heard as if the friend is saying, "Forget you. Let's talk about me." Or it can sound like she's implying that what happened to her is worse. That ambiguity arose in the following conversation, which was reported by a student in a field note written for my class.

The student, whom I'll call Helen, while studying with a friend I'll call Brooke, initiated a bit of troubles talk. Here's how Helen recalled the exchange:

> Helen: This is ridiculous. Everyone is getting to check things off, and I won't be done with a single class until next Thursday.
> Brooke: I would take that over my schedule! I have almost a hundred pages of papers to write by Monday. Please tell me how I'm supposed to not fail chemistry!
> Helen: At least it'll be over soon. Think about it. You'll have been home for three days before I've taken a single exam. It'll be so nice when it's over.
> Brooke: Yeah but I literally have no time to study!
> Helen: Yeah but you'll make it through. God, I'm so ready for finals to be over.
> Brooke: At least you have the whole week to prepare!

In commenting on this exchange in her field note, Helen explained that she felt Brooke wasn't matching her troubles but topping them, by insisting that her situation was worse. She also explained that she herself was responding to Brooke in a way intended to provide comfort—and therefore connection—by reassuring Brooke that she'd be fine, because her situation wasn't so bad. Helen convincingly supported this interpretation by reference to the exchange. However, Brooke's comments are arguably indistinguishable from Helen's: both can be seen as one-upmanship—or, more accurately, one-downmanship. In comforting Brooke by pointing out the positive (Brooke's ordeal would be over soon), Helen was saying that her situation was worse (her own ordeal would go on longer). I don't believe there is any "real" meaning here; the friends' comments aren't "really" about connection or competition. Both friends' words could be seen as either competition or connection—or both at once. Given that inescapable ambiguity and potential polysemy, it's common for friends to feel, as Helen did, that their attempts to establish connection are somehow twisted into competition. And it's common for women to feel that competition is unpleasant and unseemly, especially if their intention is connection. The ambiguity and polysemy of connection and competition are always at play in conversations among friends, as they are in email exchanges between professors and students.

I have tried herein to demonstrate that examining exchanges between professors and students adds to our understanding of the ambiguity and polysemy of power and solidarity, and that the ambiguity of power and solidarity explains how I could assume I was reflecting solidarity by omitting the elements of a formal missive but come across to students as rude. Examining professor-student email exchanges sheds light in turn on the polysemy of power and solidarity: when I send bare-bones email responses to students, I am both being friendly by being casual and also reflecting my higher rank in the university. It is because of my professorial power that I can answer quickly, omitting elements because I am busy, whereas students, no matter how busy they are, generally feel they have to spend as much time as necessary to include all the elements of formal letters. I have further suggested that considering conversational style differences in everyday conversations between women friends also affords insight into the ambiguity and polysemy of power and solidarity: ambiguity because what one friend intends in the spirit of connection can be interpreted as competition, and polysemy because, as occurred in the example of two students studying for finals, a friend might establish connection by matching troubles and reassuring her friend that her plight isn't so bad, yet also be topping her friend's troubles by claiming that her own are worse.

By calling attention to this ambiguity and polysemy, I am striking a note of caution for scholars of interaction who are inclined to interpret a way of speaking as reflecting a specific motive or seeking a particular effect, because any comment or gesture intended to show solidarity or create connection can come across as—and simultaneously be—an expression of power, and any utterance or move that seems obviously to express power can instead, or simultaneously, be an expression of solidarity.

I will conclude where I began, with emails I send to students. I still find myself composing cryptic responses to students' email queries, but I now frequently stop myself before pressing Send, and go back to add "Dear Student Name," a friendly opening greeting, and a closing such as "Best." But I don't sign off with a solidarity-reflecting (but potentially condescending) first name, nor the solidarity-reflecting first initial, but generally end with the polysemously solidarity and power-inflected initials "DT."

Notes

1   Though this first email exchange is fabricated, the next email example I present is real, as is the name of the student who signed it: Kate Thompson. I have used the email, and her name, with her permission, for which I thank her. Although I do not identify him here, I remain grateful to the student who

raised my consciousness about, and set me on the path of examining, professor-student emails. I am also grateful to the other students whose comments on professors' emails I quote here: Elizabeth Miller and Delaney Dietzgen. Examples of conversations among friends, and my analysis of them, come from Tannen (2017), and are also used with permission. The names in the last example are pseudonymous.
2 I am grateful to Didem Ikizoglou for calling this cartoon to my attention.
3 The quote from Anna Hahner, and my account of their marathon performances, are drawn from Christopher Clarey, "Hand in hand: Did their finish cross a line?," *New York Times* August 17, 2016, B10.

References

Bella, Spyridoula and Maria Sifianou. 2012. Greek student e-mail requests to faculty members. In Leyre Ruiz de Zarobe and Yolanda Ruiz de Zarobe (eds.), *Speech acts and politeness across languages and cultures*. Bern, Switzerland: Peter Lang. 89–113.
Biesenbach-Lucas, Sigrid. 2007. Students writing emails to faculty: An examination of e-politeness among native and non-native speakers of English. *Language Learning & Technology* 11 (2): 59–81.
Bolkan, San and Jennifer Linn Holmgren. 2012. "You are such a great teacher and I hate to bother you but…": Instructors' perceptions of students and their use of email messages with varying politeness strategies. *Communication Education* 61 (3): 253–70.
Boshrabadi, Abbas Mehrabi and Sepideh Bataghva Sarabi. 2016. Cyber-communic@tion etiquette: The interplay between social distance, gender and discursive features of student-faculty email interactions. *Interactive Technology and Smart Education* 13 (2): 86–106.
Brown, Penelope and Stephen Levinson. (1978) 1987. *Politeness: Some universals in language usage*. Cambridge: Cambridge University Press.
Brown, Roger and Albert Gilman. 1960. The pronouns of power and solidarity. In Thomas Sebeok (ed.), *Style in language*. Cambridge, MA: MIT Press. 253–76.
Chejnová, Pavla. 2014. Expressing politeness in the institutional e-mail communications of university students in the Czech Republic. *Journal of Pragmatics* 60: 175–92.
Chen, Yuan-shan. 2015. Developing Chinese EFL learners' email literacy through requests to faculty. *Journal of Pragmatics* 75: 131–49.
Costello, Robert. 2011. *Uses and perceptions of e-mail for course-related communication between business faculty and undergraduates*. Unpublished PhD dissertation, Johnson & Wales University. ProQuest LLC.
Deveci, Tanju and Ikhlas Ben Hmida. 2017. The request speech act in emails by Arab university students in the UAE. *Journal of Language and Linguistic Studies* 13 (1): 194–214.
Dickinson, Amber. 2017. Communicating with the online student: The impact of e-mail tone on student performance and teacher evaluations. *Journal of Educators Online* 14 (2): 36–45.
Economidou-Kogetsidis, Maria. 2011. "Please answer me as soon as possible": Pragmatic failure in non-native speakers' e-mail requests to faculty. *Journal of Pragmatics* 43: 3192–3215.
Ewald, Jennifer. 2016. *The inbox: Understanding and maximizing student-instructor email*. Sheffield, UK: Equinox.
Grice, H. P. 1967. Logic and conversation. William James Lectures, Harvard University. Reprinted in Peter Cole and Jerry Morgan (eds.), *Syntax and semantics* (vol. III): *Speech acts*. New York: Academic Press (1975). 41–88.
Hartford, Beverly S. and Kathleen Bardovi-Harlig. 1996. "At your earliest convenience": A study of written student requests to faculty. In Lawrence F. Bouton (ed.), *Pragmatics and language learning*. Urbana-Champaign: University of Illinois, Division of English as an International Language (DEIL). 55–69.
Jones, Janet S., Shelley R. Tapp, Barry W. Evans and Ralph J. Palumbo. 2016. Gender differences in online communication in higher education. *Academy of Business Research Journal* 4: 45–52.
Kim, Do-Hwan, Hyun Bae Yoon, Dong-Mi Yoo, Sang-Min Lee, Hee-Yeon Jung, Seog Ju Kim, Jwa-Seop Shin, Seunghee Lee and Jae-Joon Yim. 2016. Etiquette for medical students' email communication with faculty members: A single-institution study. *BMC Medical Education* 16 (129): 1–11.

Knupsky, Aimee C. and Natalie M. Nagy-Bell. 2011. Dear professor: The influence of recipient sex and status on personalization and politeness in e-mail. *Journal of Language and Social Psychology* 30 (1): 103–13.

Lakoff, Robin. 1973. The logic of politeness, or minding your p's and q's. In Claudia Corum, T. Cedric Smith-Stark and Ann Weiser (eds.), *Papers from the Ninth Regional Meeting of the Chicago Linguistics Society*. Chicago: Chicago Linguistics Society. 292–305.

Lam, Phoenix W. Y. 2014. Professional e-mail communication in higher education in Hong Kong: A case study. *Text & Talk* 34 (2): 143–64.

———. 2016. Academic email requests: A pragmalinguistic and sociopragmatic comparison between faculty and students. *Utrecht Studies in Language and Communication* 29: 127–46.

Merrison, Andrew John, Jack J. Wilson, Bethan L. Davies and Michael Haugh. 2012. Getting stuff done: Comparing e-mail requests from students in higher education in Britain and Australia. *Journal of Pragmatics* 44 (9): 1077–98.

Mohamadi, Zeinab. 2014. A comparative study of apologetic e-mails used by male and female Iranian EFL learners compared to English native speaking students. *Theory and Practice in Language Studies* 4 (1): 192–205.

Níkleva, Dimitrinka. 2018. Markers of politeness and impoliteness in student-teacher interaction in the discourse genre of emails. *Revista Signos* 51 (97): 214–35.

Oates, Joyce Carol. 2015. *The lost landscape: A writer's coming of age*. New York: HarperCollins.

Salazar Campillo, Patricia. 2018. Student-initiated email communication: An analysis of openings and closings by Spanish EFL learners. *Sintagma* 30: 81–93.

Savić, Milica. 2018. Lecturer perceptions of im/politeness and in/appropriateness in student e-mail requests: A Norwegian perspective. *Journal of Pragmatics* 124: 52–72.

Stephens, Keri K., Marian L. Houser and Renee L. Cowan. 2009. R U able to meat me: The impact of students' overly casual email messages to instructors. *Communication Education* 58 (3): 303–26.

Tannen, Deborah. 1990. *You just don't understand: Women and men in conversation*. New York: William Morrow.

———. 1994. The relativity of linguistic strategies: Rethinking power and solidarity in gender and dominance. In *Gender and discourse*. Oxford: Oxford University Press. 19–52.

———. 2017. *You're the only one I can tell: Inside the language of women's friendships*. New York: Ballantine.

Thomas-Tate, Shurita, Timothy J. Daugherty and Timothy K. Bartkoski. 2015. Experimental study of gender effects on language use in college students' email to faculty. *College Student Journal* 51 (2): 222–26.

Zhu, Wuhan. 2017. A cross-cultural pragmatic study of rapport-management strategies in Chinese and English academic upward request emails. *Language and Intercultural Communication* 17 (2): 210–28.

5

What Do Discourse Markers Mark? Arabic *yaʕni* (It Means) and Hebrew *ya'ani* across Modalities and Sociolinguistic Systems

MICHAL MARMORSTEIN

ANY ATTEMPT TO DEFINE discourse markers (DMs) requires caution. The task is made challenging by the structural heterogeneity of items classified as DMs and the multiplicity of functions they fulfill (Jucker and Ziv 1998; Schourup 1999). Moreover, while a wealth of data from many languages has accumulated over the last decades, a wide diversity of approaches has also emerged, resulting in many different understandings of the form-function coupling of DMs (Fedriani and Sansò 2017; Fischer 2006; Maschler and Schiffrin 2015). Commonly accepted are nevertheless the observations that DMs constitute text-level rather than clause-level structure, and that they indicate meanings that are not referential but reflexive and metalingual (Maschler 2009). The contribution of DMs, often elusive within the confines of a single clause, becomes fully evident only in discourse, that is, in contextualized and situated stretches of language.

But, *in* discourse, what is the particular work of DMs? In her foundational study on DMs and in subsequent work, Schiffrin (1987, 2006) suggested that DMs are a subclass of indexicals, similar to deictic expressions of space, time, and person. Like other indexicals, DMs point to different aspects of the context, which may involve the participants, their actions, and the text they produce. While often having "default contextual 'homes,'" DMs can "extend their reach as different domains come into simultaneous play during a discourse or as the marker itself is metaphorically extended over time" (Schiffrin 2006, 335). The multifunctionality of DMs is thus occasioned by the (synchronic) multidimensionality of discourse and is established through (diachronic) processes of meaning change.

Schiffrin pinpoints one of the most essential properties of DMs, namely, their indexical force that makes explicit the context in which language is embedded. However, the discourse model she proposes, based on her study of casual monolingual conversations drawn from sociolinguistic interviews, does not cover the entire range of possibilities for the operation of DMs, for DMs obviously operate in other

communicative contexts in which the relevant aspects to be indexed may be different and sometimes more complex, including the evocation of other discourses. The
functional extension of a marker is therefore not only induced by the simultaneous
play of certain discourse domains but is an always open possibility when the surrounding context is changed.

This chapter explores the question of how markers extend their reach by
tracking the use of the Arabic DM *yaʕni* (lit. "it means") across modalities and sociolinguistic systems. The analysis is based on three previous studies that I discuss
in what follows. The first focuses on conversational language, the natural habitat of
yaʕni, and examines its uses in Egyptian-Arabic (Marmorstein 2016). The second
examines the employment of *yaʕni* in two genres of written Egyptian-Arabic (Marmorstein, forthcoming). The third explores the transfer of this item into Modern
Hebrew, where it takes the form *yaʾani/yaʾanu* (Marmorstein and Maschler 2020).
Considering all three contexts together provides insight into the ever-renewing
meaning potential (Norén and Linell 2007) of *yaʕni*, which is arguably a general
property of DMs (cf. Aijmer 2013). As I show subsequently, in conversational language *yaʕni* serves mainly to facilitate and optimize the production of speech.
Adapted to written language, *yaʕni* acquires symbolic meanings and is used to
indicate textual cohesion. When migrating to Modern Hebrew, *yaʾani/yaʾanu* assumes an additional social function as a marker of Arabness. Overall, the analysis
illustrates how DMs are repurposed when put into new contexts of use: while they
keep a relation to their original provenance, this relation is not necessarily straightforward, but often involves a shift to higher intertextual and social frames of meaning (cf. Traugott 2010).

The Marker *yaʕni* in Conversational Egyptian Arabic

The DM *yaʕni* is one of the most frequently used words in Egyptian Arabic (as in
other Arabic dialects; cf. Kanaan et al. 2015). Formally, it is an imperfect verb form
derived from the verbal root *ʕanā* (to mean/intend) and inflected for the third-person
masculine singular. As a DM, it is never inflected for number or gender, nor does it
take agreement marking with a personal agent. Literally, then, it is interpreted as the
impersonal "it/that means."

While some of the occurrences of *yaʕni* can be interpreted according to its literal
meaning, the bulk of its uses in conversational language reflect the emergence of a
metalingual function of the DM. This observation comes from my study of a corpus
of interviews that I conducted and recorded in Cairo in 2011. My consultants were
women, native speakers of the Cairene dialect, who worked at the time as housekeep-
ers and nannies in the Israeli community in Cairo. The interviews mostly revolved
around personal accounts and descriptions of daily life. For the purpose of the study
of *yaʕni*, I sampled twenty minutes from five different interviews (thus a total of one
hundred minutes) yielding 297 tokens of *yaʕni*.

I define the core function of *yaʕni* as follows: *yaʕni* is a *point marker*, serving
to facilitate or cue the speaker's efforts to produce the locally most satisfying—i.e.,

Table 5.1. Classification of *yaʕni* in the Interview Corpus

	Preceding unit	Framed utterance		Pre-framing *yaʕni*		Post-framing *yaʕni*
A	Incomplete utterance	Assertions	+	53 (18%)	–	
B	Complete utterance	Assertions	+	193 (65%)	+	32 (11%)
		Questions	+	10 (3%)	+	2 (0.6%)
C	Introduction of speech	Assertions	+	7 (2.4%)	–	
	Total				297	

complete, correct, elaborated—expression of his/her intended message. This basic function is variously particularized in different prosodic, syntactic, and pragmatic environments. I distinguish three main groups of cases. Group A contains tokens of *yaʕni* that follow incomplete utterances and pre-frame assertions. Group B contains tokens that are hosted by complete utterances and can either pre-frame or post-frame assertions or questions. Group C contains cases where the utterance pre-framed by *yaʕni* is embedded within a higher frame of reported speech, or what Tannen (2007) calls constructed dialogue. Table 5.1 presents the classification of the tokens into these three groups. Because these are the most prevalent uses of *yaʕni* in my corpus, and for space considerations, in the remainder of this section I will focus on groups A and B, specifically on assertions framed by *yaʕni*. My goal is to demonstrate how *yaʕni* is tightly adapted to conversational interaction.

Group A: Facilitating Effortful Processing

In this group of cases, *yaʕni* occurs after a syntactically and pragmatically incomplete unit marked by a nonfinal terminal contour (i.e., continuous or truncated). This pattern is found in two subsets of cases. In the first subset, *yaʕni* prefaces a new (previously inactive; cf. Chafe 1994) idea, typically a predicate or a predicative complement, which completes the unit that came before *yaʕni*. Consider, for instance, (1), in which H complies with the request to tell the story about the engagement of her daughter N:[1]

(1) *The engagement story*

```
H:   1     hiyya N,
           she   N

     2     yaʕni--,

     3     (0.6)  ga-lha                    ʕarīs,
                  come.PRF.3SG.M-to.her     bridegroom
                  a bridegroom   came to [ask for] her [hand]
```

```
4    (0.8)  fī  šahri  talāta.
            in  month  three
            in  March
```

H starts by verbalizing her daughter's name, the topical anchor that is readily available to her from previous discourse. This hanging fragment is followed by *yaʕni*, which
precedes the narrative happening "a bridegroom came to [ask for] her [hand]." The
marker *yaʕni* thus helps to introduce a larger chunk of new information, which is
under configuration.

In a second subset of cases, *yaʕni* serves to initiate self-correction. The unit preceding *yaʕni* is abandoned midway and replaced by another, more appropriate or
accurate one. In (2), G provides an answer to the question "why are private lessons
needed?":

(2) *Quotidian life*

```
G:    1    il-madrasa,
           the-school

      2    fī-ha,
           in-it

      3    il  e--h,
           the uh

      4    yaʕni--,

      5    il-klas,
           the-class

      6    fī    wilād    kitīr.
           in-it children many
           there are many children in it
```

G starts by verbalizing the noun *il-madrasa* (the school); however, right after verbalizing the prepositional phrase *fī-ha* (in-it), she tries to correct herself and after a false
start introduces via *yaʕni* the more accurate term *il-klas* (the class).

In both examples *yaʕni* helps to overcome challenges induced by the real-time
processing of face-to-face conversation. It allows speakers more time to shape or
reshape their utterances on the fly, specifically in cases demanding more effortful
processing, such as the design of long sequences (1) or repair (2). It is no surprise that
group A *yaʕni* is often clustered with silent or filled pauses ([1] line 3 and [2] line 3),
which also display effort to resume fluent verbalization of ideas.

Group B: Elaborating on Prior Talk

Group B subsumes a larger variety of cases in which *yaʕni* either pre-frames or
post-frames assertions and questions (the latter category is not dealt with in the

present discussion). Following units ending in either continuous or falling tone, the utterances framed by *yaʕni* present various types of elaboration of previous talk. Thus, as opposed to group A *yaʕni*, group B *yaʕni* frames information that is grounded in previous discourse and is now repeated, reformulated, or expanded in order to increase participants' mutual understanding and involvement (Tannen 2007).

The next example presents a relatively simple case in which a concept, *ʕišra* (cohabitation), is elaborated. Notice that *ʕišra* is introduced via the formula "they [i.e., Egyptians] call it." In using this formula, Hb displays the recognition that this concept may be culturally specific, and hence requires further elaboration:

(3) *Customs*

Hb: 1   baʕdi fatra ma-b-yibʔā-š   fī   ḥubb.
         after period NEG-HAB-remain.IMPF.3SG.M-NEG in.it love
         after a while, there is no longer love [involved] in it

    2   bi-yʔūlu   ʕalē-ha ʕišra.
         HAB-say.IMPF.3PL about-it cohabitation
         they call it cohabitation

    3   (1.0) ʕišra.
             cohabitation

    4   **yaʕni** tnēn saknīn   fi bet-hum,
         yaʕni two live.PTCP.PL.M in house-their
         yaʕni two [people] live in their house

    5   mixallifīn ʔawlād,
         bear.PTC.PL.M children
         have children

    6   bi-yaklu,
         HAB-eat.IMPF.3PL
         eat

    7   bi-yišrabu,
         HAB-drink.IMPF.3PL
         drink

    8   (0.7) ʕišra.
             cohabitation

Elaborations are usually self-initiated in the interview's corpus, as in this example, thus disclosing the speaker's constant attendance to the way they come across. However, elaborations can also be other-initiated. In the next example, extracted from the engagement story, H relates about the initial agreement on the engagement. In line 1 she uses an idiom with which I was not familiar:

(4) *The engagement story*

H: 1   kull-ina   ʔulna   ʕala   xērit   illāh.
           all-us   say.PRF.1PL according_to choice   God
           we all said 'God grant success'

M: 2   ʕala   xēri   ʔē?
           according_to choi-   what
           grant what?

H: 3   ʕala   xērit   illāh   **yaʕni.**
           according_to choice   God   yaʕni
           God grant success yaʕni

      4   **yaʕni** bi-t-tawfīʔ.
           yaʕni with-the-success
           yaʕni with success

      5   **yaʕni** xalāṣ.
           yaʕni that's it

      6   **yaʕni** iḥna   mašyīn   fi da   ṭ-ṭarīʔ? **yaʕni.**
           yaʕni we   walk.PTCP.PL   in this the-way yaʕni
           yaʕni we are proceeding in this way yaʕni

"God grant success" is a ritual announcement of the family consent to the engagement of the young couple. Not able to make sense of this idiom, I partially reproduce
it in line 2 in rising tone, thereby flagging a problem in hearing and understanding.
H then goes on to implement a repair sequence. She first produces a repetition of the
idiom, post-framed by *yaʕni*. Then, via an aggregate of three *yaʕni*-initiated utterances, she reformulates and explains it. The sequence culminates in the utterance "we
are proceeding in this way," flanked on both sides by *yaʕni*. Evidently, at this point
the elaboration reached its locally most sufficient formulation, and thus the sequence
comes to its end.

Interlocutors are engaged not only in the elaboration of prior contents, but also
in clarifying their stance toward them. The following example is also excerpted from
the engagement story. The speaker relates how the fiancé broke off the engagement
the morning after it was announced. She argues that this inconceivable course of
action was due to a spell put on her daughter. In response to my question, whether
this was indeed the case, she says:

(5) *The engagement story*

H: 1   (0.6) ʔāh.
                 yes

      2   huwwa da.
           it   this
           this is [the case]

3   ma ma-fīš ḥāga.
    NEG NEG-EXIST thing
    there is nothing [else]

4   ..huwwa kān   bi-l-lēl   kān   e--h wakil,
    he   be.PRF.3SG.M in-the-night be.PRF.3SG.M uh   eat.PTCP.SG.M
    he was at night [at our place] uh eating

5   maʕā-na,
    with-us

6   wi-- kān   bi-yiḍḥak,
    and be.PRF.3SG.M HAB-laugh.IMPF.3SG.M
    and he was laughing

7   wi-- ḍiḥik   ?awi.
    and laugh.PRF.3SG.M very_much
    he laughed a lot

8   (0.6) **yaʕni** kān   bi-yiḍḥak   bi-yiḍḥak.
    yaʕni be.PRF.3SG.M HAB-laugh.IMPF.3SG.M HAB-laugh.IMPF.3SG.M
    yaʕni he was really laughing

The speaker repeats three times that her daughter's fiancé was laughing (lines 6–8), which serves to portray a positive atmosphere and marks the breakup the morning after as unexpected and unexplained. The third repetition, pre-framed by *yaʕni* (line 8), does not provide a clarification of the literal content just produced, but of the speaker's conviction of her position (which could be paraphrased as "it could not be anything else but the spell, for he was laughing!"), in contrast to the doubt implied by my question ("was it only the spell?"). Thus, the elaboration is carried out to enhance mutual understanding in case of potential disalignment.

Elaborations, as noted, can also be post-framed by *yaʕni* (see [4] lines 3 and 6). Post-framing *yaʕni* commonly occurs with short segments or increments containing alternative wordings, repetitive evaluations, and metadiscursive comments. In the next example, G is telling about the time when she worked at a hospital. She provides a translation into English of the Arabic word for hospital:

(6) *Quotidian life*

G: 1   ištaġalti   fi l-mustašfa.
        work.PRF.1SG   in the-hospital
        I worked in the hospital

M: 2   uhm

```
G:     3    il-mustašfa   ṭabʕan      e--h hozbital.
            the-hospital  naturally   uh   hozbital
            il-mustašfa is obviously uh  hospital


       4    (0.7) fi l-ingliš    yaʕni.
            in the-English yaʕni
            in English yaʕni
```

Translations are rarely employed in the interviews. Rather, Arabic is interpreted as a rule via Arabic (see [3], where "cohabitation" was explained). It could be that the switch to English in this case was motivated by reasons other than plain concern with intelligibility. In fact, the speaker displays the recognition that the switch to English is unusual, and even awkward in the immediate context, by providing an account for it post-framed by *yaʕni*. This account is not aimed to secure understanding as to what has been said, but as to the fact that English was (and can be) used.

To summarize this section, the DM *yaʕni* serves to facilitate both self-directed efforts to produce speech under temporal pressure (group A), and other-directed efforts to increase understanding and involvement (group B). Given the reflexive relations between language and context, *yaʕni* becomes an index of two key dimensions of conversation, temporality and interactionality. Thus, *yaʕni* has both a *facilitative* function and an *indicative* function in disclosing the workings of the sociocognitive forces that shape conversation.

The Marker *yaʕni* in Written Egyptian Arabic

The above discussion stressed the tight relation between *yaʕni* and spoken conversation. However, *yaʕni* is also found in various types of written discourse. The question then is what functions does *yaʕni* fulfill in writing and in what ways are these functions related to their "originals" in spoken discourse?

The Arabic-speaking world is well known for its diglossia, i.e., the ideologically driven division between the Arabic vernaculars, to be used in informal contexts of speech, and Standard Arabic, to be used in formal contexts and writing. Up until recently, this principle was also observed to a large extent in Egypt. However, in the last twenty-five years the balance has changed, so that Egyptian, mostly Cairene Arabic, is in ever-increasing use in a wide range of personal and public, print and digital forms of written communication (Høigilt and Mejdell 2017; Rosenbaum 2012).

My study of *yaʕni* in written Egyptian Arabic was based on two types of materials: casual-personal prose and expository writing as manifested in the Egyptian version of Wikipedia. Both types of writing largely differ in their generic constellation. What I dub "casual-personal prose" is a type of writing, typical of blogs but also very popular in printed books, which is reminiscent of everyday conversation in some important aspects. First, writing is almost entirely in the colloquial and often presents a casual, jocular, or satirical tone. Second, this type of text includes as a rule a first-person writer and a designated audience, to whom the writer constantly appeals. Third, these texts deal with issues relevant (or made relevant) to everyday life. In contrast, Egyptian Wikipedia builds on conventions of expository writing. Although designed to be "an encyclopedia that is written in the language that Egyptians use in their everyday lives,"[2] Egyptian Wikipedia is quite remote from ordinary speech. Contributors employ as a rule an objective voice and a serious tone and do not address a specific audience. In fact, the topics and overall organization are very similar to those found in the Standard Arabic version of Wikipedia.

Casual-personal prose and Wikipedia present a different distribution and use of the DM *yaʕni*. In what follows I will deal with each constellation separately and compare it to my observations from the conversational material. My goal is to examine the adaptation of *yaʕni* to the written modality.

Yaʕni in Casual-Personal Prose

My data comes from a sample of three hundred (50 × 6) printed pages of books (including blogs made into books). These featured 299 tokens of *yaʕni*, almost identical in range to the spoken corpus. Table 5.2 presents the distribution of tokens, based on the classificatory criteria of the spoken data. For the sake of comparative analysis, I focus in this section on the same groups of cases that were discussed above in relation to conversational Egyptian Arabic, namely, group A and group B assertions. A quick glance at tables 5.1 and 5.2 reveals two points of significant difference: group A presents far lower numbers in casual-personal prose than in spoken conversation (1.7%:18%), while group B post-framing *yaʕni* is used over twice as much in writing as in speech (23%:11%). How can these differences be explained?

Starting with group A, the low frequency of these cases is rather expected. As noted earlier, *yaʕni* serves to facilitate effortful processing of speech by allowing more time to retrieve and shape information. In written discourse, where temporality constraints are relieved, the need for such a device is largely obviated. Nevertheless, examples where *yaʕni* is used to introduce "hard-to-activate" information are not completely absent. For instance, in (7), the writer refers to the "sounds" that a pregnant woman's body occasionally produces:

Table 5.2. Classification of *yaʕni* in Casual-Personal Prose

	Preceding unit	Framed utterance		Pre-framing *yaʕni*		Post-framing *yaʕni*
A	Incomplete utterance	Assertions	+	5 (1.7%)	–	
B	Complete utterance	Assertions	+	149 (50%)	+	69 (23%)
		Questions	+	52 (17.3%)	+	17 (5.7%)
C	Introduction of speech	Assertions	+	7 (2.3%)	–	
	Total			299		

(7) al-Kayyāl (2014, 34)

```
bass di    yaʕni... li-ha  tafsirāt     ʕilmiyya waḍḥa
but  this  yaʕni    to-it  explanations scientific clear
But these [voices]  yaʕni... have clear scientific explanations
```

The fact that the topic is considered sensitive, and thus hard to communicate, is marked by the use of *yaʕni* after the topical entity "these" and before the newly introduced information "have clear scientific explanations." The marker *yaʕni*, followed by three dots, serves to *act out* hesitation, that is, a processing difficulty. Unlike typical conversational interaction, where *yaʕni* and delay markers help to overcome temporality challenges induced by a variety of cognitive and interactional reasons, in writing they serve the goal of evoking the situation of dealing with a problematic issue, thereby indexing its social sensitivity.

Instances of self-correction introduced by *yaʕni* were not found in the corpus. However, the corpus does contain pseudo-corrections introduced via verbal or nominal expressions derived from the root q-ṣ-d (to intend), sometimes followed by *yaʕni*. This is the case in the next example, in which the writer uses the verb *ʔaʔṣud* (I mean) several times and lastly adjoins *yaʕni* to it:

(8) Miʕawwaḍ (2010, 58)

```
ḥamāt-i            ma-tuʔʕud-ši        maʕā-na fi nafsi š-šaʔʔa..
mother_in_law-my   NEG-sit.IMPF.3SG.F-NEG with-us in same   the-apartment
My mother-in-law will not stay with  us in the same apartment...

ʔaʔṣud        fi  nafsi l-ʕimāra..  yuuh ʔaʔṣud       fi  nafsi
mean.IMPF.1SG in  same  the-building yuuh mean.IMPF.1SG in same
I mean in the same building... yuuh... I mean in the same

l-ḥayy             la ʔaʔṣud        yaʕni fi  nafsi l-balad..
the-neighborhood   NEG mean.IMPF.1SG yaʕni in same  the-country
neighborhood... no I mean yaʕni in the same country...
```

The seemingly universal joke about keeping one's mother-in-law distant is built up through a series of corrections introduced by *ʔaʔṣud*, and lastly also by *yaʕni*. Unlike face-to-face conversation, where the mechanism of repair serves to "fix" the irreversibility of speech (Auer 2009), pseudo-repair, and specifically pseudo-correction, exploits the co-presence of an error and its correction to reach a comic rhetorical effect.

Group A, then, is highly rare and marked in writing. Group B cases, on the other hand, abound in writing. However, here we observe a significant difference in the frequency of use of post-framing *yaʕni* vis-à-vis speech, which is more than doubled in assertions (69:32), and over eight times more in questions (17:2). Segments/fragments post-framed by *yaʕni* present short alternative wordings, evaluations, and metadiscursive comments. The latter is illustrated in (9). The writer describes how as a pregnant woman trying to lie down comfortably, she has to use pillows "in the plural" (referencing the grammatical form):

(9) al-Kayyāl (2014, 18)

```
ʔāxud        maʕā-ya l-mixaddāt   ʔāh mixaddāt gamʕ   yaʕni
take.impf.1sg with-me the-pillows yes pillows    plural yaʕni
I take with me the pillows, yes pillows, [in the] plural yaʕni
```

The writer draws attention to the grammatical form of the word, rather than to the notion it embeds ("many"). This display of metalinguistic awareness is indeed very common in the examined corpus and is likely to be related to the persistence of the written record, which invites more reflection on the linguistic product (cf. Herring 1999). In casual-personal prose, then, both group A and group B *yaʕni* are observed; however, they present structural, functional, and distributional differences compared to speech.

Yaʕni in Egyptian Wikipedia

In Wikipedia, *yaʕni* is overall non-frequent. In a corpus of 150 entries, I counted only 61 tokens of *yaʕni*. Moreover, the structural patterns in which *yaʕni* occurs and the functions it fulfills are far more limited. First, *yaʕni* never occurs in final position but is always pre-positioned to the utterance it frames. Second, *yaʕni* never frames questions but only assertions. Third, *yaʕni* does not occur with quotations (group C), or with incomplete utterances (group A), which are generally not attested in Wikipedia, but only with elaborations (group B). In Wikipedia, *yaʕni* is only used to pre-frame definitions and explanations of concepts and facts. This is the case, e.g., in (10), where *yaʕni* introduces a translation of the Greek word *Aígyptos* (Αἴγυπτος), "Egypt":

(10) https://arz.wikipedia.org/wiki/مصر_بين

```
egiptos    yaʕni maṣr  ʕand   il-yunaniyyīn
Aigyptos   yaʕni Egypt among  the-Greeks
Aigyptos   yaʕni Egypt in the Greeks [language]
```

Compared to both conversational language and casual-personal prose, then, Wikipedia presents not only a low frequency of tokens, but also a limited range of patterns in which *yaʕni* is used.

Yaʕni in Conversational versus Written Egyptian Arabic

Considering the three corpora together, as presented in table 5.3, it becomes evident how *yaʕni* is differently adapted to each modality and genre. In its natural habitat, *yaʕni* helps interlocutors to overcome temporality challenges and enhance interactionality by facilitating the effortful verbalization of ideas (group A) or by optimizing their formulation (group B). In casual-personal prose, both types of *yaʕni* are attested; however, their domains of use are shifted. Group A tokens, far rarer, are depleted of their problem-solving function, while their indexical force, as markers of processing difficulties, is heightened. Group B tokens occur in large numbers, especially when post-positioned. This may also be indicative of the high stylistic utility of *yaʕni* in casual writing, as an element tightly associated with casual conversational interaction.

Table 5.3. *Yaʕni across Modalities and Genres*

	Spoken conversation (100 min)	Casual-personal prose (300 p)	Wikipedia (150 entries)
Tokens (total)	297	299	61
Group A	53	5	0
Group B	$193_{pre}/32_{post}$	$149_{pre}/69_{post}$	$61_{pre}/0_{post}$
Domain	Cognitive-interactional	Symbolic-stylistic	Textual

Why is conversationality desired in writing? Metadiscourse passages provide insight into this question. For example, in the introduction to his book *Kitāb malūš ʔism* (*A Book with No Name*) composed in the colloquial, Aḥmad al-ʕAsīlī writes: "Literary Arabic (*Fuṣḥā*) has greater rhetorical force, but colloquial Arabic (*ʕĀmmiyya*) is closer to the heart. Literary Arabic may win the admiration of the lovers of Arabic and the educated, but colloquial Arabic addresses all people" (2009, 9). This short bit of text elucidates the perceived interactional values of Egyptian Arabic vis-à-vis Standard Arabic, namely, better self-expression ("closer to the heart") and greater intersubjectivity ("addresses all people"). At the macro level, these values indeed feed into "pro-ʕĀmmiyya" language ideologies (Aboelezz 2017). Thus, the increased use of *yaʕni*, while not motivated by practical needs, fulfills the important symbolic-stylistic function of marking the text as interpersonally engaging and as a local-national cultural product.

Designed even more deliberately as a purely Egyptian-Arabic artifact, Egyptian Wikipedia nevertheless presents a very limited use of *yaʕni*. In Wikipedia, *yaʕni* completes the transition from the interactional to the textual: it is not only depleted of a major part of its microfunctions, but it is also emptied of much of its macrosocial meaning, as a marker of conversationality.

The Marker *ya'ani/ya'anu* in Conversational Modern Hebrew

Not only within the confines of a single language, but also across languages, DMs provide insight into the workings of different sociolinguistic systems. Arabic *yaʕni* found its way also to neighboring languages such as Hebrew, Turkish, and Persian. In Modern Hebrew, it is likely that contact with the local Palestinian communities has induced the borrowing of *yaʕni*, although it could have also been introduced by immigrant speakers of Judeo-Arabic vernaculars. Either way, this transfer accords well with the high borrowability of DMs in general (Matras 2009, 193), and the high utility of *yaʕni* in particular.

Adapted to standard Hebrew phonology, *yaʕni* is depharyngealized and can take one of several forms; the most common are *ya'ani* or *ya'anu*. In most cases, the prosodic shape follows the Arabic original, thus the stress lies on the first syllable, viz. *ya'ani/ ya'anu*. However, a prosodic variant has also emerged, in which the stress is placed on the second syllable, viz. *ya'ani/ya'anu* (this variant is discussed in a later section).

For most speakers of Modern Hebrew, the lexical meaning of Arabic *yaʕni* is unknown. Rather, it is the metalingual function of the DM that is replicated (Matras 2009) in Hebrew *yaʾani/yaʾanu*. Dissociated from its lexical source, however, *yaʾani/ yaʾanu* is also open to assume new lexically unmotivated meanings, once it becomes associated with the ecology of Hebrew DMs.

Unlike Arabic *yaʕni*, Hebrew *yaʾani/yaʾanu* is used rather infrequently. Our analysis was based on the *Haifa Corpus of Spoken Hebrew* (Maschler et al. 2017), which includes audio-recorded conversations between students, their relatives, and friends. In this corpus we located only 38 tokens of *yaʾani/yaʾanu*, equally distributed (19:19), in over eleven hours of talk (compared to 297 tokens in one hundred minutes of conversational Arabic).

In the next subsections I will focus on two functions of *yaʾani/yaʾanu*: the first is inherited from Arabic; the second presents an innovation. My goal is to examine how the transition to a new sociolinguistic system affects the distribution and function of *yaʾani/yaʾanu*.

Replication: Elaborating on Prior Talk via *yaʾani/yaʾanu*

We observe that *yaʾani/yaʾanu* (prosodically unmarked *yaʾani/yaʾanu*) presents for the most part the same patterns of use that are found in Arabic. Specifically, *yaʾani/yaʾanu* can serve to facilitate effortful processing (group A), frame elaborations of prior talk (group B), and introduce constructed dialogue (group C). The same as in Arabic, framing elaborations is the most common function of *yaʾani/yaʾanu* in Hebrew (24 out of 38 tokens, 63%). For instance, in (11) *yaʾanu* pre-frames a specification of a preceding sequence of emotive expressions:

(11) *Intrusion of privacy*

```
166    Alon:   ....'az 'e--h,
                    so u--h,

167            ..'amarti,
               said.1sg
               I said,

168            ...gad!
               God!

169            ..'ashkara!
               really!

170            ..ke'ilu,
               like,

171            ...pashut keta   madhim!
               simply piece amazing!
               simply an amazing thing!

172            ...ya'anu,
```

```
173          'ex    'anashim do'agim        lexa,
             how    people      care.PL.M about-you
             how    people care about you,

174          ..veze,
             and-this
             and so on,
```

Alon expresses his amazement at receiving a phone call from a woman he barely knows, who called to check on him after hearing he was in a bad mood. His amazement is expressed in a sequence of emotive utterances which becomes progressively more specific. The first two utterances "God! really!" are plain interjections. Next comes a more specific depiction "simply an incredible thing!" Finally, explicit reference to the stance object (Du Bois 2007) is pre-framed by "ya'anu how people care about you." Notice that the utterance preceding ya'ani is introduced via ke'ilu (lit. "like"), a Hebrew DM which shares the same functional territory as ya'ani/ya'anu. In the next section we shall see how this association might have affected the functional extension of ya'ani/ya'anu.

Innovation: Double-Voiced Ironic Modification via ya'ani/ya'anu

Unattested in Arabic, the prosodic variant ya'ani/ya'anu serves as a modifier in Modern Hebrew. Specifically, ya'ani/ya'anu indicates that the association between the utterance it frames and the concept or state of affairs to which it refers is a loose, pretentious, or false one. The modification marked by ya'ani/ya'anu thus implicates an ironic stance, i.e., a contrastive double-voiced (Bakhtin 1981) evaluation or perspectivation (Kotthoff 2002) of the idea alluded to by the modified segment.

In the next example, two secular Jewish men, Beni and Uri, are co-telling a woman, Michal, about a gathering of newly "converted" ultra-Orthodox Jews to which they were invited. Uri and Beni ridicule the people at this gathering, who had taken various actions in an attempt to "convert" them too. In lines 107–109, Uri relates how he had told the rabbi taking such actions to leave him alone:

(12) _Back to God_

```
107 Uri:    ...'amarti      lo,
                say.PST.1SG to.him
                I said to him,

108         ..ma   'ata rotse          mimeni,
                what you  want.PRS.2SG.M from.me
                what do you want from me,

109         ..'azov            'oti be-sheket.
                leave.IMP.2SG.M me   in-peace
                leave me alone.

110 Beni:   ....kitsur,
                anyways,
```

```
111              ..kol    ha-'erev        nisu--,
                 all      the-evening     try.PST.3PL
                 all      night people    tried,

112              ..lehaxzir      'otanu be-tshuva.
                 bring_back.INF us       in-repentance
                 to 'convert' us.

113 Uri:         ...ya'ani.

114 Beni:        ya'ani,

115              ..ki      hem lo.
                 because they NEG
                 because they didn't.

116 Michal:      'al telxu    la-mifgashim      ha'ele,
                 NEG go.IMP.2PL to.the-meetings these
                 don't go to these meetings
```

Beni continues and sums up the episode by saying "anyways, all night they tried to 'convert' us," which is subsequently modified by Uri's *ya'ani*, indicating that the "conversion" attempts were not real. Beni then repeats *ya'ani* in agreement with the suggested modification, and explicitly states: *ki hem lo* "because they didn't (really try to 'convert' us)". In employing *ya'ani* to modify the specific, concrete attempts at "conversion," the speakers mark them as loosely and not-really equivalent to genuine attempts at conversion. This is a double-voiced ironic *ya'ani*, by which the speakers' stance is superimposed over the referential dimension of the utterance, indicating that they are intending the opposite of what they are saying.

How did this functional extension of *ya'ani/ya'anu* come about? It is highly likely that the association of *ya'ani/ya'anu* with the Hebrew DM *ke'ilu* has induced this change. Formally, *ke'ilu* is composed of the similative/approximative preposition *ke-* "as" and the irrealis conditional conjunction *'ilu*. As a DM, it occupies a functional territory very similar to that of Arabic *ya'ni*. Specifically, the functions subsumed under groups A, B, and C are carried out by both markers. However, *ke'ilu* in addition functions as a hedge, i.e., as an indicator of "loose fit" between what is said and what is intended (Maschler 2009, 137). Since Arabic *ya'ni* does not provide for this meaning, it is very probable that Hebrew *ya'ani/ya'anu* has accumulated its hedging function by analogy to *ke'ilu*. The shift in stress placement from *ya'ani* to *ya'ani* is also indicative of the association between both markers, which induced the prosodic assimilation of *ya'ani* to *ke'ilu*. Unlike *ke'ilu*, though, which is used as a hedge in a variety of contexts, *ya'ani/ya'anu* is scarcely used in our corpus and where it does it only serves as a double-voiced ironic hedge. These differences may well be related to the social meanings that *ya'ani/ya'anu* has come to assume for some speakers of Modern Hebrew.[3]

The Sociolinguistic Value of ya'ani/ya'anu

As noted earlier, *ya'ani/ya'anu* (of both variants) presents a low rate of use in our corpus (38 tokens), especially in comparison to the high rates in which *ke'ilu* is found

(1,102 tokens). Moreover, while *ke'ilu* is common in casual Hebrew, *ya'ani/ya'anu*—like many other Arabic-imported lexemes—is considered slang, that is, a socially marked style of speech indicating alignment with nonstandard or nonmainstream culture (Allen 2001).

What is the social import of Arabic slang in current Israeli discourse? While this question obviously does not have a simple answer, it has been widely acknowledged that the status of Arabic is in constant decline in Israel (e.g., Henkin-Roitfarb 2011; Rosenthal 2001). In the early days of pre-statehood (before 1948), Arabic, especially Palestinian, was a much-favored source for enriching the lexicon of reviving Modern Hebrew. As the language of the native inhabitants, Arabic was laden with positive values such as indigenousness and authenticity, which were crucial to the recon-struction of Jewish identity in the land of Zion (Henkin-Roitfarb 2011). However, this favoring ideology drastically changed after the state of Israel was established and in the decades that have transpired since. The ongoing political conflict and the adoption of Westernizing ideologies have had a crucial effect on the current domi-nant conception of Arabic as the "language of the enemy" (Spolsky and Shohamy 1999, 118), and more broadly, of inferior culture. This has resulted in a sharp de-crease in the number of new Arabic loans and in the social devaluation and with-drawal of previous borrowings.

Despite this, *ya'ani/ya'anu* is slang that did not go out of fashion altogether. The speakers who use it in our corpus seem to treat it as an organic (unmarked or stereo-typed) part of their vocabulary. However, the fact that overall *ya'ani/ya'anu* is infre-quent suggests that other speakers may avoid using it as a "negative identity practice" (Bucholtz 1999), through which they reject the values associated with *ya'ani/ya'anu* according to their view. Explicit articulation of these values is provided in metadis-course on *ya'ani/ya'anu*, especially in online discussions on the meaning of this term. For example, in the quick-question forum *Stips*,[4] users evaluate *ya'ani/ya'anu* as "street language" and ascribe it to the speech style of *'arsim*, a pejorative referring to a lout persona, used predominantly for Mizrahi men, i.e., Jews of Middle Eastern and North African descent. On the *Fxp* website,[5] users express even more scornful attitudes in discussing the question "Do you say *ya'ani* or *ya'anu*?" For example, one user declares that he does not say this "inferior" (*tat-rama*) word, and another user comments, "A word of Arabs. I don't say it" (*mila shel 'aravim. lo 'omer*). Interestingly, while the lexi-cal meaning of *ya'ani/ya'anu* is lost, speakers are well aware of its Arabic source. Their negative evaluations of this term disclose their depreciative stance toward marginal-ized ethnic and religious groups, such as Mizrahi Jews and Arabs, with which *ya'ani/ya'anu* is associated.

Symbiosis, Indexicality, and the Extension of Reach of *ya'ni*

Language and context are mutually constitutive. This basic tenet finds one of its clear-est representations in the phenomenon of DMs. Östman (1982) uses the term *symbio-sis* to refer to the relation between what he calls "pragmatic particles" and the context of "impromptu speech." This type of symbiosis, he argues, does not carry the usual sense of mutual dependency; rather, pragmatic particles and impromptu speech are effects of the same situation of casual conversation (1982, 164). I find symbiosis, as a term evoking mutuality, to be quite apt for describing the relation between DMs and their contexts: while both are not mutually dependent for their existence, they do co-shape each other. More specifically, particular contextual conditions call for the use of facilitating devices such as DMs, and these in turn become indexical of the contextual frame in which they occur. Importantly, what abides there implicitly in the context to be made evident via DMs is not predetermined or restricted to certain domains. Rather, by virtue of their indexical force, DMs can embody any meaning or aspect carved from the context, which is interactionally and socially pertinent in a particular type of communication.

Social indexicality is not fixed and static but, as Eckert (2008, 463) writes, "a continual interpretation of forms in context." More specifically, indexical items are immanently reconstruable because their values pertain to a system of social values that is constantly in flux (Eckert 2008; Silverstein 2003). Importantly, reconstrual does not entail the replacement of one meaning for another, but results in a stratification of meanings. Thus a first-order index, effected by and reflective of its basic context of use, acquires under certain conditions an "overlay of contextualization" (Silverstein 2003, 194), a metapragmatic interpretation of its basic use, thereby becoming a second-order, or more generally, a higher-order index.

Going back to *yaʕni*, it has been shown that the transfer of this DM to other modalities and sociolinguistic systems results in its reconstrual and acquisition of higher-order indexical values. In conversational Egyptian-Arabic, *yaʕni* is a first-order index, facilitative and indicative of the conditions and goals of *face-to-face interaction*. When used in written Arabic, *yaʕni* becomes a second-order index of *conversationality* itself, either endorsed or rejected. Its high rate of use in casual-personal prose reflects a strong stylistic-ideological link to conversationality, whereas its low rate of use in Wikipedia reflects departure from conversational conventions. Incorporated into Modern Hebrew, *ya'ani/ya'anu* becomes associated with the metapragmatic value of *Arabness*. Specifically, the limited use of *ya'ani/ya'anu* among some groups of Hebrew speakers appears to indicate a lesser social utility of this term driven by a depreciative ideology of *Arabness* in current mainstream Jewish-Israeli culture. Extending its reach to other contextual constellations, then, *yaʕni/ya'ani* assumes higher-order values, as interactional and social meanings, reflexively associated with this term, become pertinent for indexing. This high availability for reconstrual is arguably a general property of DMs as a subclass of indexicals extending from the structural to the social, thus marking discourse in its fullest scope.

Appendix: Transcription Conventions

The transcription of the Arabic excerpts follows closely the conventions of the *Encyclopedia of Arabic Language and Linguistics* (Versteegh et al. 2006–10), with the minor change of representing the pharyngeal and glottal stop using the IPA symbols ʕ and ʔ, respectively. The glottal stop in Hebrew is represented by ', the uninverted quotation mark.

Other transcription conventions are:
...   half second pause
..   perceptible pause of less than half a second
(1.2)   measured pause
--   elongation of preceding vowel sound
.   utterance-final falling intonation
?   utterance-final rising intonation
,   continuing intonation
        truncated intonation unit (no final marking)
!   utterance-final exclamatory intonation

Notes

1 See appendix for transcription conventions.
2 https://en.wikipedia.org/wiki/Egyptian_Arabic_Wikipedia
3 The patterns of use observed in *The Haifa Corpus* may be different in other populations of Hebrew speakers, especially bilinguals and heritage speakers of Arabic. This issue, however, awaits further investigation.
4 https://stips.co.il/ask/2929734/אומרים-יעני-או-יעני-סלנג
5 https://www.fxp.co.il/showthread.php?t=9811796

References

Aboelezz, Mariam. 2017. The politics of pro-ʕāmmiyya language ideology in Egypt. In Jacob Høigilt and Gunvor Mejdell (eds.), *The politics of written language in the Arab world*. Leiden: Brill. 212–38.

Aijmer, Karin. 2013. *Understanding pragmatic markers: A variational pragmatic approach*. Edinburgh: Edinburgh University Press.

al-ʕAsīlī, Aḥmad. 2009. *Kitāb malūš ʔism* (A book with no name). Cairo: Dār al-šurūq.

Allen, Irving L. 2001. Slang: Sociology. In Rajend Mesthrie (ed.), *Concise encyclopedia of sociolinguistics*. Amsterdam: Elsevier. 265–70.

Auer, Peter. 2009. On-line syntax: Thoughts on the temporality of spoken language. *Language Sciences* 31: 1–13.

Bakhtin, Mikhail M. 1981. *The dialogic imagination* (trans: Carl Emerson and Michael Holquist). Austin: University of Texas Press.

Bucholtz, Mary. 1999. "Why being normal?": Language and identity practices in a community of nerd girls. *Language in Society* 28 (2): 203–23.

Chafe, Wallace. 1994. *Discourse, consciousness, and time: The flow and displacement of conscious experience in speaking and writing*. Chicago: University of Chicago.

Du Bois, John W. 2007. The stance triangle. In Robert Englebretson (ed.), *Stancetaking in discourse: Subjectivity, evaluation, interaction*. Amsterdam: John Benjamins. 139–82.

Eckert, Penelope. 2008. Variation and the indexical field. *Journal of Socioloinguistics* 12 (4): 453–76.

Fedriani, Chiara and Andrea Sansò. 2017. Pragmatic markers, discourse markers and modal particles: What do we know and where do we go from here?. In Chiara Fedriani and Andrea Sansò (eds.), *Pragmatics markers, discourse markers and modal particles: New perspectives*. Amsterdam: John Benjamins. 1–33.

Fischer, Kerstin. 2006. Towards an understanding of the spectrum of approaches to discourse particles: Introduction to the volume. In Kerstin Fischer (ed.), *Approaches to discourse particles*. North Holland: Elsevier. 1–20.

Henkin-Roitfarb, Roni. 2011. Hebrew and Arabic in asymmetrical contact in Israel. *Lodz Papers in Pragmatics* 7 (1): 61–100.

Herring, Susan C. 1999. Interactional coherence in CMC. *Journal of Computer-Mediated Communication* 4 (4).

Høigilt, Jacob and Gunvor Mejdell. 2017. Introduction. In Jacob Høigilt and Gunvor Mejdell (eds.), *The politics of written language in the Arab world*. Leiden: Brill. 1–17.

Jucker, Andreas H. and Yael Ziv. 1998. Discourse markers: Introduction. In Andreas H. Jucker and Yael Ziv (eds.), *Discourse markers: Descriptions and theory*. Amsterdam: John Benjamins. 1–12.

Kanaan, Layal, Véronique Traverso, Loubna Dimachki and Joseph Dichy. 2015. Marqueurs de discours en arabe parlé en interaction: Le cas de *ja'ni*. *Faits de Langues* 45: 199–225.

al-Kayyāl, Muna. 2014. *Mabrūk il-madām ḥāmil* (Congratulations! The lady is pregnant). Cairo: Dār uktub.

Kotthoff, Helga. 2002. Irony, quotation, and other forms of staged intertextuality: Double or contrastive perspectivation in conversation. In Carl F. Graumann and Werner Kallmeyer (eds.), *Perspective and perspectivation in discourse*. Amsterdam: John Benjamins. 201–30.

Marmorstein, Michal. 2016. Getting to the point: The discourse marker *ya'ni* (lit. "it means") in unplanned discourse in Cairene Arabic. *Journal of Pragmatics* 96: 60–79.

———. Forthcoming. Discourse markers as a lens to variation across speech and writing: Egyptian Arabic *ya'ni* (lit. "it means") as a case study. *Functions of Language*.

Marmorstein, Michal and Yael Maschler. 2020. Stance-taking via *ya'ani* /*ya'anu*: A discourse marker in a Hebrew-Arabic language contact situation. *Language in Society* 49 (1): 1–30.

Maschler, Yael. 2009. *Metalanguage in interaction: Hebrew discourse markers*. Amsterdam: John Benjamins.

Maschler, Yael, Hilla Polak-Yitzhaki, Stav Fishman, Carmit Miller Shapiro, Netanel Goretsky, Gallith Aghion and Ophir Fofliger. 2017. *The Haifa Corpus of Spoken Hebrew*. http://weblx2.haifa.ac.il/~corpus/corpus_website.

Maschler, Yael and Deborah Schiffrin. 2015. Discourse markers: Language, meaning, and context. In Deborah Tannen, Heidi E. Hamilton and Deborah Schiffrin (eds.), *The handbook of discourse analysis* (2nd ed.). Malden, MA: Blackwell. 189–221.

Matras, Yaron. 2009. *Language contact*. Cambridge: Cambridge University Press.

Mi'awwaḍ, ʔĪhāb. 2010. *Barḍu hatgawwiz tāni* (Still I'll get married again). Cairo: Dār Kayān.

Norén, Kerstin and Per Linell. 2007. Meaning potentials and the interaction between lexis and contexts: An empirical substantiation. *Pragmatics* 17 (3): 387–416.

Östman, Jan-Ola. 1982. The symbiotic relationship between pragmatic particles and impromptu speech. In Nils E. Enkvist (eds.), *Impromptu speech: A symposium* (Meddelanden från Stiftelsens för Åbo Akademi Forskiningsinstitut 78). Åbo: Åbo Akademi. 147–77.

Rosenbaum, Gabriel M. 2012. Modern Egyptian Arabic: From dialect to written language. In Mohamed Meouk, Ángeles Vicente and Pablo Sánchez (eds.), *De los manuscritos medievales a internet: La presencia del árabe vernáculo en las fuentes escritas*. Zaragoza: Universidad de Zaragoza. 359–74.

Rosenthal, Ruvik. 2001. *hazira haleshonit* (The language arena). Tel Aviv: Am Oved.

Schiffrin, Deborah. 1987. *Discourse markers*. Cambridge: Cambridge University Press.

———. 2006. Discourse marker research and theory: Revisiting *and*. In Kerstin Fischer (ed.), *Approaches to discourse particles*. North Holland: Elsevier. 315–38.

Schourup, Lawrence C. 1999. Discourse markers: Tutorial overview. *Lingua* 107: 227–65.

Silverstein, Michael. 2003. Indexical order and the dialectics of sociolinguistic life. *Language and Communication* 23: 193–229.

Spolsky, Bernard and Elana Shohamy. 1999. *The languages of Israel: Policy, ideology and practice*. Clevedon: Multilingual Matters.

Tannen, Deborah. 2007. *Talking voices: Repetition, dialogue, and imagery in conversational discourse* (2nd ed.). Cambridge: Cambridge University Press.

Traugott, Elizabeth C. 2010. Revisiting subjectification and intersubjectification. In Kristin Davidse, Lieven Vandelanotte and Hubert Cuyckens (eds.), *Subjectification, intersubjectification and grammaticalization*. Berlin: Mouton de Gruyter. 29–70.

Versteegh, Kees (chief ed.) and Mushira Eid, Alaa Elgibali, Manfred Woidich and Andrzej Zaborski (eds.). *Encyclopedia of Arabic language and linguistics* (vols. I–V). Leiden: Brill. 2006–10.

6

Reconsidering the Concept of "Total Institutions" in Light of Interactional Sociolinguistics: The Meaning of the Marker "Here"

BRANCA TELLES RIBEIRO AND DIANA DE SOUZA PINTO

IN A RESEARCH INTERVIEW at a Brazilian forensic psychiatric hospital, an inmate/patient (Maria)—who is about to be discharged—refers to her institution while talking to Glaucia, a psychologist/researcher (the extract has been translated from Portuguese):

```
Maria:        yes, but I wanted to leave,
              I hope to leave,
              I don't want to die here, not here.
Glaucia:      right.
Maria:        I am afraid of dying here.
Same interview, some 40 seconds later:
Glaucia:      now there's something,
              I've noticed that everyone knows you around here, Maria,
              everyone kids you when they see you,
              everyone likes you,
              you are very much liked around here, right?
Maria:        they like me … I don't wanna leave here any more.
Glaucia:      don't wanna (leave) any more?
Maria:        don't wanna [crying]
```

To what extent would a close analysis of talk and interaction in a forensic psychiatric hospital contribute to a better understanding of what is considered a "total institution" as defined by Erving Goffman (1961)? And how would such understandings be considered in light of Foucault's (1975, 2006a) discussion on the relationship between power and institutions? This chapter places language and communication within interactional contexts and discusses how such focus would contribute to the understanding of institutional discourse.

In revisiting Goffman's discussion of total institutions, as well as Foucault's analysis of regimes of practices in institutions such as psychiatric hospitals and prisons, our present study analyzes how small-scale interactions (situated discourse practices) and large-scale effects (sociological and historical constructs) are combined and produced through talk. Central to our discussion is the notion that context emerges from a given social situation. Interactants help create the very context in which they act; they "dynamically reshape the context that provides organization for their actions within the interaction itself" (Duranti and Goodwin 1992, 5). Participants use what they know about the social situation (the location and participants' goals, expectations, intentions, and effects) to co-construct who they are (performed identities) and what they do (what activity they engage in). Identities are hence produced through discourse practices and are experienced rather than just represented in a given context.

Specifically, we will discuss how participants in a total institution, such as a forensic psychiatric institution, may display ambiguous and uncertain positions in a variety of alignments to self and other. For example, in our data, an inmate/patient[1] may shift from giving credence to the institution (and thus aligning herself with the institutional discourse) to promoting distance (and displaying contradictory and ambivalent stances); also the data indicates that mental health-care providers may act confused when the psychiatric institution fails to provide clear norms for certain behaviors, such as patients' sexual practices in a hospital setting.

Two types of interactions, situated in very different settings, are discussed in this chapter. First, we examine a conversation between a psychiatric inmate/patient and a researcher conducted in a forensic hospital. The research interview takes place a few years after the inmate/patient Maria was discharged after thirty years of institutionalization. Rather than leaving the forensic hospital Maria decided to stay, because she no longer had any social or family support. The institution provided her room and board, which she accepted for lack of other living options. Our discussion focuses on how this inmate/patient refers to herself and others as it relates to where she is. Indexical processes (particularly the use of the deictics "you," "I," and "here") capture the dynamics of identity performance and social participation in a specific location that she viewed both as a prison and a home. Short segments of data analysis attest to Maria's sharp ambiguity about staying at the institution. Second, we examine an excerpt from a focus-group discussion among mental health-care providers on sexuality, sexual practices, and HIV prevention in a psychiatric hospital. While providers acknowledge that sexual practices take place within the hospital, most do not know how to cope with the sexual activities of patients or how to position themselves. Some shift their understanding of what constitutes privacy in a psychiatric hospital. Specific locations (a room, a ward, a garden) may index different understandings (a therapist approves of a patient having sex in a private room but not in a ward). Also, the same location may be seen as either a private or a public space. Ambivalence regarding acceptance or denial of sexual practices emerges in the data. Examining the use of certain markers, such as the deictic "here," is particularly interesting in discussing how a provider relates to location. Both sets of data highlight that a total institution can be interpreted as either a public or a private space and viewed alternatively as a safe and a tough space. This discussion contributes to Goffman's (1961) research on the notion of total institutions in capturing clear identity shifts and ambiguity in an inmate/patient or among mental health-care professionals.

Despite Goffman's and Foucault's different perspectives on institutional practices, mainly to what extent global processes (or social forces) and local practices (or human agency) are interrelated, for the present discussion some of their concepts are helpful to the analysis of talk and interaction in such institutions. Goffman's (1961) analysis of total institutions, particularly asylums, and Foucault's (1975) investigation of the regimes of practices and discourses that embody disciplinary power present important perspectives to understand the complex processes that underlie institutionalization, especially the stripping of identities (so-called "normal" identities) that a patient or inmate/patient undergoes at admittance to a total institution. Both Goffman and Foucault dissect many processes of institutionalization. Goffman sees social interaction as strategic conduct; he focuses on disclosing the tacit knowledge used by social actors when enacting social encounters. He provides rich descriptions of strategies patients often use in a total institution to resist and to maintain their personal worlds, the so-called primary and secondary adjustments (discussed below). Foucault dissects the relationship between power and knowledge, and discusses how disciplinary technology aims and succeeds in controlling patients' bodies, time, and activities, and produces docile bodies.

Interactional sociolinguistics (IS) is well suited to examining the (re)production of the identities and power relations among those who live and work in total institutions. IS embraces "a comprehensive framework for engaging with the empirical specifics"—in this case, the everyday activities of specific institutions—required for any theoretical social science that is aligned with practice theory (Rampton 2019, 13). At its core, IS proposes a link between small-scale interactions and large-scale sociological systems. It analyzes the use of language in society through situated speaking practices (Schiffrin 1994). The following discussion presupposes that language is ubiquitously indexical, which has been central to IS (Gumperz 1982, 1999). It examines indexical communication processes in light of participants' expectations and actions (about themselves and others) and the sociological/historical systems at play in situated institutional contexts.

Interactional Sociolinguistics: Contextualization Process

When Goffman (1964, 1974, 1981) highlights the study of the social situation, he points to the construction of meaning by all participants. The question he asks is both semantic and pragmatic: "What is going on here?" In other words, meaning and sense-making are determined by what is being communicated and metacommunicated by participants as they interact. Hence, context may change from moment to moment: a situational perspective shares with an ethnomethodological perspective (e.g., Atkinson and Heritage 1984) and symbolic interactionism (e.g., Dennis and Martin 2005) the assumption that context is not given a priori but is continually renewed and modified. As Erickson and Shultz (1982, 147) note, "the capacity to assess *when* a context is as well as *what* it is" is an essential part of social and communicative competence. Interactants signal and recognize transition points in activities to produce behavior appropriate to each stage. In this regard, Gumperz's (1982, 1992) "contextualization cues" are crucial. These may include code, register, style, topic, tempo, rhythm, voice quality, formulaic expressions, and nonverbal behavior (eye gaze, postural shifts, laughing, etc.). They are conventionally associated with particular settings, events, and participants, and generally function as cues to a change in the situation.

Deictics as Contextualization Cues

In order to understand language and communication in a total institution—particularly the notion of representation of a given location (a room, a ward, a hospital), and inferencing (how to understand what the interactants mean and do)—our analysis will discuss the use of specific contextualization cues, such as referential deictics ("I," "you," "Maria," "patients"), and location deitics (specifically the explicit and implicit use of "here"). Social identities and multifaceted roles are discursively constructed and embedded in given locations. Unless we know where speakers are, we will not be able to assign meaning to a discourse marker expressed as a *locator* (Schiffrin 1987, 322). For example, what would the contextual coordinator "here" mean to an inmate/patient and a researcher as a subjective locator, or as what Hymes (1974) calls a psychological scene or geographical physical place or setting? Our analysis discusses these multiple contextual layers.

Schiffrin (1987, 322) points out that the speaker holds the "deictic center" of an utterance by which other coordinates are established (speaker, hearer, time, and place) and assigned a context-specific interpretation. In our analysis we examine how participants hold this deictic center by positioning themselves and others as it relates to where they are. Positioning is an intricate (and sometimes elusive) characteristic of interactive talk (Davies and Harré 1990). Positioning shifts occur when participants adopt different alignments or stances in interaction, and can themselves be (re)positioned by others. Goffman calls these nuanced moves shifts in footing and reframings (1974, 1981). In our discussion, linguistic deixis—a marker for self or an indicator for a location—helps signal positionings. Analyzing the use of deixis reveals how contextualization develops in communication, that is, how interactants point to self or others in talk exchanges or how they refer to settings in various communicative acts.

Summarizing, the IS approach highlights the moment-by-moment construction of meaning where context is ever shifting. Such contextual redefinitions are crucial to understand how inmates/patients or health-care providers locate themselves and others within complex social structures such as total institutions.

Total Institutions and Regimes of Practice

Foucault (1975, [1975] 2006b) and Goffman (1961) provided powerful frameworks for analyzing interactions in mental health institutions. Two concepts are particularly relevant: Foucault's concepts of power and resistance and Goffman's notion of adjustments. For Foucault, power is enacted/practiced at the micro-levels of social relations and is ubiquitous; resistance is coextensive with power. Whenever there are power relations—including in the most common everyday talk—patterns of resistance frequently emerge.

Foucault's investigations provide detailed descriptions of how discourses and theories about the social world relate to power and the ways in which knowledge and power produce regimes of truth: knowledge and power play a role in the creation of specific historical mechanisms that produce discourses and implement what is seen as "truth" at a given location and during a given period of time (Foucault, 1972). In his examination of psychiatry, Foucault asked what types of knowledge and power have created the conditions for a new discipline by which "insane"[2] individuals are the object of scrutiny.

In a second phase, Foucault is primarily concerned with the "archaeology of power." He seeks to understand how discursive practices produce individuals who are subject to a disciplinary society that classifies, categorizes, and determines who are and are not normal. Relevant to our study, Foucault focuses on how psychiatric practices produce truth-value statements regarding those classified as "insane." He conceived of the asylum as the place where order and power dominate; where the constant regulation of activities, gestures, and, particularly, time, takes place. Rules of all sorts run through the bodies. Psychiatric power relies on disciplinary order. Therefore, the asylum is a socially constructed apparatus that produces discursive practices, that in turn constitute representations of madness. In asylums, as in other disciplinary institutions such as prisons, power is meticulously planned and calculated.

Goffman (1961) entered the enclosed world of the clinic, and specifically psychiatry, from an ethnographic and sociological perspective. *Asylums* describes an American psychiatric institution in the 1960s and examines some of the institution's purposes, namely to control and discipline inmates. The total institution defines contexts where all human activities (sleeping, eating, showering, comingling) become visible to one another and are conducted under the same single authority. A total institution—such as the forensic psychiatric hospital in our study—comprises an isolated enclosed social system whose primary purpose is to control most aspects of its inmates'/patients' lives. It is a place where physical barriers separate the external from the internal world and where all activities of human life (sleeping, eating, working) are conducted in the same place.

Becker (2003) asserts that Goffman proposes a terminology still important today that points to his theoretical and empirical positions: patients' "moral career," "mortifications of the self," and "total institutions" are specific terms of the Goffmanian universe of mental illnesses or inmates. The term "career" relates to "a trajectory that the individual covers along his/her life" (Goffman 1961, 111). When hospitalized, the mentally ill person's behavior is ordered by pattern changes that result in modifying ways of interpreting and evaluating oneself and others (112). While examining the intimate life of a public institution, Goffman points out that the institution expects patients to behave according to the established norms. Individuals adopt a "primary adjustment" when they identify with and cooperate with the goals of a social organization.

However, individuals confront disciplinary expectations by enacting "secondary adjustments." These adjustments represent forms where the individual may behave in nonprescribed ways (Goffman 1961, 189). They represent the "individual's bondage to other types of social entity" (1961, 197). Such practices, known as "distancing practices," are referred to by Goffman as the underlife of an institution (1961, 199). In the context of a mental hospital, it "consists of adjustments that patients make using resources of the institution, officially designed for other purposes to re-establish territories of the self, spheres of autonomy, separate social structures, and separate system of status" (1961, 201–3).

Following Goffman (1961, 183), it seems to us reasonable to consider that sexual practices within a psychiatric institution illustrate such adjustments. Sexual practices are the main subject of the mental health-care providers' focus-group discussion. Also it seems reasonable to consider secondary adjustments as an equivalent to "practices of resistance," in Foucault's terms. If power is exercised over individual bodies through a set of discursive practices (whose final aim is to maintain individuals under control and surveillance), sexual practices in psychiatric institutions might be enacted as a way to resist discipline. As Branaman (1997, lx) puts it, "certain stances are available to even the more marginalized members of society." Goffman himself adds "a certain recalcitrance to complete social determination is an essential constituent of the self" (1961, 319). The data discussion captures these shifts and acts of resistance.

The Research Setting: The Brazilian Institutions

Our discussion is prompted by Brazilian Portuguese research interviews conducted at a forensic psychiatric institution and a psychiatric hospital in the city of Rio de Janeiro, Brazil. We conducted ethnographic field observations, audio-recorded interviews and focus-group discussions, and transcribed, translated, and analyzed talk in these institutional settings (Pinto, Ribeiro and Dantas 2005; Ribeiro, Pinto and Mann 2014; Wainberg et al. 2016). Ethnographic descriptions of the interview contexts and its participants informed our analysis. This research examined inmates/patients' and mental health-care providers' ambivalence, mobility, and relative agency, as well as ongoing changes in the institutions themselves.

The first setting—the forensic psychiatric hospital—was a custody and treatment institution that admitted mentally ill patients convicted of crimes ranging from misdemeanors to serious felonies.[3] It was the first forensic psychiatric hospital in Latin America. In 2013, following a process of deinstitutionalization of the mentally ill, the institution became responsible for the psychiatric examinations for all convicted criminals in the state of Rio de Janeiro.[4]

Forensic psychiatric hospitals are hybrid institutions that primarily treat and confine adult inmates/patients. However, given the Brazilian deinstitutionalization process (Hirdes 2009) these institutions took on other institutional roles, such as sheltering a few ex-inmates/patients who lacked social support and structure for basic care, safety, and independence.

At the time data was collected in 2011, the institution had three main buildings: the administration, the male ward, and the female ward. Besides a cafeteria and a small soccer court, there were two renovated one-bedroom houses that served as shelters for a couple of male and female ex-inmates/patients. The institution offered some support to help inmates/patients adapt to a semi-independent life. However, progressively a culture of imprisonment prevailed, where inmates/patients would still comply with unstated rules and norms that again ordered their daily lives. As a consequence, these patients would negotiate adjustments with the staff over institutional requirements and prohibitions, consistent with Goffman's (1961) definition of a "total institution."

The second setting—the Institute of Psychiatry—is a mental health teaching and research hospital in Rio de Janeiro. Admittance to the psychiatric wards, the daycare hospital, and the outpatient clinic are institutional resources available to all patients. As a public hospital, it serves patients who typically come from the adult working and lower-middle classes. Ward policies have shifted over the last forty years from strictly male/female to mixed wards (between 1996 and 2002, following psychiatric European guidelines) and then back to separate wards (Wainberg et al. 2007).

Total Institutions and Disciplinary Practices in Light of Discourse Analysis

In analyzing total institutions, Goffman (1961, 180) focused on the different stances participants take that are often dialectal; it is through a "dialectic of identification and distancing that the identity of a participant in a social organization is defined." Such stances are particularly interesting when analyzing language and communication in a psychiatric setting. They capture the multifaceted notion of institutional discourse (Sarangi and Roberts 1999) and how psychiatric patients, inmates/patients, and mental health-care providers may express contradictory and ambivalent positions regarding the institution.

Ambivalent Positionings and Contradictory Wants

In the research interviews, some discharged inmates/patients had ambivalent responses about their confinement in a forensic psychiatric hospital ("Is it a place for treatment or for custody?"). Maria—a fifty-year-old working-class single woman who had lived at the institution for thirty years (see the opening of this chapter)—clearly performs such ambivalent positionings (Davies and Harré 1990). In addressing a twenty-minute research interview conducted by Glaucia, a forty-year-old clinical psychologist and also a researcher, Maria presents ambivalent positionings about her confinement: the institution can be seen as "good. You can eat, you can sleep, you have everything" and it can also be viewed negatively "[crying] but I hope I can leave."

These contradictory positionings were often the case for Maria, who had a long history of hospitalization in different mental institutions that had started when she was eighteen. After she had been discharged, she spent some time wandering around the city, mainly in her old neighborhood. However, she voluntarily asked to return to the institution. As she would tell the team of researchers afterward, "this (i.e., the forensic psychiatric hospital) is the place I belong to." This episode illustrates the importance of the institutional space to the inmate/patient's sense of self and to her sense of belonging. It is also a discursive and identification practice that is co-constructed with many others (staff, researchers, and inmates/patients) through social interaction in situated contexts.

In our data, certain markers, such as the word "here," not only encode the spatial-temporal location in relation to where participants are but also capture processes of identity shifts. In the interview, the marker "here" is reiterated by both interlocutors, but "here" can assume different interactional meanings. Also the recurrent use of such deictics conveys a sense of involvement (Tannen 1989) and sometimes intense emotions felt by the interviewees and inmates/patients:

Segment 1: At the onset of the interview (in this and other extracts, our English translation appears on top and the original Portuguese appears underneath in italics):

1. Glaucia: and how do you like it here?
               e o que que você acha daqui?
2. Maria: here it's good for me,
               aqui pra mim é bom,
               you can eat, you can sleep, you have everything but (not audible), [she cries]
               que tem onde comer, tem onde dormir, tem tudo, mas (transcrição impossível) [Maria chora]
3. Glaucia: um hum, today you have here a place of your own, isn't it?
               uhum, hoje você aqui tem seu cantinho, é isso?
4. Maria: [crying] but I'm hoping I can leave.
               [chorando] mas eu tô com a esperança de ir embora.

This interview takes place at a time when Maria is no longer a convict. However, she has opted to stay at the forensic psychiatric hospital as an intern, where she has her own room. In turn 1, Glaucia asks Maria an open question (and introduces a new topic) "and how do you like it here?" where the deictic "here" may have several meanings: a hospital, a shelter, and a home. Maria responds by juxtaposing a sequence of actions that enables us to interpret "here" as home. She first evaluates "here" positively ("it's good for me") and then explains her previous assessment by describing very basic needs ("you can eat, you can sleep") being fulfilled by the institution. She closes with an encompassing statement that reinforces how good "here" is: "you have everything" (shelter, care, and food). Two aspects need to be discussed in her response. First, Maria uses a third-person indefinite reference marked by the verb in Portuguese, signaling detachment, as if she were an observer of this scene rather than an actual participant. Second, she shifts to a contrastive position ("but"), repositions herself, and uses a semiotic sign of distress (crying).

As a sequence, the interviewer uses "here" a third time in a yes/no question ("um hum, today you have here a place of your own, isn't it?" in turn 3); the expression "a place of your own" adds a personal and emotional connection to the location. Some background information helps contextualize this utterance: in 2010, the hospital leadership approved the development of a shelter to house previous inmates who had no family ties or any other social support and needed to remain at the institution. Maria was the first to live in this location—a small one-bedroom house, built at the back of the institution to function as a temporary shelter—along with two other female inmates/patients. Ethnographic observations indicate that Maria was extremely happy to have "a place of her own," as she initially told many people. She was particularly proud that her living space was tidy and attractive. In turn 3, the interviewer echoes Maria's prior positive assessment and initial positioning about having everything. Maria was known to be helpful and thoughtful. She was sympathetic to others, whom she would frequently ask how things were going, if people (selected staff and inmates/patients) were upset, and if so, why. She was eager to help prepare for holiday events and even work on repairs of the facilities. In discussing the forensic institute as "location," it is evident how social and cultural sources of selfhood provide room for the co-construction of identities: Maria as empathetic, as resourceful, as interested in the well-being of others. However, in turn 4, Maria reassesses her present situation by crying (signaling a lament or complaint), repositions herself, and closes the conversation by stating that she hopes she can leave. Although implicitly acknowledging that she has a place of her own, it seems that having such a place is no longer enough. She reframes the location as a place (she) hopes to leave, connoting a painful reference to the hospital where she has been kept away from the world for most of her adult life (thirty years).

In the next segment, the interviewer reminds Maria how popular she is in this institution. Location ("here") refers to the place where Maria has co-constructed her identity with many others over the years and where she has been ratified, accepted, and appreciated by many others.

These positive responses contrast sharply with how she was perceived in her early years of confinement, when staff and inmates stated that she was aggressive and feared by everyone.

Segment 2: Ten minutes into the interview (following opening except):

1. Glaucia: now there's something,
            agora uma coisa,
            I've noticed that everyone knows you around here, Maria,
            eu observei que todo mundo aqui dentro conhece a Maria,
            everyone kids you when they see you,
            todo mundo passa e brinca com você,
            everyone likes you,
            todo mundo gosta de você,
            you are very much liked around here, right?
            você é muito querida aqui, né?
2. Maria: they like me ... I don't wanna leave (from) here any more.
            gostam... eu não quero mais ir embora daqui não...
3. Glaucia: don't wanna (leave) any more?
            não quer mais não?
4. Maria: don't wanna [crying]
            quero não. (choro)

Maria responds affirmatively to Glaucia's repositioning and claims that other inmates/patients appreciate her ("they like me") and concludes after a brief pause "I don't wanna leave here any more." Once again, she expresses an ambivalent position toward her location, but this time she does so consistent with the way Glaucia positions her. It seems that recognizing herself as the object of attention and care of others gives Maria some comfort and provides her with a positive assessment of self, which shifts her position "I don't wanna leave here any more." Being reminded of the many others in her life triggers a shift from a position of pain to a position of some comfort. The closing emotional statement of crying works as a contextualization cue of her ambivalence and distress in recognizing her objective and subjective locations: how misplaced she might feel as a former inmate for whom "here"—the forensic psychiatric hospital—has been the sole location where she can truly relate and construct herself, and while staying in this location, now more of a shelter than a prison, she can be appreciated by many others. Conflicting social and psychological interpretations take place: Maria touches on both the isolation of an inmate (removed from the wider world), and the appreciation of many others (including the interviewer and researcher) with whom one has cocreated important relationships in this specific location. Language and communication anchor sociological and psychological information.

Mental Health-Care Professionals: Ambivalent Responses to Psychiatric Patients' Sexual Practices

Ambivalent positionings can also be observed when mental health-care professionals (MHCPs)—doctors, psychologists, social assistants, and nurses—attempt to define the psychiatric hospital. Is it a place for treatment? A place for counseling? A place to control psychiatric patients' emotions? These contradictory definitions are particularly problematic when MHCPs confront taboo practices—such as sexual activities—at the institution (Wainberg et al. 2007; Wainberg et al. 2016). Ribeiro, Pinto, and Mann (2014) investigated how MHCPs voice their perceptions and positions regarding the sexuality of psychiatric patients particularly when they have to deal with sexual activities in the institutional context. In a multidisciplinary focus-group discussion in 2003, thirteen MHCPs discussed how the group viewed issues of sexuality, mental health, and HIV/AIDS.[5] The MHCPs often expressed a variety of positionings and feelings ranging from caring to perplexity, from a duty of repressing and enforcing the prohibition of sex to counseling clients/patients on sexually transmitted disease prevention. Professionals said they were uncertain about the goals of the institution (caring? protecting? controlling?) and what enforcement actions were required.

Indexing location signals a shifting relationship by professionals to the institution, which ultimately implies the performance of multiple identities (such as a caregiver, a counselor, or a guardian). In the following segment from a focus-group discussion among health-care professionals, a nurse technician narrates an event that attests to her conflicted position over sexual practices "here." Faced with two patients having sex in a standard bedroom that accommodates up to four patients in a male/female ward, she inquires—using "constructed dialogue" (Tannen, 1989) to animate her utterance in the story—"what's happening here?"

Segment 3

```
Nilma:  I got in the ward, not thinking much,
        Eu entrei de bobeira na enfermaria,
        two patients were having sex,
        dois pacientes transando,
        then I put my hands up and said "what's happening (here)?"
```

> *aí eu botei a mão na cintura e falei "que que é isso?"*
> (laughter) (...) but that was the only reaction I had.
> *(risos) (...) mas foi a única reação que eu tive.*
> then they left and I didn't know what to say,
> *aí eles saíram e eu não sabia o que dizer,*
> either "you can't do this" or "can do this but not (here)."
> *ou "não pode fazer isso" ou "faz isso mas não (aqui)."*
> you're not ready when it happens, you know it happens,
> *na hora você não espera, você sabe que acontece,*
> yet you don't expect to see it (here).
> *mas você não espera ver (isso aqui).*

Nilma's reported reaction is to gesture ("put my hands up") and then shout, "what's happening here?"; both phrases point to her shock. Nilma has unwillingly become a witness to a private relationship. Additionally, sexual practices among in-patients are prohibited in Brazilian clinical institutions. Thus, in the rhetorical question she puts forward ("what's happening (here)?"), the implicit deictic "here" points to a personal system of moral beliefs—which activities of patients are seen as right or wrong in a ward—that seems to guide her institutional performance. It also highlights the inappropriateness of the activities in a place where individuals' actions are assumed to be controlled by the power relationships engendered through disciplinary practices (Dennis and Martin 2005; Dreyfus and Rabinow 1983). Thus, it seems that the marker "here" captures multiple interrelated contextual layers: the subjective psychological scene (the effect on the nurse as a witness to a private event), the moral event (the nurse deciding whether this event is morally acceptable in this location), the clinical institutional scene (the assessment and prohibition by the health-care provider), and the physical setting (private events in a public domain: a room in a ward in a psychiatric hospital).

Nilma's words indicate that she lacked the interactional competence to deal with the unexpected situation (she explains, "I didn't know what to say"). Her ambivalence is then reinforced when she links two alternative statements ("either ... or") that point to the prohibition of sexual practices at the hospital: "either 'you can't do this' or 'can do this but not (here).'" Thus, by redirecting actions to specific locations in terms of scenes and settings (Hymes 1974), Nilma affirms the asylum as a productive power apparatus (Foucault 2006a), which sustains a set of statements that are taken as legitimate/rightful: as psychiatric patients are deprived of reason, they cannot take agency for their own actions—having sex, for instance—instead, patients should be mentored and guided psychologically, morally, and clinically. Disciplinary practices produce docile bodies. Yet, these practices also leave room for resistance to take place.

Finally, Nilma moves from the self ("I") and uses the general, indeterminate "you" to acknowledge that despite ongoing sexual activities in the institution, professionals lack expertise and guidance on how to cope with it. She constructs herself and her peers as perplexed and sometimes frustrated professionals trying to understand such complex topics and activities.

This focus-group discussion illustrates perspectives seldom explored when it comes to the investigation of total institutions. The discussion examines sensitive topics about psychiatric patients' sexuality and sexual practices within the institutional space. In Goffman's terms, the staff is a small class that supervises and controls the patients. The staff is also socially integrated with the outside world and in general conceives the other members, inmates or patients, in a stereotypical way. Moreover, the staff tends to feel righteous and knowledgeable, while patients are commonly perceived as instances of embodied pathologies who are not able to make decisions on their own and are treated likewise.

However, our discussion in this chapter (and in a prior analysis; Ribeiro, Pinto and Mann 2014) portrays professionals whose discourses point to an alternative assessment and understanding of the institutional context. Sexual practices among psychiatric patients in the institutional space are acknowledged and could be interpreted not as acts of disobedience, but as practices of resistance (Foucault 2006a) against the so-called stripping process that results from the mortification of the self (Goffman 1961). Additionally, while reflecting upon the function of the institution, the MHCPs question themselves about the extent of their responsibilities and duties in a hybrid institutional context (is it a place of care, treatment, or confinement?). They acknowledge their lack of interactional skills to cope with these challenges, positioning themselves as lacking competence in decision-making in delicate matters. Instead of relying on their institutional and official authority, conforming to the social and normative expectations, they express anxiety, distress, and discomfort by assuming a perplexed position that emphasizes their uncertainties.

IS assumes that language is ubiquitously indexical, that it is "continuously pointing to persons, practices, settings, objects and ideas" (Rampton 2019). Our discussion has focused on the use of deictic markers, and specifically how the so-called total institutions are conceived and interpreted in patients' and health-care providers' discourse. We discuss two types of discourse processes, namely participants' inferential process and their process of contextualization, key to the construction of a theory of social practice (Gumperz 1982; Jacquemet 2011; Rampton 2019; Schiffrin 1994). Such sociolinguistic theory examines the connection between dynamic interactive processes and large-scale sociological effects that "combine to create or to eliminate social distinctions" (Gumperz 1982, 29).

A few common themes emerge when looking at location as it relates to self and other in total institutions. First, location may be a private place, a "place of one's own" (where the place is kept tidy for one's own use and one is proud of that space). For Maria, it is the only place where she has spent most of her adult life: a ward, but later also her home and shelter, where she now feels protected and cared for. This private space of care, safety, and relationships is, however, contrasted with the public space, a second theme. In public locations such as total institutions, there are physical barriers, as Foucault (1975) and Goffman (1961) describe. Separation can be used as a disciplinary strategy. The effects of accumulated social practices of exclusion and difference emerge in the data. There is loneliness (Maria cries) and limitations as others with more power (staff, guards, researchers, MHCPs) control and limit time, practices, and habits.

Ambiguous positions clearly emerge in how an inmate/patient indexes location. Having a sense of the private space (a room, a home) versus the public space (a ward, a hospital) provide for very different positionings of self and other. In such cases, it seems that it is not one position versus another, but rather both or sometimes ambivalent positions at the same time: one is sad and happy, as Maria cries of sadness and happiness in her processes of institutionalization and deinstitutionalization; she also wishes to leave and stay at the same time. Thus, the analysis of deictics, specifically locators, in discourse among those who reside in a forensic psychiatric hospital brings to light a set of social and normative expectations of the institution; however, it also connotes where Maria, as an individual, performs various aspects of her social identities (as empathetic, resourceful, and interested in others' well-being) that distances her from an essentialized and static identity of a forensic psychiatric hospital inmate.

Ambivalent and contradictory positions are also present among MHCPs, mostly when they relate to practices that have yet to be fully examined and regulated, such as patients' rights to exert their sexuality within hospital settings (Ribeiro, Pinto and Mann 2014). Professionals shift positions according to their perception of the hospital; is "here" a place for treatment and care, or is it a place where patients should obey rigid rules? Is it a public or a private place? How much privacy can inmates/patients have within a public space? MHCPs often display a lack of interactional competence, ambiguity, and perplexity in their relationship to inpatients and to themselves when indexing location as it relates to practices, such as sex acts in wards, that are not yet fully understood and accepted. These practices challenge unstated conventional rules that sustain power relations in such institutions.

Goffman (1961) explored the implications of total institutions upon the construction of self for patients and inmates. He focuses on degrading procedures and reduced opportunities for interactions with others in the outer world. However, in both institutions under investigation in this discussion, some of the "adjustment strategies" have played an important role. Nilma's statements above challenge the expected and homogeneous values of the staff, as well as the set of attitudes and knowledge that the staff takes for granted. Professional teams face institutional dilemmas of their own. MHCPs seem to distance themselves from "regimes of truth" that give structure and constitute the disciplinary institution; consequently these professionals also distance themselves from the position of authority and guardians. It is reasonable to affirm that by practicing sex openly within a psychiatric institution, patients are transgressing a set of norms designed to control and discipline their bodies. These transgressive practices then suggest a subjective dimension and relative autonomy. Patients seem to consent to restrictions on their freedom by not practicing sex openly, but rather privately (in a room), removed from public scrutiny, and thus creating forms of resistance.

Investigations grounded in microanalysis of talk and interactions among inmates/patients, psychiatric patients, caretakers, and researchers contribute to a better understanding of the complexity of total institutions, such as a forensic psychiatric institution and a psychiatric hospital, which have not been sufficiently investigated. In analyzing transcripts of co-constructedness of situated social practices (such as a research interview or a focus-group discussion), studies that utilize interactional sociolinguistic theory help clarify the complex processes of identity construction and challenge the notion of essentialized identity in institutional discourses (Ribeiro 1994). While total institutions are characterized by power relations often engendered to discipline bodies, they are also part of complex social units, where human beings (re)create themselves in everyday talk and activities, and where they learn how to affect others and are also affected by others discursively.

Appendix: Transcription Conventions

Transcription Convention	Meaning
.	Sentence-final falling intonation
,	Sentence-final rising and fall intonation; more to come
?	(Brazilian Portuguese question pattern)
…	Pause (length of time was not assigned)
(…)	Short text omitted
(not audible)	Transcription impossible
(words)	Uncertain transcription
[ ]	Description of nonverbal behavior

Notes

1   In this chapter, the term "inmate/patient" is employed for those who were confined in the forensic psychiatric institution because it captures the institution's hybrid nature of both prison and hospital (our first site). We use the term "patient" for research subjects who were interns undergoing treatment in the psychiatric hospital (our second site).
2   Foucault uses the term "insane" in *History of Madness* ([1975] 2006b), where he investigates how historical, economic, and cultural forces determine that a derailed person should be perceived as dangerous and as such should be confined.
3   Ethical norms in Brazil require anonymity related to participants and institutions. We are grateful to national research agencies (CNPq, FAPERJ, among others) that have encouraged and sponsored interdisciplinary studies in psychiatric hospitals, prisons, and related "enclosed" institutions.
4   Pinto and associates (Pinto 2011; Pinto and Nascimento 2012; Santos, Farias and Pinto 2015) coordinated an interdisciplinary research project on narrative studies at this institution. This project investigated the social-historical memory of this forensic psychiatric hospital by focusing on the narratives of inmates, reports from the management team, and the analysis of institutional documents so as to understand how the institution was perceived and portrayed by its users and the public at large.
5   Taping, transcribing, and analyzing focus-group discussions by MHCPs at the Institute of Psychiatry was part of *The Interdisciplinary Project in Sexuality, Mental Health, and AIDS* (PRISSMA) that anchored the creation of a Brazilian provider-delivered HIV prevention for severely mentally ill patients (Wainberg et al. 2007; Wainberg et al. 2016).

References

Atkinson, J. Maxwell and John Heritage (eds.). 1984. *Structures of social action: Studies in conversation analysis.* Cambridge: Cambridge University Press.

Becker, Howard S. 2003. The politics of presentation: Goffman and total institutions. *Symbolic Interaction* 26 (4): 659–69.

Branaman, Ann. 1997. Goffman's social theory. In Charles C. Lemert and Ann Branaman (eds.), *The Goffman reader.* Malden: Blackwell. xlv–lxxxii.

Davies, Bronwyn and Rom Harré. 1990. Positioning: The discursive construction of selves. *Journal for the Theory of Social Behaviour* 20 (1): 43–63.

Dennis, Alex and Peter J. Martin. 2005. Symbolic interactionism and the concept of power. *The British Journal of Sociology.* 56 (2): 191–213.

Dreyfus, Hubert L. and Paul Rabinow. 1983. *Michel Foucault: Beyond structuralism and hermeneutics.* Chicago: University of Chicago Press.

Duranti, Alessandro and Charles Goodwin (eds.). 1992. *Rethinking context: An introduction.* Cambridge: Cambridge University Press.

Erickson, Frederick and Jeffrey Schultz. 1982. *The counselor as a gatekeeper: Social interaction in interviews.* New York: Academic Press.

Foucault, Michel. 1972. *Power/Knowledge: Selected interviews & other writings 1972–1977.* Colin Gordon (ed.). Colin Gordon, Leo Marshall, John Mepham, and Kate Soper (trans.). New York: Random House.

———. 1975. *Discipline and punish: The birth of the prison* (trans: Alan Sheridan). London: Penguin.

———. 2006a. *Psychiatric power: Lectures at the Collège de France, 1973–1974.* New York: Palgrave Macmillan.

———. (1975) 2006b. *History of madness.* New York: Routledge.

Goffman, Erving. 1961. *Asylums.* New York: Anchor Books.

———. 1964. The neglected situation. *American Anthropologist* 66 (6): 133–36.

———. 1974. *Frame analysis.* New York: Harper and Row.

———. 1981. *Forms of talk.* Philadelphia: University of Pennsylvania Press.

Gumperz, John J. 1982. *Discourse strategies.* Cambridge: Cambridge University Press.

———. 1992. Contextualization and understanding. In Alessandro Duranti and Charles Goodwin (eds.), *Rethinking context: Language as an interactive phenomenon.* Cambridge: Cambridge University Press. 229–52.

———. 1999. On interactional sociolinguistic method. In Srikant Sarangi and Celia Roberts (eds.), *Talk, work and institutional order. Discourse in medical, mediation and management settings.* New York: Mouton de Gruyter. 453–71.

Hirdes, Alice. 2009. The psychiatric reform in Brazil: A (re)view. *Ciência & Saúde Coletiva* 14 (1): 297–305.

Hymes, Dell. 1974. *Foundations in sociolinguistics: An ethnographic approach.* Philadelphia: University of Pennsylvania Press.

Jacquemet, Marco. 2011. Crosstalk 2.0: Asylum and communicative breakdown. *Interdisciplinary Journal of Language and Discourse Communication Studies* 31 (4): 475–97.

Pinto, Diana de Souza. 2011. Discourse analysis, the use of images and the health field: Theoretical-methodological aspects. *RECIIS: Electronic Journal of Communication Information and Innovation in Health* 5 (2): 8–15.

Pinto, Diana de Souza, Claudio Gruber Mann, Milton Wainberg, Paulo Mattos and Suely Broxado de Oliveira. 2007. Vulnerability to HIV, and mental health: An ethnographic study of psychiatric institutions. *Cadernos de Saúde Pública* Fiocruz 23 (9): 2224–33.

Pinto, Diana de Souza and Uriel Massalves de Souza do Nascimento. 2012. Caminhos da memória social do Hospital de Custódia e Tratamento Heitor Carrilho: Uma investigação filosófica. *Psicanálise & Barroco em Revista* 10 (1): 1–22.

Pinto, Diana, Branca Telles Ribeiro and Maria Tereza Lopes Dantas. 2005. "Let the heart speak out": Interviewing practices by psychiatrists from two different traditions. *Communication & Medicine* 2 (2): 177–88.

Rampton, Ben. 2019. Interactional sociolinguistics. In Karin Tusting (ed.), *The Routledge handbook of linguistic ethnography*. London: Routledge.

Ribeiro, Branca Telles. 1994. *Coherence in psychotic discourse*. Oxford: Oxford University Press.

Ribeiro, Branca Telles, Diana de Souza Pinto and Claudio Gruber Mann. 2014. Mental healthcare professionals' role performance: Challenges in the institutional order of a psychiatric hospital. In Heidi E. Hamilton and Wen-ying Sylvia Chou (eds.), *The Routledge handbook of language and health communication*. New York: Routledge. 389–406.

Santos, Ana Luiza Gonçalves dos, Francisco Ramos de Farias and Diana de Souza Pinto. 2015. Por uma sociedade sem hospitais de custódia e tratamento psiquiátrico. *História, Ciências, Saúde-Manguinhos* 22 (4): 1215–30.

Sarangi, Srikant and Celia Roberts (eds.). 1999. *Talk, work and institutional order: Discourse in medical, mediation and management settings*. New York: Mouton de Gruyter.

Schiffrin, Deborah. 1987. *Discourse markers*. Cambridge: Cambridge University Press.

———. 1994. *Approaches to discourse*. New York: Blackwell.

Tannen, Deborah. 1989. *Talking voices: Repetition, dialogue, and imagery in conversational discourse*. Cambridge: Cambridge University Press.

Wainberg, Milton L., Francine Cournos, Melanie M. Wall, Andrea Norcini Pala, Claudio Gruber Mann, Diana Pinto, Veronica Pinho and Karen McKinnon. 2016. Mental illness sexual stigma: Implications for health and recovery. *Psychiatric Rehabilitation Journal* 39 (2): 90–96.

Wainberg, Milton L., M. Alfredo Gonzáles, Karen McKinnon, Katherine S. Elkington, Diana Pinto, Claudio Gruber Mann and Paulo E. Mattos. 2007. Targeted ethnography as a critical step to inform cultural adaptations of HIV prevention interventions for adults with severe mental illness. *Social Science & Medicine* 65 (2): 296–308.

7

The Expression of Authority in US Primary Care: Offering Diagnoses and Recommending Treatment

JOHN HERITAGE

AMONG THE LEAST DISPUTED claims among observers of American medicine is the notion that medical practice centrally involves the exercise of legitimate authority (Freidson 1970; Parsons 1951; Shorter 1985; Starr 1982). According to sociologist Paul Starr, medical authority involves the patient in what he calls "the surrender of private judgment" (Starr 1982, 13). By this he means that when patients get a recommendation from their doctor, they end up abandoning or at least suppressing whatever doubts, uncertainties, and misgivings they may have about their condition and its treatment and accept the recommendation. The origins of this authority, according to Starr, are *social*, arising from the dependence of the patient on expert intervention to address disease, and *cultural*, arising from the ascendency of modern science. It is the cultural authority of medicine—enshrined in the likelihood that "particular definitions of reality and judgments of meaning will prevail as valid and true" (Starr 1982, 13)—that enables physicians to make definitive pronouncements about the nature of medical symptoms and the causal processes underlying them, and to recommend treatment regimens for their alleviation and cure.

The authority that physicians wield comes in two flavors: epistemic and deontic. The former, perhaps most obviously manifest in the diagnostic phase of the medical consultation, relies strictly on physicians' cultural authority. The latter, deontic authority, most clearly embodied in treatment recommendations, rests on both the cultural authority of medicine and its social authority based in the perceived powerlessness of patients to improve without medical intervention of some kind. The purpose of this argument is to examine how these forms of authority are verbally expressed in American primary care consultations, drawing both on research from the past and on more recent studies published in the past year or so.

Background: Medical Authority

The development of medical authority has come about slowly, emerging from the late nineteenth-century reforms of US medical education that culminated in the Flexner Report of 1910. This inaugurated a period of growth, power, and prestige for the medical profession that continued uninterrupted for at least half a century. The reforms implemented a standard medical curriculum supported by the certification of physicians by medical schools and state-run professional medical boards and resulted in clinicians whose judgment and authority could be relied upon by patients who were increasingly prepared to defer to physician expertise (Freidson 1970; Shorter 1985; Starr 1982). By the 1960s, medicine was established as a "sovereign profession" (Starr 1982) and was experiencing a "golden age" of prosperity and influence (McKinlay and Marceau 2002). Indeed, Freidson (1988, 384) comments that during the period 1945–65, US medicine "was at a historically unprecedented peak of prestige, prosperity and political and cultural influence—perhaps as autonomous as it is possible for a profession to be."

During this same period, physicians were trained to deliver diagnoses and clinical judgments as definite and certain, and to minimize expressions of doubt or indecision (Fox 1957). Subsequent research on diagnoses and treatment recommendations by Byrne and Long (1976) showed that most diagnoses and treatment recommendations were expressed in a "doctor-centered" fashion, using a "plain assertion" format (Peräkylä 1998) without hedges, mitigation, or other qualifications.

Later in the century, the individual clinician's cultural authority and clinical autonomy started to come under threat from what sociologist Donald Light (2000) has termed "countervailing powers." The patients' rights movement of the 1970s resulted in legislation requiring patient informed consent for treatment regimens. Patients themselves became more knowledgeable, demanding, and consumerist in their stance toward health-care providers (Light 2000; Shorter 1985). The development of the internet enabled patients to evaluate medical recommendations against up-to-date research and practice guidelines. In this more proactive stance, patients were greatly abetted by the drug companies through direct-to-consumer advertising. Drug companies are spending many billions of dollars annually to reach patients, and the insistent message to "Ask your doctor if X is right for you" is highly influential. A recent study showed that requests for antidepressant medications very greatly increased the odds of a prescription being written (Kravitz et al. 2005). Treatment decisions are evidently decreasingly autonomous and increasingly co-constructed.

On the other side of the equation, rising health-care costs have motivated government, third-party payers, and for-profit medical service corporations to take measures to control them (Gray 1991; Waitzkin 2000, 2001). Managed-care organizations have built incentive structures that reward minimized care (Waitzkin 2001) and have designed review processes that regulate the exercise of clinical judgment, reaching deeply into the citadel of medical autonomy (Light, 2000), albeit with varying degrees of success (Heritage, Boyd and Kleinman 2001; Kleinman, Boyd and Heritage 1997).

This chapter focuses on the interactional management of two key sites of social action in primary-care visits where medical authority is expressed: offering diagnoses and recommending treatment. By describing how these actions are designed and how patients respond to them, we can gain important insights into how medical authority is expressed and managed in contemporary primary care.

Preliminary Observations

As a general rule, patients respond to diagnoses and treatment recommendations quite differently. With few exceptions, they respond to diagnoses as "informings" coming from a more to a less knowledgeable person, and thus treat diagnoses as within the physician's territory of knowledge and epistemic responsibility. By contrast, patients orient to treatment recommendations as proposals to be accepted or rejected: in the case of acceptances, they defer to the deontic authority that may be expressed in the recommendation and also accept the associated deontic responsibility involved in implementing, or cooperating with, the treatment recommendation.

These contrasting stances are easily recognizable in primary-care interactions. For example, in (1) a pediatrician diagnoses a child with an ear infection (line 1) and then details some clinical exam findings associated with the diagnosis (lines 3–5). Across this series of utterances, the parent remains silent, though there are three points at which he could have made a response (indicated with ≠>).

(1) [Stivers 2006, 282]

```
1   Doc:        .hhh Uh:m his- #-# lef:t:=h ea:r=h, is infected,

2          ≠>   (0.2)

3   Doc:        .h is bulging, has uh little pus in thuh

4          ≠>   ba:ck,=h

5   Doc:   ≠>   Uh:m, an' it's re:d,

6   Doc:        .hh So he needs some antibiotics to treat tha:t,

7   Dad:   =>   Alright.

8   Doc:        Mka:y, so we'll go ahead and treat- him: <he has

9               no a- uh:m, allergies to any penicillin or anything.
```

It is only after the pediatrician moves to the treatment recommendation (line 6) that the parent finally responds with "Alright." (line 7), whereupon the pediatrician moves toward other aspects of the treatment (Koenig 2011), in this case determining the specific antibiotic to be used for the treatment (lines 8–9).

The next case exhibits a similar pattern. The pediatrician's diagnosis (lines 1–2) attracts a minimal response (Gardner 1997)—a continuer (Schegloff 1982)—which acknowledges the diagnosis as an action, but without taking a stance on its information content. The treatment recommendation, by contrast, is addressed more substantively:

(2) [Stivers 2006, 283]

```
1  Doc:      Well I think what's happened is is that she

2            ha:s this: uh- (.) .h ear infection in her left ear?,

3  Mom: ≠>   [Mm:.

4  Doc:      [And we'll put her on some medicine and she'll [be fine.

5  Mom: =>                                                 [Okay.
```

Here the mom's "Okay." with its falling intonation (Heritage and Clayman 2010, 113–5) treats the doctor's recommendation "as a proposal to be accepted/rejected" (Stivers 2006, 283), rather than as an action to be simply acknowledged.

In both these cases, the physician, having received no or minimal uptake in response to the diagnosis, simply proceeds to the treatment recommendation as the upshot of the diagnosis and gets acceptance in response. As it turns out, overt acceptance is associated even with cases in which the treatment decision is to rule out the need for antibiotics, as in (3) and (4):

(3) [17-08-13]

```
1  Doc:      But it's #hmh# one uh these things that antibiotics

2            would be uh absolute waste of ti:me.

3  Mom:      Yeah,

4            (.)

5  Mom: =>   I- I know_ I agree.
```

(4) [1074 (Dr. 1)]

```
1  Doc:      An:d I think what's happened is he had uh co:ld_

2            an' it kinda triggered off thee:=

3  Mom:      =An' that'[s what happens u[sually. [Ri:ght.

4  Doc:               [wheezing?,       [.hh      [#::#=

5  Doc: ->   =An:d=uh: but I don't think he needs an antibiotic,

6  Mom: =>   O[kay. Good.

7  Doc:      [Right now,
```

Acceptance of treatment recommendations generally permits physicians to proceed to a discussion of the arrangements associated with the treatment (Koenig 2011), as in (5), where the treatment concerns wrist pain. Following the patient's acceptance of two treatment recommendations (Rx> indicates a treatment recommendation in the transcript), the physician moves on to various next actions (NA>).

(5) [PCT 20-06 Wrist pain]

```
1                (13.0) ((DOC writing in PAT's chart)) [04:33]
2  Doc: Rx> U::m, (3.0) I would give you::, (.) anti-
3            inflammatories, which is Bextra(p),
4  Pat: => °Okay,
5  Doc: NA> Ten milligrams. and you take one pill, (.)
6            a da:y.wis' food always.=
7  Pat:     =°nkay.
8                (2.0)((DOC leaning over PAT's chart))
9  Doc: Rx> And I'll give you also, (1.0) um, (0.8) wrist
10           supports.
11               (0.2) ((DOC holds gesture))
12 Pat: => M'kay.
13 Doc: NA> And you will be wearing them, as much as
14           pos[sible.
15 Pat:        [(°Okay,)
16 Doc: NA> Night time including. (.) okay:?
17               (1.5) ((DOC looks down, starts writing in
18           PAT's chart))
```

Given this pervasive orientation to treatment recommendations as something to be accepted or rejected, failure to respond to them, or minimal treatments of them merely as
information, frequently finds doctors in pursuit of acceptance. In (6) below, there is a
minimal pursuit. Receiving no uptake for his recommendation of "Bactrim" (lines 1–2),
the physician recycles the recommendation at line 4, and gets an acceptance (line 6).

(6) [PCT 14-03 Urinary Tract Infection]

```
1  Doc: Rx>  Okay. so, (.) uhm:, (1.0) <I'm going to>
2             start you on Bactrim.
3        ≠>   (.)
4  Doc: Rx'> We can do a three day course of Bactrim,
5             [uhm:, ]=
6  Pat: =>    [unkay.]
7  Doc:       =and uh, (0.2) I need to know how you're
8             feeling=.hh=>uh<
```

A more elaborate case involves a physician's recommendation of a cream to treat cold sores in (7). In the transcript, Dx>refers to diagnosis.

(7) [PCT 14-01 Cold sores]

```
 1  Doc:        Oka:y:,=hh

 2              (3.4)

 3  Doc: Dx>    Well you got <<pre::ty clearly>> he:re two:

 4              (.) aphthous ulcers:. ((said deliberately))

 5              (0.6)

 6  Doc:        They h(h)::urt¿ (.) li:ke [h(h)e:ck.

 7  Pat:                                 [((nods slowly))

 8              (0.4)

 9  Doc:        Fortunately they're f:airly easy to treat

10              if we catch 'em early#.

11              (.)

12  Doc: Rx'>   <munna give you a cream for your mouth.=

13              =it's like a paste.

14       ≠>     (.)

15  Pat: ≠>     mm[hm,

16  Doc: Rx'>   [(that) you put on=there¿ .hh 't's a-

17              steroid crea[m.=

18  Pat: ≠>     [((PAT nods))

19  Doc: Rx">   =it- (.) it's- healthy for your mouth.

20       ≠>     (.)

21  Pat: =>     °°Mm(kay). ((PAT nods slightly))

22  Doc: NA>    .h and you put it on there twice a day.
```

Here across several turns at talk, the physician expands the treatment recommendation (lines 16–17, 19) in search of a response that expresses acceptance, receiving it finally at line 21, whereupon she moves on to the next step in the recommendation, which concerns the frequency of application (line 22).

There is an important conclusion to be drawn from these observations. Because patient response to diagnosis is not required as a next action (Heath 1992; Heritage and McArthur 2019; Peräkylä 1998, 2002, 2006), physicians can move on to next actions such as treatment recommendations without waiting for patient response. This has the further implication that if patients wish to question diagnoses, they must do so proactively—normally by asking questions about them. The situation in the context of treatment recommendations is quite otherwise. Because treatment recommendations are understood by clinicians and patients alike as requiring responses in next turn, absent these responses physicians cannot move forward to next actions, including moving to visit closure. A corollary of this is that patients can resist treatment recommendations passively, by withholding response (Koenig 2011; Stivers 2005a, 2006, 2007; see also Heritage and Lindström 2012; Heritage and Sefi 1992). And in their efforts to secure patient acceptance (a condition for moving ahead with the visit), clinicians may modify their recommendations so as to align their proposals more closely with what they take to be patients' desires or preferences (Heritage and Sefi 1992; Stivers 2005a, 2006, 2007).

With this backdrop, we now proceed to the central task: analysis of the linguistic design of contemporary diagnoses and treatment recommendations, and patient responses to these actions in the context of US primary care. For this analysis, the primary data corpus is 255 video-recorded consultations that were gathered from thirty-three clinics involving seventy-one physicians across Southern California (2003–05). Original collection of the data, and its reuse for this study, was approved by UCLA's Institutional Review Board. For a detailed description of the procedure originally used to gather the data, see Robinson and Heritage (2006). Of the 255 patients recorded, 212 presented at least one new and/or acute problem and some visits contained more than one new and/or acute medical problem, resulting in 244 observations in the 212 recordings under investigation.

It should be noted that the study involves a cross-sectional snapshot of primary care in one country—the United States. Because every such study is performed at a particular time and place, these observations should ideally be considered in contexts that are both comparative and historical. Some efforts are made to this end in the present discussion, but there are very significant limitations in the historical data record, and few comparative studies to draw upon.

Diagnoses

One of the earliest considerations of diagnoses was Byrne and Long's (1976) analysis of British medical visits. Based on over twenty-five hundred consultations, the study focused on the predominantly "doctor-centered" behaviors that characterized the visits they studied, finding that the provided diagnostic information was limited, when it was given at all. Noting that doctors switch quickly from the examination to the treatment phase of consultations "with hardly a word to the patient *en route*," they also observed that information about the condition was given as a prelude to closing the visit, and "in explanation of the nature of the prescription they are about to hand over" (Byrne and Long 1976, 50–1). These observations dovetail with Fox's (1957) discussion of medical training aimed at reducing expressions of uncertainty and, like Fox's, they relate to a period when the authority of physicians was at its apogee, and informed consent, shared decision-making, and patient-centered care were far from general consideration. Indeed, Byrne and Long's study was one of the earliest to employ the term "patient-centeredness," and was in fact designed to promote its advocacy.

Heath's (1992) study, based on data collected later than Byrne and Long's, documented a widespread tendency for diagnoses to be couched as "factual, monolithic assertions" (Heath 1992, 246) that attracted few responses other than minimal ones. More substantial responses were infrequent and tended to emerge only if diagnoses were framed as questions ("If I was to say you had X, how would you feel about that?"), were presented as uncertain, or were in conflict with the patient's own belief about the condition, including its legitimacy as a basis for seeking care (cf. also Heritage 2005, 2009; Heritage and Robinson 2006). Heath argued that the minimal responses of British patients to their doctors' diagnoses reflected the informational asymmetry of the medical visit and the belief that doctors' diagnoses were not appropriate targets for comment, let alone agreement or confirmation.

Subsequently, using Finnish primary-care data collected in the 1990s, Peräkylä showed that Heath's "factual monolithic assertions," which he termed "plain assertions," were used in 44% of diagnoses. However, a further 17% were evidentialized ("This looks like X") and a further 39% were accompanied by descriptions of evidence and reasoning in support of the diagnosis. Peräkylä's study echoed Heath's in the observation that when evidence and reasoning were offered—often in cases where the diagnosis involved doubt or controversy—the patient was considerably more likely to respond to the diagnosis, sometimes quite expansively (Peräkylä 2002, 2006). While only 19% of plain and evidentialized assertions received expansive responses, 57% of diagnoses that explicated evidence were so received (Peräkylä 2002, 224).

Notwithstanding the fact that the two older of these studies are based on British data while the more recent is from Finland, it appears that they document a trend toward a more "patient-centered" approach to diagnosis in which there is less reliance on the linguistic expression of medical authority in diagnosis delievery. Indeed, Peräkylä (1998) argues that in the Finnish data medical authority is somewhat counterbalanced by clinical accountability in which, as he later put it, "the doctors treat themselves as accountable for the evidential basis of the diagnosis, thereby not claiming unconditional authority vis-à-vis the patients" (Peräkylä 2002, 221).

Incidence of Diagnoses

The US dataset from the 2000s described here embodies elements that are comparable with each of the main studies described earlier (Heritage and McArthur 2019). A first observation concerns the prevalence of diagnoses and has something in common with Byrne and Long's finding that diagnoses were uncommon within primary care. Focusing on conditions for which a treatment recommendation was offered, we found that full-fledged diagnoses were offered in support of only 53% of these recommendations, with a further 12% offered as justifications during the course of the treatment recommendation (Heritage and McArthur 2019). This apparent infrequency may be unavoidable. As Heneghan et al. (2009) among others note, there are obstacles in arriving at diagnoses in primary care: patients who visit the doctor early in the course of their illness often present symptoms that are not sufficiently developed to enable a clear diagnosis (Green and Holden 2003; Silverston 2016), even fully developed symptom clusters may be ambiguous as to the underlying disease process (Heneghan et al. 2009), and symptomatic treatment may not require full diagnostic evaluation where conditions are minor and self-limiting. Indeed, in a study of diagnostic strategies used by primary-care physicians, Heneghan et al. (2009, 338) found that "less than 50% of the cases resulted in the certainty of a 'known diagnosis' without further testing." Here, as the authors observe, there is a contrast to be drawn between primary-care and secondary-care contexts. In the latter, diagnostic specificity may be of paramount importance, whereas in the former symptomatic treatment accompanied by reassurance that the condition is not serious may be entirely adequate.

Design of Diagnostic Utterances

In our approach to the design of turns that communicate a diagnosis, we focused on diagnostic utterances that named (e.g., "this is bronchitis"), described (e.g., "you have a nerve that's pinching"), or provided an explanation for the patient's problem (e.g., "my suspicion is it's related to the smog"). We did not include treatment recommendations—for example, for antibiotics that may imply a (bacterial) infection, but do not name, describe, or explain the condition. Following Heath (1992) and Peräkylä (1998), we distinguished between plain assertions—simple declarative announcements of diagnostic information—and utterances in which those assertions were mitigated using epistemic modality (Kärkkäinen 2003; Palmer 2001), evidentialization (Cornillie 2009; Peräkylä 2006), or epidemiologic generalization. These are exemplified in table 7.1.

The three mitigated forms are hearably "cautious." In diagnoses employing epistemic modality, expressions like "could be," "maybe," "probably," etc. are used to present a diagnosis as uncertain to a greater or lesser extent. Evidentialized diagnoses index the source of the information in which the diagnosis is grounded (Cornillie 2009; Peräkylä 2006), but do not specify the evidence, and do not make an explicit evaluation of the likelihood that the claim is true. This can communicate a lack of commitment to the evidentialized proposition and may be associated with later patient doubt about the diagnosis (McArthur, unpublished). Diagnoses that are

Table 7.1. Examples of Diagnostic Utterance Formats

Format type	Example from data
Plain assertion	You have a throat infection.
Epistemic modality	You might have cracked one of your ribs over there.
Evidentialized	It feels like an early plantar fasciitis, you know like a heel spur.
Epidemiologic generalization	It's like the lining is irritated. The most common reason for the lining to be irritated is because of the acid from your stomach.

Table 7.2. Distribution of Diagnostic Utterance Designs

Design type	Frequency	Percent
Plain assertions	36	34%
Mitigated assertions*	70	66%
Epistemic modality	41	39%
Evidentialized	29	27%
Epidemiologic generalization	11	10%
Total	106	100%

*Subcategories of mitigation are not mutually exclusive.

communicated epidemiologically do not explicitly tie a diagnosis to the patient's symptoms, but rather imply it through the generalized claim of linkage between the symptoms and the condition.

As table 7.2 shows, 66% of the diagnoses in our data were presented in a mitigated fashion, communicating some element of uncertainty about the conclusion.

With this 2003–05 dataset, we are a long distance away from Fox's observation that physicians are trained to avoid expressions of uncertainty, and also Byrne and Long (1976) and Heath's (1992) confirmation that "plain assertions" were the most frequent diagnostic format in the period up to the 1980s. The present findings also represent a reduction in plain assertions from Peräkylä's data from the 1990s (from 44% to 34%). This data may thus illustrate a progressive moderation in the assertiveness of diagnostic utterances across the past forty years, perhaps reflecting a move toward a less paternalistic stance on the part of providers and a more inclusive orientation to patients.

Patient Response to Diagnoses

In examining patient responses to diagnoses, we distinguished between several classes of response: (1) simple nods, unaccompanied by verbal response; (2) minimal acknowledgments functioning as "continuers" that acknowledge acts of speaking as incomplete, but not the acts, or their content, as such; (3) accepting responses such as "I see" or "Okay"; (4) news acknowledgments such as "Oh, really, is it," that treat the diagnosis as "news," and sometimes as counter to expectations; and (5) expanded responses, such as assessments and questions. Table 7.3 describes the distribution of these responses.

Table 7.3 confirms the findings of earlier studies by Heath (1992) and Peräkylä (1998, 2002, 2006) that patients tend to respond minimally to physicians' diagnoses. In addition to the 26% of diagnoses that did not receive a verbal response, a further 33% received a minimal "continuative" response. Thus, only 40% of diagnoses receive a substantive response of any kind, including acknowledging/accepting responses such as "okay." Our study also confirmed Heath's and Peräkylä's observations that plain assertions of a diagnosis have a chilling effect on patient response, decreasing the likelihood of patient response by 66%. Some 30% of diagnoses were also delivered

Table 7.3. Distribution of Patient Responses to Diagnostic Utterances

Response type	Example	Frequency	Percent
No response		16	15%
Nod (only)		12	11%
Minimal response	Mm hm, uh huh	35	33%
Accepting response	Okay, I see	19	18%
News response	Oh, Really, Is it	10	9%
Expanded response	That's good, Is there a cure	14	13%
Total		106	99%

*Percentage totals subject to rounding effects.

without gazing at the patient, and the absence of gaze also decreased the likelihood of patient response by 83% (Heritage and McArthur 2019).

Considering these results, a reasonably clear trend away from "plain assertions" as the currency of diagnosis can be discerned across the data points reviewed here. From circumstances in which physicians were actively trained to suppress the expression of diagnostic uncertainty to a situation in which a two-thirds majority of diagnoses involve such expression represents a remarkable shift in diagnosis design. Recent findings also underscore the earlier established connections between diagnoses that express doubt or uncertainty and more substantive patient responses.

It might therefore be tempting to argue that physician authority has been reduced in the era of patient-centered care. However, although diagnoses are *expressed* with less authority than previously, it would be premature to conclude that the epistemic authority of physicians as diagnosticians has also declined. Patient responses to diagnoses, while clearly influenced by aspects of their design, still tend to be minimal and nonsubstantive. Some of this minimality may arise from an interest in a treatment solution for their problem that overrides an interest in its diagnosis (Freidson 1970, 22). Minimal responses treat the diagnosis as "on the way to" a desired treatment objective and facilitate rapid transition to that objective. However, it would perhaps be unwise to rule out the significance of patients' continuing orientations to the epistemic authority of the physician. This orientation may inhibit not only questioning and commentary on a diagnosis, but also reactions to the diagnosis as "news" and even "agreeing" acknowledgments, all of which may be taken as intruding on the physician's epistemic domain of expertise. Thus, even absent the presentation of diagnoses as *ex cathedra* assertions, patients may still find themselves in an "epistemic vise" (Heritage and McArthur 2019) that inhibits responses to diagnoses that could be construed as conveying a "knowing" stance toward medical conclusions. In sum, while the expression of medical authority in the design of diagnosis may be substantially reduced, the underlying orientation to its existence by patients may not be undergoing a corresponding change.

Treatment Recommendations

As previously noted, treatment recommendations bring a distinct form of medical authority into play. As directives (Craven and Potter 2010; Ervin-Tripp 1976; Stevanovic and Svennevig 2015), treatment recommendations express deontic authority, concerned with "the right to determine others' future actions" (Stevanovic and Peräkylä 2012, 297; see also Lindström and Weatherall 2015). As in other professions, deontic authority is dependent upon, and interwoven with, epistemic authority (Abbott 1988), and this is clearly the case at the interactional level in medicine (Lindström and Weatherall 2015; Stivers et al. 2018). Deontic authority is also rarely absolute, particularly in primary care where patients are responsible for accepting and implementing most treatment recommendations. Even in cases where it is recommended that patients should undergo a procedure, they have the right to "informed consent" and to reject the recommendation (Katz 1984; Rodwin 1994), a right that has been consolidated in American case law (Nelson-Marten and Rich 1999).

Despite their obvious importance, treatment recommendations have remained understudied in primary care. Perhaps the most significant of contemporary studies have focused on recommendations that are resisted by patients or their caretakers, for example, for nonantibiotic treatment regimens for upper respiratory infections (Mangione-Smith et al. 2006; Stivers 2002a, 2002b, 2005a, 2006, 2007) and vaccination recommendations (Opel et al. 2012, 2013, 2015). The present discussion of treatment recommendations is based on Stivers et al.'s (2018) analysis of different forms of recommendation and on an enlarged version of the US dataset described previously (n = 304 treatment recommendations), augmented by a large dataset from British primary care (n = 393 treatment recommendations), for a total of 697 instances. The primary focus of this study is treatment recommendations considered as social actions.

Clearly, treatment recommendations can vary considerably in their expression of deontic authority. As Stivers et al. (2018, 1335) note, "There are clear differences between *I'm going to start you on X*, *We can give you X to try*, and *Would you like me to give you X*. Yet little is known about this variation, its contexts, or its consequences." Basing their study on the 697 instances of initial treatment recommendations mentioned above, Stivers et al. developed a taxonomy of treatment recommendations by classifying them as distinctive kinds of social actions. They distinguished between five major classes of recommendations broadly embodying a cline in the expression of deontic authority from first to last: (1) pronouncements, (2) proposals, (3) suggestions, (4) offers, and (5) assertions. These categories are summarized in table 7.4.

As table 7.4 suggests, the coding categories were based on two major dimensions of the design of the recommending turn: (1) who is presented as the instigator of the recommendation, and (2) who is presented as the decision maker. In a pronouncement such as "I'll start you on X," the formulation presents the physician as the occupant of both roles, to the point that the patient is apparently occluded from a decision-making role. The conjoining of these two elements in the design of the turn

Table 7.4. Recommendation Action Types

Action type	Description	Example
Pronouncement	Physician asserts recommendation as instigator, decision maker and presents it as already determined.	"I'll start you on X"
Proposal	Physician recommends as instigator, but decision making is treated as shared by doctor and patient. Proposals highlight the recommendation as speculative.	"Let's try X and see how that goes"
Suggestion	Physician recommends as instigator but treats patient as decision maker and medication as optional.	"You could try X"
Offer	Physician treats patient as having instigated recommendation and as the decision maker, thus treating the recommended medicine as having been occasioned.	"Would you like me to give you X?"
Assertion	Physician asserts a generalization about a treatment's benefit implying a recommendation but not proffering an overt directive.	"X is good for this"

Source: Adapted from Stivers and Barnes 2018, 1333.

results in a strong expression of physician authority. In proposals and suggestions, the physician retains the role of instigator, but treats the decision-making role as shared between doctor or patient (proposals), or as the patient's decision (suggestion). In the case of offers (e.g., "Would you like me to give you X"), the physician treats the patient as both instigator (cf. Curl 2006) and decision maker, effectively abrogating deontic authority for the recommendation in the process. Finally, in assertions, physicians offer generalizations that express epistemic authority but that are not translated into overt directives with deontic content.

While it may be tempting to view these five action types as embodying a cline in the expression of authority from maximal to minimal, this generalization should be treated with caution. The action categories described here are quite broad and, as Stivers and Barnes (2018, 1333) note, can subsume many variations. Arguably, the most important of these is the strength with which the physician's turn endorses the recommendation. For example, in the following pairs of recommendations, the second case embodies a stronger endorsement than the first:

(8) [Stivers and Barnes 2018, 1333]

(Pronouncement)

(a)   I'd like to start you on X

(b)   I'll start you on X

```
(Suggestion)

(a)     You might want to try X

(b)     You really ought to try X

(Offer)

(a)     I'd be willing to let you try X

(b)     I could give you X
```

It is safer to conclude, then, that although the action categories do represent a general cline in the expression of authority, variations in their formulation can create some degree of overlap at the margins.

Considering the distribution of these treatment recommendation formats (see table 7.5), it is immediately apparent that American clinicians predominantly use pronouncements, and to a lesser extent suggestions, as vehicles for their recommendations, with all other categories being weakly represented in the aggregate. This distribution, however, is likely to be particular to primary care and to the US context for, as table 7.5 also shows, British physicians show a much more even spread of recommendation types, with the pronouncement category only somewhat larger than other categories. Despite these differences, physicians from both countries tended to use pronouncements when prescribing anti-infective medications (most prominently, antibiotics). Anti-infectives were prescribed using pronouncements 93% of the time in the United States and 62% of the time in the United Kingdom.

It is important to repeat at this point that primary-care physicians are, for the most part, treating minor, self-limiting illnesses, and that the associated treatment recommendations frequently carry low risks to the patient and a relatively low treatment burden. In contexts where patient risks and burdens are higher, physicians' treatment recommendations tend to assume a more cautious design. For example, there are relatively few pronouncements among such recommendations in psychiatry, where new medications can have potentially adverse consequences (Thompson and McCabe 2017). In oncology, where treatments can carry significant risk and patient burden, recommendations for new treatments are rarely, if ever, presented in the

Table 7.5. Distribution of Treatment Recommendation Types in US and UK Primary Care

	US primary care	UK primary care
Pronouncement	65%	29%
Proposal	4%	16%
Suggestion	21%	24%
Offer	5%	15%
Assertion	5%	16%
Total (N)	304	393

form of pronouncements, although midcourse adjustments and treatments for ancillary problems are quite frequently presented in pronouncement form (Tate 2018).

Patient Responses to Treatment Recommendations

As noted earlier, patients tend to respond to treatment recommendations, and physicians tend to build their recommendations in search of explicit acceptance and work to achieve such acceptance when it is not immediately forthcoming (Koenig 2011; Stivers 2005a, 2005b, 2007; Stivers et al. 2018; see also Heritage and Sefi 1992).

In analyzing patient responses to treatment recommendations, we grouped responses into four categories: (1) no response, (2) acknowledging responses (including nods), (3) accepting responses ("okay"), and (4) resistant responses that questioned the recommendation or otherwise presented obstacles to its acceptance. Whereas earlier we noted that patient responses to diagnoses were strongly influenced when the latter were epistemically downgraded, patient responses to treatment recommendations, by contrast, were only mildly influenced by the design of the recommendation itself (and not to a level of statistical significance; see Stivers et al. 2018, 1336, table 1). In general, 85% of patients responded in some way to the treatment recommendation, with offers attracting a slightly higher level of response and assertions a slightly lower rate. While these mild variations are predictable enough, it is striking that pronouncements attracted the same level of response as suggestions and proposals. This demonstrates the consistency of the deontic landscape of treatment recommendations: because patients will necessarily have to cooperate in the management of their treatment, some acknowledgment of this obligation is a characteristic feature of the treatment recommendation sequence.

While there were no between-country differences in the general rate of response to treatment recommendations, there were some differences in how patients from the United States and the United Kingdom responded within these broad categories (Bergen et al 2018). Broadly speaking, American patients were significantly more likely to overtly accept treatment recommendations (38% vs. 19%), while British patients were more likely to resist them (18% vs. 10%). However, while British patients resisted prescription and nonprescription medications in equal measure, American patients were significantly more likely to resist nonprescription recommendations, and did so mainly on the basis of perceived inefficacy (Bergen et al. 2018).

Discussion

What do the various findings reported tell us about the expression of authority in American primary care? We began with a distinction between the expression of two forms of authority—epistemic and deontic—and it will be appropriate to maintain this distinction in the following discussion.

Considering the primarily epistemic authority that is expressed in diagnoses, we appear to be witnessing a long-term secular decline in its expression. The story begins with a historic high point in medical authority in the mid-twentieth century—the "golden age" of American medicine—in which physicians were trained to present diagnoses as undoubted assertions of fact, admitting little or no doubt or uncertainty. Across a series of studies, albeit from different countries and distinctive health-care systems, there has been a steady decline in the certainty with which diagnoses are generally expressed, and with it a decline in the expression of authority accompanying the diagnosis itself. This decline in the expression of authority may not reflect a decline in the "real authority" of physicians as patients see it. Physicians are arguably more knowledgeable about disease and its diagnosis than they were in times past. In fact, patients continue a long-term pattern of muted response, verging on nonresponse, that has been in place for decades. Thus, while physicians' deliveries of diagnoses have changed, patients' overall responsiveness has not. Patient responses continue to embody respect for the epistemic authority of the medical profession, and certainly an unwillingness to challenge that authority immediately and outright.

Turning to the deontic context of treatment recommendations, we unfortunately lack the historical guidance that can come from earlier studies. At the present time, we see a clear bifurcation between treatment recommendations in primary care, which are mainly delivered as pronouncements *ex cathedra* as it were, and treatment recommendations in secondary care (e.g., psychiatry and oncology) that predominantly do not take this form. This points to an important underlying generalization: high-risk, high-burden treatments are recommended using proposals and suggestions while, at least in the United States, low-risk, low-burden treatments are not. This bifurcation emerges *within* secondary care and primary care as well as *between* them. In the United States, antibiotics are recommended through pronouncements around 90% of the time, while antidepressants are so recommended only about 55% of the time (Stivers et al. 2018). In oncology, new treatments are almost never recommended through pronouncements, but treatments for problems that are ancillary to the treatment process frequently are so presented (Tate 2018).

These observations may be associated with a further consideration. Primary-care patients with upper respiratory symptoms very frequently present with antibiotics in view and find a variety of ways to communicate this objective to their providers (Mangione-Smith et al. 1999, 2004, 2006, 2015; Stivers 2002a, 2005a, 2005b, 2006, 2007; Stivers et al. 2003). It is certainly conceivable therefore that, in recommending an antibiotic prescription with a pronouncement—the most authoritative form of treatment recommendation—physicians are pushing on an open door, recommending a treatment that, at the individual level at least, is a minor inconvenience and is already seen to be agreeable to the patient. In societies where patients are generally less favorable to prescription medications, such as the United Kingdom, their recommendation is approached with a greater degree of caution (Bergen et al. 2018; Stivers et al. 2018). Perhaps what is common to all the settings in which medical treatment is at issue is the trade-off between physician expertise on the one hand and patient preferences and beliefs on the other—a trade-off that is itself expressed in the design of treatment recommendations.

References

Abbott, Andrew. 1988. *The system of the professions: An essay on the division of expert labor*. Chicago: University of Chicago Press.

Bergen, Clara, Tanya Stivers, Rebecca K. Barnes, John Heritage, Rose McCabe and Laura Thompson et al. 2018. Closing the deal: A cross-cultural comparison of treatment resistance. *Health Communication* 33: 1377–88.

Byrne, Patrick S. and Barrie E. L. Long. 1976. *Doctors talking to patients: A study of the verbal behaviours of doctors in the consultation*. London: Her Majesty's Stationery Office.

Cornillie, Bert. 2009. Evidentiality and epistemic modality: On the close relationship between two different categories. *Functions of Language* 16: 44–62.

Craven, Alexandra and Jonathan Potter. 2010. Directives: Entitlement and contingency in action. *Discourse Studies* 12: 419–42.

Curl, Traci S. 2006. Offers of assistance: Constraints on syntactic design. *Journal of Pragmatics* 38: 1257–80.

Ervin-Tripp, Susan. 1976. Is Sybil there? The structure of American English directives. *Language in Society* 5 (1): 25–66.

Fox, Renee C. 1957. Training for uncertainty. In Robert K. Merton, George G. Reader and Patricia L. Kendall (eds.), *The student-physician*. Cambridge, MA: Harvard University Press. 207–41.

Freidson, Eliot. 1970. *Profession of medicine: A study of the sociology of applied knowledge*. Chicago: University of Chicago Press.

———. 1988. Afterword 1988. In Eliot Freidson, *Profession of medicine: A study of the sociology of applied knowledge*. Chicago: University of Chicago Press.

Gardner, Rod. 1997. The conversation object Mm: A weak and variable acknowledging token. *Research on Language and Social Interaction* 30: 131–56.

Gray, Bradford H. 1991. *The profit motive and patient care*. Cambridge, MA: Harvard University Press.

Green, Caroline and John Holden. 2003. Diagnostic uncertainty in general practice. *European Journal of General Practice* 9 (1): 13–15.

Heath, Christian. 1992. The delivery and reception of diagnosis and assessment in the general practice consultation. In Paul Drew and John Heritage (eds.), *Talk at work*. Cambridge: Cambridge University Press. 235–67.

Heneghan, C., P. Glasziou, M. Thompson, P. Rose, J. Balla, D. Lasserson, C. Scott and R. Perera. 2009. Diagnostic strategies used in primary care. *BMJ* 338: b946.

Heritage, John. 2005. Revisiting authority in physician-patient interaction. In Judith Felson Duchan and Dana Kovarsky (eds.), *Diagnosis as cultural practice*. New York: Mouton De Gruyter. 83–102.

———. 2009. Negotiating the legitimacy of medical problems: A multi-phase concern for patients and physicians. In Dale E. Brashers and Daena J. Goldsmith (eds.), *Communicating to manage health and illness*. New York: Routledge. 147–64.

Heritage, John, Elizabeth Boyd and Lawrence Kleinman. 2001. Subverting criteria: The role of precedent in decisions to finance surgery. *Sociology of Health and Illness* 23: 701–28.

Heritage, John and Stephen Clayman. 2010. *Talk in action: Interactions, identities and institutions*. Oxford: Blackwell-Wiley.

Heritage, John and Anna Lindström. 2012. Advice giving: Terminable and interminable. In Holger Limberg and Miriam A. Locher (eds.), *Advice in discourse*. Amsterdam: John Benjamins. 169–94.

Heritage, John and Amanda McArthur. 2019. The diagnostic moment: A study in US primary care. *Social Science and Medicine* 228: 262–71.

Heritage, John and Jeffrey D. Robinson. 2006. Accounting for the visit: Giving reasons for seeking medical care. In John Heritage and Douglas W. Maynard (eds.), *Communication in medical care: Interactions between primary care physicians and patients*. Cambridge: Cambridge University Press. 48–85.

Heritage, John and Sue Sefi. 1992. Dilemmas of advice: Aspects of the delivery and reception of advice in interactions between health visitors and first-time mothers. In Paul Drew and John Heritage (eds.), *Talk at work*. Cambridge: Cambridge University Press. 359–417.

Kärkkäinen, Elise. 2003. *Epistemic stance in English conversation: A description of its interactional functions, with a focus on* I think. Amsterdam: John Benjamins.

Katz, Jay. 1984. *The silent world of doctor and patient*. Baltimore: Johns Hopkins University Press.
Kleinman, Lawrence C., Elizabeth A. Boyd and John C. Heritage. 1997. Adherence to prescribed explicit criteria during utilization review: An analysis of communications between attending and reviewing physicians. *Journal of the American Medical Association* 278: 497–501.
Koenig, Christopher J. 2011. Patient resistance as agency in treatment decisions. *Social Science and Medicine* 72: 1105–14.
Kravitz, R. L., R. M. Epstein, M. D. Feldman, C. E. Franz, R. Azari, M. S. Wilkes, L. Hinton and P. Franks. 2005. Influence of patients' requests for direct-to-consumer advertised antidepressants: A randomized controlled trial. *Journal of the American Medical Association* 293: 1995–2002.
Light, Donald W. 2000. The medical profession and organizational change: From professional dominance to countervailing power. In Chloe E. Bird, Peter Conrad and Allen M. Fremont (eds.), *Handbook of medical sociology*. Upper Saddle River, NJ: Prentice Hall. 201–16.
Lindström, Anna and Ann Weatherall. 2015. Orientations to epistemics and deontics in treatment discussions. *Journal of Pragmatics* 78: 39–53.
Mangione-Smith, R., M. N. Elliott, T. Stivers, L. L. McDonald and J. Heritage. 2006. Ruling out the need for antibiotics: Are we sending the right message? *Archives of Pediatric and Adolescent Medicine* 160: 945–52.
Mangione-Smith, R., M. N. Elliott, T. Stivers, L. L. McDonald, J. Heritage and E. A. McGlynn. 2004. Racial/ethnic variation in parent expectations for antibiotics: Implications for public health campaigns. *Pediatrics* 113 (5): e385–94.
Mangione-Smith, R., E. McGlynn, M. N. Elliott, P. Krogstad and R. H. Brook. 1999. The relationship between perceived parental expectations and pediatrician antimicrobial prescribing behavior. *Pediatrics* 103: 711–18.
Mangione-Smith, R., C. Zhou, J. D. Robinson, J. A. Taylor, M. N. Elliott and J. Heritage. 2015. Communication practices and antibiotic use for acute respiratory tract infections in children. *Annals of Family Medicine* 13: 221–27.
McArthur, A. Unpublished. Communicating uncertain diagnoses in primary care: The impact of wording on patient confidence. Unpublished Ms, Department of Sociology, UCLA.
McKinlay, John B. and Lisa D. Marceau. 2002. The end of the golden age of doctoring. *International Journal of Health Services* 32: 379–416.
Nelson-Marten, P. and B. A. Rich. 1999. A historical perspective of informed consent in clinical practice and research. *Seminars in Oncology Nursing* 15 (2): 81–88.
Opel, D. J., J. Heritage, J. A. Taylor, R. Mangione-Smith, H. S. Salas, V. DeVere, C. Zhou and J. D. Robinson. 2013. The architecture of provider-parent vaccine discussions at health supervision visits. *Pediatrics* 132: 1–10.
Opel, D. J., R. Mangione-Smith, J. D. Robinson, J. Heritage, V. DeVere, H. S. Salas, C. Zhou and J. A. Taylor. 2015. The influence of provider communication behaviors on parental vaccine acceptance and visit experience. *American Journal of Public Health* 105: 1998–2004.
Opel, D. J., J. D. Robinson, J. Heritage, C. Korfiatis, J. A. Taylor and R. Mangione-Smith. 2012. Characterizing providers' immunization communication practices during health supervision visits with vaccine-hesitant parents: A pilot study. *Vaccine* 30 (7): 1269–75.
Palmer, F. R. 2001. *Mood and modality*. Cambridge: Cambridge University Press.
Parsons, T. 1951. *The social system*. New York: Free Press.
Peräkylä, Anssi. 1998. Authority and accountability: The delivery of diagnosis in primary health care. *Social Psychology Quarterly* 61: 301–20.
———. 2002. Agency and authority: Extended responses to diagnostic statements in primary care encounters. *Research on Language and Social Interaction* 35: 219–47.
———. 2006. Communicating and responding to diagnosis. In John Heritage and Douglas W. Maynard (eds.), *Communication in medical care: Interactions between primary care physicians and patients*. Cambridge: Cambridge University Press. 214–47.
Robinson, Jeffrey D. and John Heritage. 2006. Physicians' opening questions and patients' satisfaction. *Patient Education and Counseling* 60: 279–85.

Rodwin, M. A. 1994. Patient accountability and quality of care: Lessons from medical consumerism and the patients' rights, women's health and disability rights movements. *American Journal of Law and Medicine* 20: 147–67.

Schegloff, Emanuel A. 1982. Discourse as an interactional achievement: Some uses of 'uh huh' and other things that come between sentences. In Deborah Tannen (ed.), *Analyzing discourse: Text and talk (Georgetown University Roundtable on Languages and Linguistics 1981)*. Washington DC: Georgetown University Press. 71–93.

Shorter, Edward. 1985. *Bedside manners: The troubled history of doctors and patients*. New York: Viking.

Silverston, Paul. 2016. Teaching patient-centered safety-netting in primary care. *Journal of Community Medicine & Health Education* 6 (3).

Starr, Paul. 1982. *The social transformation of American medicine*. New York: Basic Books.

Stevanovic, Melisa and Anssi Peräkylä. 2012. Deontic authority in interaction: The right to announce, propose, and decide. *Research on Language & Social Interaction* 45: 297–321.

Stevanovic, Melisa and Jan Svennevig. 2015. Introduction: Epistemics and deontics in conversational directives. *Journal of Pragmatics* 78: 1–6.

Stivers, Tanya. 2002a. Participating in decisions about treatment: Overt parent pressure for antibiotic medication in pediatric encounters. *Social Science and Medicine* 54: 1111–30.

———. 2002b. Presenting the problem in pediatric encounters: "Symptoms only" versus "candidate diagnosis" presentations. *Health Communication* 14: 299–338.

———. 2005a. Parent resistance to physicians' treatment recommendations: One resource for initiating a negotiation of the treatment decision. *Health Communication* 18: 41–74.

———. 2005b. Non-antibiotic treatment recommendations: Delivery formats and implications for parent resistance. *Social Science and Medicine* 60: 949–64.

———. 2006. Treatment decisions: Negotiations between doctors and patients in acute care encounters. In John Heritage and Douglas W. Maynard (eds.), *Communication in medical care: Interactions between primary care physicians and patients*. Cambridge: Cambridge University Press. 279–312.

———. 2007. *Prescribing under pressure: Parent-physician conversations and antibiotics*. New York: Oxford University Press.

Stivers, Tanya and Rebecca K. Barnes. 2018. Treatment recommendation actions, contingencies, and responses: An introduction. *Health Communication* 33: 1331–34.

Stivers, Tanya, John Heritage, Rebecca K. Barnes, Rose McCabe, Laura Thompson and Merran Toerien. 2018. Treatment recommendations as actions. *Health Communication* 33: 1335–44.

Stivers, Tanya, Rita Mangione-Smith, Marc N. Elliott, Laurie McDonald and John Heritage. 2003. Why do physicians think parents expect antibiotics? What parents report vs what physicians perceive. *Journal of Family Practice* 52: 140–8.

Tate, Alexandra. 2018. Treatment recommendations in oncology visits: Implications for patient agency and physician authority. *Health Communication* 34 (13): 1597–1607.

Thompson, Laura and Rose McCabe. 2017. How psychiatrists recommend treatment and its relationship with patient uptake. *Health Communication* 33 (11): 1345–54.

Waitzkin, Howard. 2000. Changing patient-physician relationships in the changing health-policy environment. In Chloe E. Bird, Peter Conrad and Allen M. Fremont (eds.), *Handbook of medical sociology*. Upper Saddle River, NJ: Prentice Hall. 271–83.

———. 2001. *At the front lines of medicine*. Lanham, MD: Rowman and Littlefield.

8

Semiotic Ideologies and Trial Discourse: Implications for Multimodal Discourse Analysis

SUSAN EHRLICH

MULTIMODAL APPROACHES TO DISCOURSE analysis are motivated by the principle that texts exploit various kinds of semiotic resources and that their meanings cannot be explained by language alone. Jewitt (2016, 69–70), for example, in a review article on multimodal analysis, identifies three theoretical assumptions that she sees as underpinning the study of multimodality:

1. While language is widely taken to be the most significant mode of communication, speech or writing are part of a multimodal ensemble.
2. Each mode is understood to have different meaning potentials...and to realize different kinds of communicative work.
3. People orchestrate meaning through their selection and configuration of modes. Thus the interaction between modes is significant for meaning-making.

In this chapter I am interested in the second of these issues, the "meaning potential" of different modes, or as Jewitt (2016, 69) says in a somewhat different way, "how choosing to represent something through an image or writing impacts on its meaning." While multimodal discourse analysts have attempted to describe the different meaning-making possibilities associated with various semiotic modes—what van Leeuwen (2015, 450), following previous work by Kress (e.g., 2003), labels the "affordances" of different modes—typically these "affordances" have been established by analysts independently of consumers of texts and their own beliefs about the meaning potential of modes. For example, van Leeuwen (2000, 335) makes a comparison between racism that is visually communicated and that which is verbally communicated and concludes that visual racism can be much more easily denied and dismissed than verbal racism because "images seem just to allude to things" and do not convey them in an explicit way. In making these claims, however, van

Leeuwen does not discuss the extent to which they may be grounded in viewers' own interpretive practices or their own ideas about the meaning-making potential of visual racism vs. verbal racism.

In a somewhat different account of the differences between visual and verbal modes, Jones and Hafner (2012, 52) argue that the spatial/simultaneous logic of images vs. the temporal/sequential logic of writing means that images tend to have a "more direct" effect on viewers (than writing or speech), eliciting an "immediate emotional reaction" in viewers. Jones and Hafner point to a time in American history when images of "dead and dying soldiers and civilians" (61) on television news and in photojournalism, historians have suggested, were instrumental in changing public opinion about the Vietnam War. In other words, the emotional reactions that images (as opposed to writing or speech) provoke in viewers "can powerfully influence our attitude towards a particular subject or event" (2012, 61). While Jones and Hafner go further than van Leeuwen in providing empirically based support for their claims (i.e., in citing evidence from historians writing about resistance to the Vietnam War), it seems to me that investigations of multimodality could move even further in this direction. How, for example, do we reconcile van Leeuwen's (2000) observations about the relative ease with which (racist) visual meanings can be denied (i.e., relative to verbal meanings) with Jones and Hafner's comments about the emotional power and resonance that visual images can have without recourse to some further kind of evidence? In posing this question, my purpose is not to argue for one of these accounts over the other, but rather to suggest that an "emic" approach to the investigation of the meaning-making possibilities of different modes may help to resolve the inconsistencies and contradictions that we see in the two accounts presented above (and others in the literature). That is, in answering Jewitt's (2016, 69) question about how representing "something through an image or writing impacts on its meaning," it may be useful to examine how participants in actual speech events view the meaning potential of images vs. writing.

Thus, departing from much previous work on multimodality, in this chapter I investigate multimodality from an "emic" perspective, demonstrating the way that semiotic ideologies (Thurlow 2017) informed participants' assessment of evidence in a particular speech event—the Steubenville rape trial. This trial was noteworthy in that the events under investigation were documented (by the defendants and their friends) on social media as they unfolded. Moreover, this "real-time" record of the events was documented in both visual (photographs, videos) and linguistic (text messages, tweets) modes. Drawing upon transcripts from the trial, I argue that the witnesses and the lawyers in the trial ascribed a veracity and evidentiary capacity to the visual evidence that was not extended to the linguistic evidence, and that this difference had a significant impact on the outcome of the trial.[1] In Thurlow's (2017, 15) terms, the visual evidence was treated as "carrying meaning" more reliably than the verbal evidence. Overall, then, this paper has important implications for multimodal discourse analysis: the semiotic ideologies of participants (in specific speech events) may be an important consideration in determining how different semiotic modes give rise to different kinds of meanings.

Description of the Steubenville Rape Trial

On March 17, 2013, a juvenile court judge found two Steubenville (Ohio) teenagers—Trent Mays and Ma'lik Richmond—guilty of raping a sixteen-year-old young woman from a neighboring West Virginia town. Richmond was sentenced to a minimum of one year in juvenile detention and Mays to a minimum of two years in juvenile detention. The rapes occurred late on the night of August 11 and in the early morning of August 12, 2012. Mays and Richmond, both sixteen years of age at the time of the rapes, were at a house party celebrating the end of summer and the upcoming football season. Both young men were members of the city's high school football team, Big Red, a team that is a source of enormous pride for the city of Steubenville and the surrounding Ohio Valley. The victim, known only as Jane Doe, was also at the party. At a certain point in the evening, Mays and Richmond decided to leave with friends to go to another teammate's house, and Jane Doe went with them. Witnesses reported that she was quite intoxicated at the time but left with the boys despite friends asking her to remain with them at the party. At the second house, Jane Doe was vomiting and had to be carried inside the house. Mays and Richmond were eventually asked to leave the second house and took Jane Doe with them to a third house, where they spent the remainder of the night. According to witnesses, Mays penetrated Jane Doe with his fingers in the backseat of the car on the way to the third house. Once at the third house, Mays and Richmond took Jane Doe into the basement, violated her with their fingers, and attempted to make her perform fellatio. Mays also slapped the complainant with his penis. Jane Doe was reportedly unresponsive to all of the young men's acts of sexual aggression, passing in and out of consciousness at the time the assaults took place. She woke up the next morning, naked and without her cell phone, and with no memory of what had transpired during the previous night and early morning.

Throughout the night and early morning, the defendants, and other football players present at the various venues (and there were a number of them), used their cell phones to document the events that occurred at the two houses. They took numerous photographs and videos of the victim and of the acts perpetrated on the victim by the defendants, uploaded many of them to social media, shared them through text messages and tweets and engaged in collective viewing of them. This record of the events allowed Jane Doe and her parents to reconstruct what had happened to her the night in question (given that Jane Doe had no memory of the events) and was also instrumental in the defendants being charged and convicted of rape.

Jane Doe's parents made a complaint to the police and, in doing so, relied upon what they had collected from social media (e.g., Instagram and YouTube): a number of photographs that showed the complainant in an apparently unconscious state, often naked, and a videotape (uploaded to YouTube) that featured one of the young men who had witnessed the events laughing and making fun of Jane Doe, seemingly as a way of entertaining some of the other young men who had also witnessed the events. On the basis of the social media material brought in by the parents, the police were able to identify many of the young men who were present at the various venues the night in question, including the two young men who were eventually charged with rape. The police issued search warrants to seize the men's cell phones. In seizing these cell phones, the police were able to access the text messages that were exchanged among the various young men while the events were taking place, including photographs and videos that had not been previously deleted by the men. The police also had access to the material on social media that had been posted and circulated more widely.

One of the photographs posted on Instagram as the events of August 11 and 12 were unfolding played a very prominent role in the trial.[2] (It was labeled the prosecution's Exhibit 1.) Many of the witnesses were asked questions about the photograph and it was projected on a large screen at the front of the courtroom while this questioning was taking place. The photograph depicts the two defendants carrying a limp and lifeless Jane Doe by her wrists and her ankles. The prosecution in its closing argument characterized the defendants in the photograph as "carrying her like a rag doll" (Trial Transcript 2013, pp. 1494–95).[3] There were many other photographs entered as exhibits by the prosecution and, based on the testimony produced by witnesses when asked about these exhibits, they all seemed to portray Jane Doe in an unconscious state. As the remainder of this paper will demonstrate, it is the way in which participants in the trial treated this photographic evidence vis-à-vis the linguistic evidence, that, I suggest, has relevance for studies of multimodality.

Entextualization, Recontextualization, and Resemioticization

In investigating texts within online environments, as this paper attempts to do, other scholars of digital discourse (see, for example, Jones 2009; Leppanen et. al. 2014) have adopted the dynamic approach to discourse advocated by Bauman and Briggs (1990). Rejecting a view of text and context as static concepts, Bauman and Briggs emphasize the process by which texts are created and then recirculated in other settings. For Bauman and Briggs (1990, 73), entextualization is "the process of rendering discourse extractable"—of demarcating and segmenting a stretch of naturally occurring discourse and turning it into a unit "that can be lifted out of its interactional setting." Once segmented and extracted, this unit—a text—takes on a life of its own and becomes available for circulation in other contexts. Indeed, when relocated in a new context, the text may bring something from its earlier context but may also take on new meanings as it is "recentered" or recontextualized in the new context (1990, 73). These transformations in meaning often have an ideological dimension to them and/ or function to shore up institutional power as, for Bauman and Briggs (1990, 76), to decontextualize and recontexualize a text is "an act of control."

While Bauman and Briggs seemed to privilege language over other kinds of semiotic modes in their original account of entextualization and recontextualization, the increasing interest in multimodality within discourse analysis and linguistic anthropology has drawn attention to what Iedema (2001) has called resemiotization— the process by which "texts" may be translated from one semiotic mode to another. As Jones (2009, 287) says, the "product of...entextualization might be a written or spoken 'text'" or alternatively "might be a drawing or a photo or a video or an audio recording" (Jones 2009, 287). In other words, as some aspect of human experience is entextualized, it can be realized in different semiotic modes as it moves into other contexts. This is especially true in online environments, given that digital technologies allow for the use of complex combinations of semiotic modes.

There are several ways in which the social media evidence in the Steubenville trial differed from the kind of evidence available in more typical sexual assault cases. Adjudicators in more typical cases do not have direct access to the disputed events; rather, they must rely on after-the-fact "he said/she said" accounts of what happened. In the Steubenville case, by contrast, there was a "real-time" record of the events under investigation and this record consisted not only of linguistic/discursive descriptions of the events (e.g., text messages and tweets) but also visual documentation (i.e., photographs and videos). Put in the terms of the previous discussion, as the events were entextualized (i.e., turned into representations of the events) and recontextualized in new settings (i.e., shared by the defendants and their friends via text messages and tweets and posted on social media sites), they were also resemiotized (i.e., they were realized in verbal and visual modes). And, the argument I am making here is that the different semiotic modes (i.e., visual vs. verbal) the evidence took had different meaning-making consequences for the trial participants, which, in turn, had an impact on the trial's outcome.

Analysis: Photographic Evidence and Semiotic Ideologies

In a recent volume investigating the role of visual evidence in the legal system (*Law, Culture and Visual Studies*, edited by Wagner and Sherwin 2014), various contributors argue that digital photography and videos tend to be accepted as evidence in a much less critical way than verbal testimony. That is, because verbal testimony is mediated by a linguistic code, it is understood as shaping or constructing our view of legal evidence as opposed to representing that evidence in a neutral and straightforward way. By contrast, there is a view of images in various areas of the legal system whereby images are indistinguishable from what they represent. According to Adler (2014, 165), visual images are so closely associated with what they depict that there is a kind of "fusing" or "merging" of the signifier and signified. As Richard Sherwin, a coeditor of the volume, says, "visual images...often get treated as 'windows' opening onto reality rather than as the visual constructions that they are.... Unlike words which are abstract and obviously constructed, photos, films and videos seem to be caused by the external world. With no obvious trace of mediation visual images seem to lack artifice. That is why visual images make for such highly persuasive evidence for what they purport to depict" (Sherwin 2014, xxxiii).

The kinds of beliefs that Sherwin and other contributors to this coedited volume identify as informing the assessment of evidence in the legal system are specific instances of what might be more generally understood as semiotic ideologies (Keane 2003; Thurlow 2017).[4] Indeed, Thurlow (2017, 15), in his work on the digital media practice of "sexting," draws attention to the operation of a similar semiotic-ideological principle to that described above: public discourse on sexting, he argues, "is grounded in a long-standing trenchant belief in the realism of photography— the idea that, in spite of so much evidence to the contrary, photographs do not lie." While Thurlow exemplifies his argument in relation to the way that sexting is "metadiscursively framed," his claim is more general—the semiotic-ideological principle he describes "necessarily shape[s] the way all digital media are understood and talked about" (Thurlow 2017, 16). Consistent with work by Sherwin (and contributors) and Thurlow, witnesses, the prosecution, and even the defense in the Steubenville case seemed to draw on the "realism of photography" ideology in assessing evidence in the trial; that is, they seemed to ascribe an evidentiary capacity to the photographs that was not ascribed to the linguistic evidence in the same way.

Excerpt 1 comes from the cross-examination of a witness for the prosecution. The witness is a friend of the complainant and was with the complainant at the first house party (see description of case above). After the complainant left that party with the two defendants, the friend continued to follow the events that took place at the two other venues. This was possible because, as I have indicated, the events were being documented on social media as they unfolded.

```
(1)  From Defense's Cross-Examination of Witness for the Pros-
     ecution⁵
```

```
1    Q: And then all of these things happen and your memory began to be
2       constructed at that time based on what you read online. Safe to say?
3    A: Yes.
4    Q: You had no idea if those things were accurate; did you?
5    A: No.
6    Q: You had no idea if they were true or someone was just playing a mean
7       joke; correct?
8    A: Yes.
. . .
9    Q: All right. In particular about her being urinated upon—
10   A: Uh-huh.
11   Q:—isn't that correct?
12   A: Yes.
13   Q: You don't know if that's true; do you?
14   A: Well, I saw the picture.
     (Trial Transcript 2013, pp. 80-81 [italics added])
```

The import of the defense lawyer's cross-examination in this excerpt is that the witness's understanding of what happened to the complainant over the course of the evening (i.e., that she was the victim of sexual acts of aggression) was shaped by, or "constructed," as he says, by what the witness had read online (lines 1–2). In fact, according to the defense lawyer, the witness had no idea whether any of the things she read online were accurate (line 4); they could have been "a mean joke," for example (lines 6–7). The defense lawyer's use of the term "constructed" in line 2 is interesting, as this is the same word that Sherwin uses in his characterization above of the "seeing is believing" ideology: "unlike words which are abstract and obviously *constructed*, photos... seem to be caused by the external world" (emphasis added). The witness seems to agree with the defense lawyer's contention that her understanding of what happened to the complainant may have been "constructed" by what she read online, as evidenced by her answers to his questions in lines 3, 5, and 8. However, when the lawyer asks in lines 9 and 11 about a specific event that was alleged to have occurred—the complainant being urinated upon—the witness's response is somewhat different. In line 13, the lawyer asserts that the witness does not know if this event actually happened ("you don't know if that's true") and then seeks confirmation for this proposition. The witness does not confirm the lawyer's proposition but instead responds in line 14 with the utterance, "Well, I saw the picture." The discourse marker "well" signals that this response is inconsistent with "the expectations of prior coherence" (Schiffrin 1987, 126); in other words, this answer departs from the witness's previous answers in which she confirms the lawyer's contention that what she has read online may not be an accurate rendition of events. Indeed, in line 14, the witness indicates that, unlike the written material online, "the picture" (i.e., the photograph) vouches for the truth-value and reliability of her belief that the complainant was "urinated upon."[6]

We see something similar in (2), which comes from the prosecution's opening statement. Here the prosecuting lawyer is putting forward a crucial part of the prosecution's case—the need to prove that the complainant was substantially impaired and therefore did not have the capacity to consent. In parsing "substantial impairment" for the court, the prosecutor states that it is not necessary to prove that the complainant was unconscious, only that there was "a reduction in her ability to act and think."

(2)   From Prosecution's Opening Statement

She could not consent and we don't have to guess and guess what substantial impairment means. The State doesn't have to prove that she was unconscious. We just have to prove there's a reduction in her ability to act and think. *The pictures prove that all.* (Trial Transcript 2013, p. 25 [italics added])

Significant for my purposes here is the fact that the prosecuting lawyer does not cite testimony from witnesses in order to "prove" the complainant's reduction in ability to act and think (and there was much that could have been cited); nor does she cite evidence from the texts or tweets the young men exchanged over the course of the evening (including the many that described Jane Doe as a "dead girl"). Rather, in the italicized lines of this excerpt ("The pictures prove that all"), the lawyer points to "the pictures" (i.e., the photographs) as providing the definitive proof for—or truth about—the complainant's substantial impairment. We see again the idea that photographs are a particularly reliable source of proof and truth.

While (1) and (2) are somewhat implicit in their ascribing of greater evidentiary capabilities to the photographs relative to the linguistic evidence, (3), from the prosecution's closing argument, explicitly privileges the photographic images of Jane Doe over the textual evidence.

(3)   From Prosecution's Closing Statement

15 There are "three distinct areas of evidence that you will use when

```
16   looking at the elements of the offenses charged in this complaint.
17   First you heard about text messages that came in through the
18   computer technician. You also heard witness testimony from albeit
19   kids, teenagers, who most of them had been drinking alcohol but then
20   you also heard and seen about pictures and photographs like this one
21   that's been spread throughout this trial⁷.... The photographs are great
22   evidence and you've seen them in this case, the victim passed out it
23   appears with semen on her stomach, her face down and spread eagle
24   while people are standing around taking pictures of her and it appears
25   she's passed out. This is evidence you will use when you look at these
26   charges."
(Trial Transcript 2013, p. 1476)
```

In line 15 of (3), there is reference made to "three distinct areas of evidence." As the remainder of this excerpt indicates, these three types of evidence are text messages, verbal testimony, and the photographs. However, the prosecutor does not grant the same kind of veracity to each of these. In particular, the accuracy/truthfulness of the witness testimony seems to be called into question when the prosecutor notes that it was produced by "albeit kids, teenagers" (lines 18–19), most of whom "had been drinking alcohol" (line 19). Moreover, this verbal testimony is separated from another kind of evidence, "pictures and photographs" (line 20), by the contrastive conjunction "but" (line 19), thereby signaling the oppositional nature of the two kinds of evidence and, seemingly, the greater trustworthiness of the photographic evidence. Indeed, the prosecutor's comments in lines 18–19 about the witness testimony suggest that it cannot be trusted. Later in this same excerpt, we again see the prosecutor assigning special significance to the photographic evidence, characterizing it as "great evidence" (lines 21–22) and then proceeding to describe two photographs that depict the complainant as "passed out," a crucial part of the prosecution's case.

There are other points in the trial, especially during cross-examination, when the prosecution appeals to the supposed "truth-value" of the photographs as a way of challenging the version of events put forward by the defense. This happens, for example, in (4), where the prosecution is cross-examining a defense expert witness, someone who is an expert on alcohol consumption. In her direct examination, this expert witness argued, based on the amount of alcohol consumed by the complainant, that the complainant was not in "passed out" mode during the events under dispute but rather in "blackout" mode. This meant that, while the complainant couldn't remember what happened, she, in the words of this expert witness, "was capable of engaging in voluntary decisions, as well as exhibiting at least some degree of behavioral capability" (Trial Transcript 2013, p. 1281). (Note that the comment here about the complainant's capacity to engage in voluntary decisions is no doubt a thinly veiled claim about the complainant's capacity to consent to the sexual "advances" of the two defendants.) When this expert witness is cross-examined by the prosecution, one line of questioning concerns the sort of evidence on which the expert witness has based her assessment of the complainant's state that night.

(4)   From Prosecution's Cross-Examination of Defense's Expert Witness[8]

```
27  Q:  Okay. And in this case you're limited to what was provided to you by
28      the Defense; correct?
29  A:  Yes, ma'am.
30  Q:  Did they give you any text messages?
31  A:  Yes.
32  Q:  Oh, they did? You didn't mention that.
33  A:  I did not. I apologize.
34  Q:  Okay. Did they have any bearing or factor into your calculations at all?
35  A:  No. I was really looking for evidence related to alcohol. It's not my
36      job to assess other information.
37  Q:  Did they show you any photos?
38  A:  No.
39  Q:  They didn't show you a photo that looked like this?
40  A:  No.
41  Q:  Okay. And they didn't show any photos that look like this. I'm going to
42      show you what's been previously marked as State's Exhibit 2.[9] Did you
43      see that photo in your assessment?
44  A:  No, ma'am.
45  Q:  Okay. I'm going to show you what's marked as State's Exhibit 24. Did
46      you see that photo?
47  A:  No.
```
(Trial Transcript 2013, p. 1284)

In line 30, we see the prosecutor asking specifically about whether the expert witness has seen the text message evidence, which she has (line 31). In a much longer sequence (lines 37–47), the prosecutor asks a series of question about whether the witness has seen the photographic evidence. In line 37, the lawyer asks a general question about the photographic evidence and in subsequent lines asks about specific photographs (line 39, lines 41–43, lines 45–46). In response to all of these questions, the expert witness responds in the negative, that is, she was not shown any of the photographic evidence by the defense. While the witness states that it is not her job to assess evidence other than that related to alcohol, I think the implication of the prosecutor's line of questioning is clear: that if the expert witness had seen the photographic evidence it may have been harder for her to claim that the complainant "was capable of engaging in voluntary decisions, as well as exhibiting at least some degree of behavioral capability." And, of course, it is significant for the argument that I am making here that the defense did show this expert witness the text message evidence but did not show her the photographic evidence. It appears that the defense, like the prosecution, imputed a certain veracity and reliability to the photographic evidence that was not imputed to the text message evidence. In other words, the defense seems to have believed that the photographic evidence might challenge the expert witness's conclusions about the complainant's condition in a way that the linguistic evidence would not, even though the text messages also supplied descriptions of the complainant's condition, albeit verbal ones.

Perhaps the most succinct expression of the semiotic ideology that, I suggest, informed the treatment of evidence in this trial was produced in the closing statement of one of the defense lawyers. This lawyer was reflecting on the nature of photography or "pictures" very generally and said about the most prominent photograph in the trial (the prosecution's Exhibit 1)—"this picture speaks a thousand words" (Trial Transcript 2013, pp. 1485–86). The defense lawyer went on to emphasize that one's perspective ("where you stand") determines what one sees (or what "this picture speaks") and that the defense held the position (i.e., perspective) that Jane Doe was "joking" when the photograph (Exhibit 1) was taken (i.e., she was feigning unconsciousness). Nonetheless, the idiom "A picture is worth a thousand words" conveys the idea that a visual image expresses meaning more effectively than a linguistic description does. And, as this section has attempted to demonstrate, it was this semiotic-ideological principle that generally structured how witnesses, the prosecution, and the defense assigned meaning to the various kinds of evidence in the trial.

Conclusions and Implications

One of the questions that arises from this analysis is the extent to which the trial participants' privileging of the photographic evidence over the linguistic evidence may have affected the outcome of the trial. The defense in the Steubenville case argued that the complainant had consented to all of the acts of sexual aggression perpetrated by the defendants in spite of her seeming passivity. Consider the most explicit articulation of this position, which comes from the defense's closing argument in the probable cause hearing, a hearing that preceded the trial.[10]

(5) From Defense Closing Statement, Probable Cause Hearing

Not once did you hear her say or any witness the State produced say she didn't want to do it. Now because she's silent, that doesn't mean she's objecting or that she was comatose or flat-lined. She didn't affirmatively say no.... The person who is the accuser here is silent just as she was that evening and that's because there was consent.
(Probable Cause Hearing 2012, p. 249)

In this excerpt the defense describes the complainant as "silent" on the evening in question but maintains that this silence "doesn't mean she's objecting" or "she didn't want to do it." In other words, silence, according to the defense, does not mean there is an absence of consent. Yet, I argue in Ehrlich (2019) that the defense's argument failed to gain traction in this particular case because the photographic evidence revealed an exceedingly passive and unresponsive Jane Doe, *and* there was an uncritical trust put in the evidentiary capacity of this evidence. In other words, because the "realism of photography" ideology seemed to determine to a large extent the way the social media evidence was assigned meaning by the trial participants, a finding of consent—in line with the defense's position—was made difficult.

In considering the implications of this analysis for multimodal discourse analysis, I return to the notions of entextualization and recontextualization introduced earlier (Bauman and Briggs 1990). In a paper that followed their original formulation of these processes, Briggs and Bauman (1992) introduced the idea of "an intertextual gap" in order to characterize the relationship between a recontextualized text and its generic type (or previous text). As noted above, once some aspect of human experience is entextualized, it can be relocated in another context (i.e., recontextualized) and a gap can arise between the text's original meaning and its recontextualized meaning. And, according to Briggs and Bauman (1992), depending on how faithful a recontexualized text is to its "original," this intertextual gap can be minimal or maximal. Following work by Gershon and Manning (2014, 542) on media ideologies, I suggest, based on the above analysis, that establishing the extent or degree of an intertextual gap across "texts" realized in different modes is not something an analyst can do independently of participants' understandings. Indeed, my analysis has demonstrated that the participants in this particular trial took the evidence when realized in a visual mode as having greater veracity than the same evidence when realized in a verbal mode. Put somewhat differently, they understood the photographic representations of the events to be more faithful and closer to the "original" events than the linguistic representations. Thus, it seems that the semiotic ideologies of participants are crucial in understanding how representing something through images or language has an impact on meaning. In a recent review article on multimodality for the second edition of *The Handbook of Discourse Analysis*, van Leeuwen (2015, 460) notes that within the domain of educational studies, multimodal analysis has been productively combined with ethnography. In a similar way, I am suggesting that convincing evidence about the meaning-making potential of different semiotic modes may come from attending to the semiotic ideologies that inform people's multimodal interpretive practices.

Acknowledgments

I thank Cynthia Gordon, the editor of this volume, and audience members at GURT 2018 for very useful feedback on this paper. All remaining errors are, of course, my own.

Notes

1   See Ehrlich (2019) for an extended version of this argument—one that explores the role of the photographic evidence in disrupting normative conceptions of female sexuality.
2   The image is available at http://a.abcnews.com/images/2020/abc_2020_rape2_130322_wg.jpg (accessed December 8, 2020).
3   Crime blogger Alexandria Goddard, a former resident of Steubenville, became aware of the assaults a few days after they occurred. Before many of the young men had deleted their posts, photographs, and videos, she took screen shots of them and posted them on her blog (Prinniefied.com). This particular photograph "went viral" after she had posted it.

4   Thurlow (2017, 15) argues that Keane's notion of semiotic ideologies, while generally concerned with beliefs about signs and meaning-making, is "essentially related to questions of multimodality, prompting the following types of questions: What is the relative importance or value of language vis-à-vis other modes of communication? Which modes are thought to 'carry' meaning better or more reliably?"

5   Q and A in (1) precede questions asked by the defense lawyer and answers provided by a witness for the prosecution, respectively.

6   The photograph referred to in (1) was the prosecution's Exhibit 2. It is apparently a photograph of Jane Doe lying motionless on the floor with a substance on her stomach. When witnesses and lawyers described this photograph within the context of the trial, some described the substance on the complainant's stomach as urine; others described it as semen.

7   The photograph described in this excerpt as "spread throughout the trial" is the prosecution's Exhibit 1, the photograph of a limp Jane Doe being carried by her wrists and ankles by the two defendants.

8   Q and A in (4) precede questions asked by the prosecuting lawyer and answers provided by an expert witness for the defense, respectively.

9   Exhibit 2 is also referred to in (1) and (3). As noted previously, it is a photograph of Jane Doe lying motionless with either urine or semen on her stomach.

10 This was a hearing in which the judge was presented with evidence in order to determine whether there were grounds to detain the defendants and hold them for trial.

References

Adler, Amy. 2014. The first amendment and the second commandment. In Anne Wagner and Richard K. Sherwin (eds.), *Law, culture and visual studies*. Dordrecht, Netherlands: Springer. 161–78.

Bauman, Richard and Charles L. Briggs. 1990. Poetics and performance as critical perspectives on language and social life. *Annual Review of Anthropology* 19: 59–88.

Briggs, Christopher L. and Richard Bauman. 1992. Genre, intertextuality and social power. *Journal of Linguistic Anthropology* 2 (2): 131–72.

Ehrlich, Susan. 2019. 'Well, I saw the picture': Semiotic ideologies and the unsettling of normative conceptions of female sexuality in the Steubenville rape trial. *Gender and Language* 13 (2): 251–69.

Gershon, Ilana and Paul Manning. 2014. Language and media. In N. J. Enfield, Paul Kockelman and Jack Sidnell (eds.), *The Cambridge handbook of linguistic anthropology*. Cambridge: Cambridge University Press. 539–56.

Iedema, Rick. 2001. Resemiotization. *Semiotica* 37: 23–40.

Jewitt, Carey. 2016. Multimodal analysis. In Alexandra Georgakopoulou and Tereza Spiloti (eds.), *The Routledge handbook of language and digital communication*. London: Routledge. 69–83.

Jones, Rodney H. 2009. Dancing, skating and sex: Action and text in the digital age. *Journal of Applied Linguistics* 6 (3): 283–302.

Jones, Rodney H. and Christopher Hafner. 2012. *Understanding digital literacies*. London: Routledge.

Keane, Webb. 2003. Semiotics and the social analysis of material things. *Language and Communication* 23: 403–25.

Kress, Gunther. 2003. *Literacy in the new media age*. London: Routledge.

Leppanen, Sirpa, Samu Kytola, Henna Jousmaki, Saija Peuronen and Elina Westinen. 2014. Entextualization and resemiotization as resources for identification in social media. In Philip Seargent and Caroline Tagg (eds.), *The language of social media*. Basingstoke, Hampshire, UK: Palgrave Macmillan. 112–36.

Probable Cause Hearing. 2012. In the Matter of Ma'lik Richmond an Alleged Delinquent Child and In the Matter of Trenton W. Mays an Alleged Delinquent Child. Transcript of Proceedings.

Schiffrin, Deborah. 1987. *Discourse markers*. Cambridge: Cambridge University Press.

Sherwin, Richard K. 2014. Introduction: Law, culture, and visual studies. In Anne Wagner and Richard K. Sherwin (eds.), *Law, culture and visual studies*. Dordrecht, Netherlands: Springer. xxxiii–xli.

Trial Transcript. 2013. In the Matter of Ma'lik Richmond an Alleged Delinquent Child and In the Matter of Trenton W. Mays an Alleged Delinquent Child. Transcript of Proceedings.

Thurlow, Crispin. 2017. "Forget about the words"? Tracking the language, media and semiotic ideologies of digital discourse: The case of sexting. *Discourse, Context & Media* 20: 10–19.

van Leeuwen, Theo. 2000. Visual racism. In Martin Reisigl and Ruth Wodak (eds.), *The semiotics of racism.* Vienna: Passagen Verlag. 333–50.

———. 2015. Multimodality. In Deborah Tannen, Heidi E. Hamilton and Deborah Schiffrin (eds.), *The handbook of discourse analysis* (2nd ed.). Oxford: John Wiley & Sons. 447–65.

Wagner, Anne and Richard K. Sherwin. (eds.). 2014. *Law, culture and visual studies.* Dordrecht, Netherlands: Springer.

9

Repair as Activism on Arabic Twitter

NAJMA AL ZIDJALY

ARABS HAVE CONTINUOUSLY APPROPRIATED new media technologies as activism tools due to lack of freedom of expression in quotidian contexts (Al Zidjaly 2017a). Given Facebook's ubiquity and prominence, a good deal of existing academic research has highlighted the role that this social media tool has played in the Arab Spring (Khondker 2011; Lewinski and Mohammed 2012; Sinatora 2019a, 2019b). Despite Twitter gaining presence among Arabs (Radcliffe and Bruni 2019), little is known to date regarding its appropriation as a cultural tool to incite change in Arabic (and non-Arabic) contexts.[1] Moreover, existing sociolinguistic studies on Twitter often foreground the function of hashtags as facilitating "ambient affiliation" (Zappavigna 2011) and organizing social actions (Blommaert 2018b). In this chapter, I examine an example from the Twitter revolution: how Arabs from various theological positions have appropriated Twitter to incite social reform by "repairing" those Islamic texts, beliefs, and practices they perceive as hindering change. By "repairing," I mean "correcting," using techniques that have certain commonalities with conversational repair. I specifically identify a new type of repair I term *multiscale repair*,[2] because it concurrently operates at three levels: grammatical, textual, and cultural. I therefore examine conversational repair as social activism in the context of Arabic Twitter.

To capture the function of multiscale repair in precipitating socioreligious change—and to arrive at the workings of repair in the Arabic activism context—I use a mediated-action approach to discourse, drawing upon the theory of mediated discourse analysis (Scollon 2001) and its accompanying methodology nexus analysis (Scollon and Scollon 2004). I collectively refer to these analyses as mediated discourse and nexus analysis (MDNA) to highlight the need for a mediated discourse approach to use an ethnographic, interdiscursive methodology, as originally intended by the Scollons (see Al Zidjaly 2019a for a discussion). In this theory, discourse is theorized as a mediated action grounded in larger discourses and as constantly acting in a dialogic, mutually constitutive, and mutually constraining relationship with social actors, mediational means, cycles of discourses, and their combined histories. Accordingly, I theorize repair as a mediated action strategically appropriated on Twitter by Arab reformers to discredit Islamic authoritative discourses (Bakhtin 1981) through the desynchronization (Blommaert 2005) or the uncovering of the multiple (and invisible) layered meanings embedded in the contested texts. In this theorization, repair is constructed as a multimodal strategy mediated by what Carbaugh (2007) calls cultural discourses, made possible by intertextual references and resulting in cultural effects, captured through grounding discourse in action. Theorizing repair as a mediated action that is appropriated strategically to generate cultural revolution demonstrates the complexity of this key linguistic strategy. The analysis also reveals repair to be a multiscale phenomenon in this context, as repairing a term concomitantly repairs the texts from which it is extracted and the larger culture in which it functions. The study also highlights human creativity and how social media help showcase meaningful uses of semiotic tools.

Background

In what follows, I contextualize the presented study by providing a synopsis of intertextuality and repair in digital discourse and by introducing my data collection with a focus on the tenets of MDNA.

Social Media and Intertextuality

Intertextuality, as coined by Kristeva ([1967] 1980), refers to the Bakhtinian (1981) theorization of meaning-making as a dialogic interaction between past, present, and future texts, discourses, and actions (Fairclough [1999] and Scollon [2007] added the notion of action).[3] Accordingly, intertextuality is an inherent part of digital action formation and identity construction (Al Zidjaly 2010, 2017b; Gordon 2006, 2015; Hamilton 1996; Hodsdon-Champeon 2010; Schiffrin 2000). Gordon (2015, 121–22) elaborates that various kinds of intertextuality have been examined online, ranging from hyperlinks (Mitra 1999) to direct or indirect reference to texts (Al Zidjaly 2010, 2017a; Hodsdon-Champeon 2010) to quotations (Hodsdon-Champeon 2010). Such research extends the large body of research examining intertextuality in everyday conversational discourse (e.g., Gordon 2009; Tannen [1989] 2007).

The identified interactional and pragmatic functions of intertextuality include bonding by creating connection and involvement (Becker 1994; Gordon 2015; Tannen [1989] 2007), constructing meaning (Gordon 2009), building family relationships (Tovares 2012), and creating diverse identities in discourse (Gordon 2006). In this chapter I identify an additional function of intertextuality: inciting cultural revolution by enabling the repair, and discrediting, of Islamic "authoritative discourses"; following Bakhtin (1981), these are taken-for-granted (cultural) discourses or texts that cannot, and should not, be questioned, in contrast to "internally persuasive discourses," which can be negotiated. I consider authoritative discourses key to examining digital religious discourse. Arab activists intertextually and digitally reference three types of authoritative discourses (which have varying degrees of authoritativeness). First is the Quran, the book of Islam; questioning the book as the word of God may lead to incarceration. Although only anonymous Twitter accounts and exiled Arab activists critique the Quran, it remained authoritative only until 2006 (by which I mean public instances of it being questioned were to that point rare or nonexistent). Second are the hadiths, the reported sayings of the prophet of Islam collected posthumously in the books of Sahih Al-Bukhari and Muslim, which vary in authoritativeness. Questioning these remains frowned upon. Third are cultural discourses (Carbaugh 2007), timeless actions and beliefs of Arabic cultures, such as women being unfit to lead or Charles Darwin being wrong about the origin of life.

My decade-long ethnographic examination of digital Arab identity (Al Zidjaly 2010, 2012, 2014, 2017a, 2017b, 2019a, 2019b, 2019c; Al Zidjaly and Gordon 2012) has demonstrated that from the inception of interactive media platforms (e.g., Yahoo chat rooms), Arabs have taken the opportunity to turn authoritative discourse into internally persuasive discourse, using digital media as tools to reconcile Islam with the twenty-first century. It was not until the era of Twitter and YouTube, however, that a group of Arabs systematically engaged in discrediting all Islamic authoritative discourses, an action prohibited by law that potentially could change the foundation of religiously based Arabic societies. This study demonstrates how this discrediting happens on a moment-by-moment basis.

Repair in Digital Discourse

Traditionally, conversational analysts theorize repair as an important mechanism by which interactants attend to problems in hearing, speaking, or understanding (e.g., Sacks, Schegloff and Jefferson 1974). Thus, repair is key to constructing intersubjectivity, defined as a display of mutual understanding of conversational activities at hand (Schegloff 1992). Further, self-initiated repairs typically are preferred and other-initiated repairs are mitigated (Sacks, Schegloff and Jefferson 1974; Schegloff 1992; Schegloff, Jefferson and Sacks 1977) to maintain conversational rapport and save face. In conflict discourse, however, Goodwin (1983) demonstrated speakers' tendency to display rather than mitigate expressions of disagreement, which involves initiating repair on another participant's discourse. Goodwin terms this type of other-initiated repair aggravated or unmodulated repair because the purpose of aggravated repair is to contest previously proposed ideas rather than to resolve misunderstandings or maintain intersubjectivity. Accordingly, Goodwin suggests aggravated repair sequences differ in organization from modulated repair sequences: repair sequences in the latter case are constructed as a disruption of the communicative act (i.e., they are a timeout act to correct a perceived error or misunderstanding prior to pursuing the conversation). In contrast, aggravated repair sequences continue the flow, as the challenge is what constitutes the prior ongoing activity. In Goodwin's (1983, 665) own words, "rather than removing participants from the business at hand in a kind of 'side sequence' (Jefferson 1974), corrections provide a solution for continuing what participants were up to all along while creating a new focus of interactive discord." In Goodwin's expansive approach, repair is constructed as a highly contextual conversational mechanism.

The contextual nature of repair has been exemplified in the scarce research on the subject in digital contexts, as noted by Gordon (2019).[4] Meredith and Stokoe (2014) explored the differences in use and function of repair in synchronous written Facebook chats, in contrast to spoken face-to-face discourse. The findings suggest that online and face-to-face repair operate similarly, a conclusion corroborated by Schegloff (2013) and Schönfeldt and Golato (2003). However, in digital contexts, unique trouble sources exist given *context collapse* (as described by Georgakopoulou 2017), which refers to the infinite audiences and multiauthored nature of texts in digital contexts. For instance, Meredith and Stokoe (2014) identified *message construction repair* as occurring before the author posts the message, making this repair type invisible to recipients and having no equivalence in face-to-face interactions. Therefore, the authors argue that despite similarities between written and spoken self-repairs, their initiation and completion during message construction provides for a systematic difference between spoken and online interaction. In identifying the user-created strategy of employing a unique morpheme (*) to correct misspellings in online discussions, Collister (2011) also demonstrated the multiplicity of repair modalities, illustrating the need to take an expansive approach to examine this phenomenon, especially in digital contexts.

Perhaps the most expansive examination of other-initiated repair online to date is Gordon's (2019) study of weight-loss blogs, which addresses how commenters repair multiple aspects of blog posts (e.g., language production errors, plus the nature and amount of included vocabulary, information, and images). Following Blommaert (2018a), Gordon (2019, 402) theorizes repair as a "local light practice through which participants engage, construct connection, and help define group expectations pertaining to the website's expert-written blogs." In initiating and completing repair, commenters "draw on (and reflect) global-level assumptions or cultural discourses (Carbaugh 2007) about blogs" (2019, 402). In addition to extending the concept of repair to images, this study identifies functions that go beyond creating interactivity in the moment: repair signals metalinguistic awareness, creates the fleeting moments of connection that work to build community, and helps establish shared meanings regarding, for instance, what types of information are important to readers of weight-loss blogs. In other words, Gordon (2019, 421) argues, repair is but "one practice among many light practices that, in facilitating interactivity in this asynchronous communication context, also construct commenters as involved in the larger activity of sharing weight loss information and support." Accordingly, the identified repair examples correct perceived errors to facilitate interaction and further draw upon larger discourses, thus unifying people by constructing and maintaining intersubjectivity—locally about the interaction and globally about larger social weight-loss and food norms.

In this chapter, I build on Goodwin (1983) and Gordon (2019) to broaden the conversation analysis-based definition of repair to include all aspects of

meaning-making or semiosis. I also explore the mechanism of repair in the hith-
erto unchartered territories of memetic actions (i.e., actions that take the form of
memes), thus enabling me to explore the complexity of repair as a multimodal
action strategically appropriated to incite cultural revolution. In this nonconven-
tional theorization, repair is constructed as a deliberate deconstructing act of cultural texts and discourses, extending beyond mere correction of a conversational
production or understanding error.

Data Collection and Theory
I use the theory of mediated discourse analysis (Scollon 2001) and the methodology of nexus analysis (Scollon and Scollon 2004) to examine repair in the context
of Arabic activism. Mediated discourse and nexus analysis (MDNA), as I term the
integration of these approaches, theorizes linguistic strategies as mediated actions
grounded in larger discourses.[5] The conceptualization of discourse as action is not
unique: many analytical approaches to discourse (e.g., pragmatics, conversation
analysis) theorize words as actions, such as those of Goodwin (1990) and Blommaert (2018b), who have stipulated that highlighting language as action is key to
understanding the process of meaning-making. How MDNA differs is that a mediated project is less concerned with *discourse as action* and more with *discourse in
action* (Norris and Jones 2005). Accordingly, MDNA as an approach to discourse
works best for activism research, as it contextualizes semiotic strategies through
ethnography and methodological interdiscursivity (i.e., collecting different types of
data; Reusch and Bateson 1968). It also highlights the dialogic relationship actions
have to the social actors who carry them out (and their histories and motives), the
mediational means (with their affordances and limitations) used to accomplish the
actions, and the larger societal discourses surrounding them. In this theorization,
the linguistic strategy of repair is not a mere communicative subprocess aimed at
organizing talk; rather, it is a unique multimodal action prohibited by Arabic governments in particular authoritative discourse contexts and appropriated by a group
of Arab activists to foment cultural revolution. Repair discredits authoritative discourses through inviting a desynchronization process of texts and actions long taken
for granted. Repair in this data thus is a revolutionary action made possible by Twitter and the creativity of Arab Twitter users.

The dataset is taken from the Arabic Reform Project section (Al Zidjaly 2019a)
of a larger longitudinal and ethnographic project on Arab identity and social media
I commenced in 2015.[6] As actions in a mediated nexus project are conceptualized
as interdiscursively rich and shaped by multiple contexts (e.g., discursive, cultural, and historical), I collected various types of data, including over fifty thousand
tweets and memes with comments by Arabs from various religious and political
backgrounds. I also gathered information about larger discourses relevant to examining the role that repair plays in the context of digital religious activism (e.g.,
the history of Islam, Islamic religious texts, cultural discourses, beliefs, and daily
practices). As an integrative theory and methodology, which encourages collecting
different types of data, MDNA allows the use of any analytical framework deemed

fit for analysis. These unique features make it an integrative theory applicable across academic fields. Therefore, to analyze the particular dataset in this paper, I draw upon interactional sociolinguistics (Tannen 2005) and multimodality (Kress and van Leeuwen [1996] 2006).

Analysis of Multiscale Repair

This section provides an analysis of what I call multiscale repair in six highly circulated Twitter posts. I consider multiscale repair as other-initiated actions that are motivated by larger repair goals and therefore operate concurrently at three levels (each with its own trouble source): grammatical, or linguistic; textual, or discursive; and cultural. Linguistic, the first and most immediate scale, is similar to conversation analysts' definition of repair and corrects an actual or perceived error in a trouble source (e.g., a verse from the Quran). By implication, linguistic repair also achieves discursive, second-scale repair because the identified trouble source is part of an authoritative text (e.g., the Quran, hadith, or cultural belief). At this second level, the problematic but traditionally unrepairable authoritative discourse is converted into a repairable, internally persuasive discourse. Although not analyzed extensively in this paper, the repair of authoritative texts initiates a desynchronizing action that unpacks discourses (e.g., Quran and hadith) into their various layers, ultimately achieving the end goal of third-scale repair of the larger Islamic culture (main trouble source) that informs such authoritative discourses.

I use "repair" to reference the discrediting actions of a group of Arab reformers on Twitter not only to connect to existing scholarly theorizing on repair, but also because this is the term used by members of the Arab reform community themselves (تعديل), as illustrated in example 1 (and not correction - تصحيح).[7] Examples 2–6 display the main types of repair found in the Arabic reform community (e.g., repairing grammatical errors, morphological choices or terms, euphemisms, and ideologies) on Twitter and the four main types of texts repaired in the community (the Quran, the hadiths, Arabic terminology, and Arabic cultural ideas about evolution). The typical format of multiscale repair actions by Arabs on Twitter often consists of two parts: (1) retweet and a comment (example 1); and (2) tweet and justification: the justification is provided either by the author of the tweet themselves (example 2) or by a follower of the tweet author (examples 3–6).

Minor Repair

A ubiquitous practice established in 2018 among Arab tweeters involved account holders of various theological positions (from believers to nonbelievers) indirectly discrediting the implied meaning (illocutionary force; Austin [1962]) of others' tweets. In this *minor repair*, as termed by the community, @NeverknowOb in example 1 retweets and comments on @Adab_a5Ia8's original tweet, which cites a famous quote ingrained in the Muslim historical body (Nishida 1958) typically voiced as a dismissive response to calls for Islamic reform. @NeverknowOb's retweet and comment form a pair that de-layers or unsynchronizes or uncovers (Blommaert 2005) the discourses referenced in @Adab_a5Ia8's original tweet. The first part of the pair is the retweet (bottom), and the second part is the response (top), which clarifies a term used in the original tweet ("errors"), thus discrediting the legitimacy of the indirect claims presented in the retweet. (Note: the vector of reading should begin with the bottom retweet, followed by the comment on top. In the translation, which follows each tweet, I have underlined both "errors" in the original tweet and the term's clarifications (and unpacking) in the response. My added comments appear in square brackets.)

Example 1: Minor repair

Retweet from @NeverknowOb, May 26, 2018

Minor repair: I am a Muslim, and Islam commands me to beat my wives at bedtime and beat my children at prayer time and that I go to Mecca to circumambulate around a stone and to kiss a stone and to throw a stone at a stone. _. Despite all that, Islam is a complete religion, and the sin is the sin of the Muslim.	تعديل طفيف: أنا مسلم والاسلام يأمرني بضرب زوجاتي عند الفراش وضرب ابنائي عند الصلاة وان اذهب لمكة حتى اطوف حول حجر وارمي حجر على حجر ثم ارجع واضرب ابنائي وزوجاتي مرة اخرى ورغم كل ذلك الاسلام دين كامل والذنب ذنب المسلم

Original tweet from @Adab_a51a8, October 10, 2017

I am a Muslim and Islam is a complete religion; but I am not a completed human being; If I have committed <u>errors</u>. Do not blame Islam; blame me. (Ahmed Deedat).	أنا مسلم و الإسلام دين كامل لكنني لست إنسانا كاملا إن ارتكبت خطأ فلا تلوموا الإسلام لكن لوموني أنا. (أحمد ديدات).

The illocutionary force of @Adab_a51a8's original tweet (which can be found at the bottom of @NeverknowOb's retweet) is that Islam does not require reform; any perceived shortcomings exist only because Muslims may commit errors. Per Ahmed Deedat, the key twentieth-century Indian Islamic figure whose image is included in the tweet, most of the problems with Islam are caused by the actions of Muslims themselves, rather than by the wholesome religion. The accompanying image of Deedat in mid-discourse with a hand gesture appropriated by Islamic cultures (especially by Muslims in India) to indicate a challenge and the end of debate (meaning something to the effect of, "What else do you want? You want a piece of me?") accentuates the dismissiveness of Deedat's quote, which indicates that Islam shares no responsibility for human errors.

@NeverknowOb takes up the challenge in his comment. Specifically, he outlines the kinds of so-called human "errors" Muslims may commit: physically assaulting women for withholding sex (indicated by the use of "at bedtime") and polygamy (indicated by the term "wives"), both sanctioned in the Quran; physically assaulting children for refusal to pray, an authoritative action sanctioned by hadiths; and Islamic pilgrimage to Mecca, a commandment in the Quran. While the first three examples can be easily constructed as deplorable yet religiously sanctioned actions, the pilgrimage is provided as a problematic Islamic action because it is historically based on paganist actions (involving ritualized activities pertaining to throwing stones at evil) that, per the retweet author, oppose Islamic monotheism. By deconstructing "errors," @NeverknowOb discredits the cultural discourse that Islam is a wholesome religion.

This type of "minor repair" (as identified by the retweeter) functions as what Schegloff (1992) terms *specification*, wherein @NeverknowOb specifies the types of errors mentioned in the original tweet, thereby reminding his followers that many problematic actions Muslims commit are sanctioned by holy texts. In so doing, he discredits Deedat's quote cited in the original tweet, asserting an illocutionary force that Islam indeed requires reform, additionally and indirectly inviting followers to rethink whether the problem lies with Islam or its followers.

In what follows, I examine five examples of multiscale repairs that involve lexical repair motivated by prepositional, semantic, morphological, or epistemic considerations. These examples present what some (like @Adab_a51a8) construct as irreparable: a verse from the Quran, the most authoritative text in Islam (example 2); a famous misogynistic hadith, the second most authoritative text in Islam (example 3); problematic Arabic euphemisms (example 4); an erroneous cultural discourse (example 5); and texts that go against free will (example 6). Collectively, the examples illustrate how identifying and rectifying (or "repairing") errors in Islamic texts enable Arab reformers to turn authoritative texts into debatable discussions in an attempt to ignite religious and social reform.[8]

Repair of the Quran

Example 2 is an oft-circulated and debated[9] representative of one of the main types of repair found on Twitter. In it, the tweet author identifies and repairs perceived production errors in the Quran, a book believed by Muslims to be written by God. This type of repair takes the form of memes where factual, historical, and scientific errors (in addition to grammatical errors) in the Quran are identified. Arabs on Twitter routinely rely on intertextual material drawn from Islamic authoritative discourses for multiscale repair actions. In this example, the original trouble source text (the Quranic verse) is notably absent, because the source is one of many verses Muslims memorize in childhood, making it part of the Islamic historical body (Nishida 1958).

The repair is presented in the following format (note that the use of checks and crosses is a common convention by laypeople when identifying and repairing perceived errors in the Quran on Twitter): First, a perceived grammatical or production error in a verse from the Quran is listed (trailed by a red **X**). Decontextualizing the authoritative text and repairing it in this way is textually striking (because the text is terse, which calls attention to the topic/content by the very sparseness of its expression) and visually striking (the text is complemented with color-coded symbols [e.g., **X**, **✓**, and =] and emoji), producing an effect of disruption. These features possibly contribute to the popularity of such repairs, regardless of their accuracy. Second, a corrected verse is provided (trailed by a red **✓**). Third, an explanation of the correction is provided (trailed by a "laughing at" or "mocking" emoji). The emoji in particular turns the repair into an extremely face-threatening action (Brown and Levinson [1978] 1987), signaling that the repair author is unapologetic and unfearful about repairing what the majority consider as the irreparable "word of God." This strengthens the repair and discourages rebuttals.

In the example below, the Quranic verse being repaired pertains to a debatable grammatical error found in the Quran (i.e., the Quran used *bi-hi* (with it) instead of *maʕ-hu* (with him) when discussing monotheism). While the English name of the account holder responsible for these kinds of actions plays off "genuine agnostic" (Ex-Muslim), their Arabic account title is "Legends of the Elders," which is itself an intertextual reference from the Quran, wherein Arab contemporaries of the prophet of Islam accused him of writing down myths of cultures past rather than the word of God. Also, note that "legends" are often not true. The tweet was additionally tagged to the popular #thesapientones used by Arabs to propose secularism and elect science over religion. Comments that explain the verse in the translation are provided in brackets.

Example 2: Repair of Quranic verse

أساطير الأولين
@Genuineagnostik

(واعبدوا الله ولا تشركوا به شيئا) ✖

(واعبدوا الله ولا تشركوا معه شيئا) ✓

تشرك به = تتقاسمه مع 😭
تشرك معه = تقاسم معه

#عقلانيون

Translate Tweet

8:22 AM · 04 Sep 18

2 Retweets **6** Likes

Tweet from @Genuineagnostik, September 4, 2018

Worship Allah and do not associate anything with it **X** [This is an actual verse from the Quran - Chapter 4:36] [Arabic original: *bi-hi*: preposition + pronoun = with it] Worship Allah and do not associate anything with him ✓ [This is the correction provided by @Genuineagnostik] [Arabic original: *maʕ-hu*: preposition + pronoun = with him] Associate with it [*tu-šrik bi-hi*] = divide him with [*ta-taqāsam-uh maʕ*] 😭 Associate with him [*tu-šrik maʕ-hu*] = to share with him [*tu-qāsim maʕ-hu*] #thesapientones	(واعبدوا الله ولا تشركوا به شيئا) **X** (واعبدوا الله ولا تشركوا معه شيئا)✓ تشرك به = تتقاسمه مع"😭 تشرك معه = تقاسم معه #عقلانيون

Goodwin (1983) termed the type of repair in the above example *replacement*, which often is found in conflict discourse. In example 2, the correction repairs a misplaced prepositional pronoun به (with it) by replacing the pronoun with معه (with him) so the "corrected" phrase now reads, "Worship God and do not associate anything with him.[10] The author elaborated that به (with it) has the added connotation of "sharing God with others," an unintended meaning of the Quranic verse, whereas معه (with him) connotes (not) associating other idols with God (i.e., encouraging monotheism), which is the intended meaning. After consulting formal Arabic dictionaries, I could find neither support to confirm this as a production error (meaning as an actual grammatical error) nor to confirm that معه (with him) more accurately advises monotheism than به (with it). However, به (with it) does construct God as inanimate, whereas معه (with him) constructs God as a human male. Although both constructions appear in the Quran, day-to-day Islamic discourse typically constructs God as a male human being, suggesting معه (with him) may be more appropriate.

The illocutionary force of this first-level, prepositional repair indirectly suggests that the Quran cannot be the word of God given its production errors. In other words, it points out that one cannot help but be skeptical about the authoritative source text given the identification of such errors. First-level repair therefore is a desynchronizing action making visible the multiple, time-bound, and often invisible layers of authoritative texts: identifying and repairing grammatical or factual Quranic errors invites Twitter users to deconstruct the multiple (and invisible) layers that go into building authoritative discourses, often leading to the identification and subsequent repair of more errors. Such desynchronization is key to claiming voice (Blommaert 2005). In turn, @Genuineagnostik encourages cultural reflexivity by reexamining and unraveling the historical practices involved in producing the holy texts of Islam, which involved collecting and recording discourses long after their initial revelation to the prophet of Islam. In other words, this accomplishes second-level repair. These actions transform the Quran into an internally persuasive discourse, reconstructing it as a historical book written by men (and I exclude "and women" on purpose) that can and should be repaired to reform Islam (third-level repair). In this way, Arab reformers de-holify the most authoritative book of Islam, arguably for the first time in public. Such discrediting actions are punished by law, and very few accounts (always anonymously) engage in this kind of repair of perceived Quranic production errors.

Repair of Hadith

Example 3 features a lexical repair of hadith, the second-most authoritative text in Islam. As in example 2, the original problematic source text (here, "The nation shall not prosper that turns its affairs over to a woman" from the Sahih Al-Bukhari book) is absent, as the hadith is one of the most popular authoritative discourses used by religious men to argue against women's rights and oppose gender reform in Islamic societies. This text also is popularly repaired on Twitter—at times sarcastically and often sternly (see Al Zidjaly 2019a). Also, like example 2, the repair (in this case, replacing the object "to a woman" with "to a man of religion") is followed by an explanation justifying and clarifying the repair. However, in this example the justification is provided by a follower of @Life__Check. As a result, this repair example includes both repair mechanisms: replacement and specification strategies.

Example 3. Repair of hadith

Tweet from @Life__Check, July 24, 2017

The nation shall not prosper that turns its affairs over to 'a man of religion'	!"لن يفلح قوم ولّوا أمرهم "رجل دين"

Reply from @MadhatAdib, July 25, 2017

Merchants of religion are worse than heroin dealers; they lie as often as they take a breath, because they are terrorists	تجار الدين أخطر من تجار الهيروين .. يكذبون مثلما يتنفسون لانهم ارهابيون

The repair in the above hadith is accented with the photos of two infamously misogynistic religious men and active opponents to gender reform in Arabia. Both men are captured mid-speech, gazing away from the camera. According to Kress and van Leeuwen's ([1996] 2006) semiotic framework, the men's averted gaze could help construct them as dishonest and untrustworthy to lead. In other words, it is not women who should be prevented from leading nations, but religious men. A subsequent post by follower @MadhatAdib further clarifies that the problem with religious men is their treatment of religion as a business: "[They] are worse than heroin dealers…because they are terrorists" (as they call for jihad against gender reform). In sum, repairing this famous cultural adage discredits the validity of the hadiths (thus accomplishing what I term second-level repair), generating a call to investigate the truth value of such authoritative discourses that stand against gender reform in Arabia. Over time, such repairs are anticipated to yield reform of Islamic culture (the ultimate "trouble source"), signaling third-level repair.

Repair of Arabic Terminology

Although euphemisms often are examined as ways of addressing face, politeness, or connection (Allan and Burridge 2006; Tannen [1989] 2007), Arab reformers in digital contexts argue that euphemisms in Arabic discourse are appropriated to conceal atrocious acts and thus require repair by simplifying the wording and removing any positive spin. Members of the Ex-Muslim community argue that discarding euphemisms, which performs a type of lexical repair (motivated in the case of this example by semantics), is needed to understand why Muslims refuse secularism (separating religion from politics), which is the main request behind reform actions in Arabia.

Example 4, one of the most popular tweets among the Arab reform community, repairs the popular euphemisms used for condoned but questionable Islamic cultural practices. Such practices oppose reform and present secularism as a direct approach that calls into question those practices that oppose human rights and values. The example consists of two parts: the first part is a popular meme tweeted by an Ex-Muslim account that provides an answer to why Muslims reject secularism; the meme is followed by an explanation of the answer by one of the anonymous followers of the account. Note: In the Arabic original, the questioned terms and their replacements were in yellow font; in the Arabic text and English translation I have underlined them.

Example 4: Repair of euphemisms

Image tweeted by @observer_2012, August 30, 2018

Why do the sheikhs and jurists reject <u>secularism</u>?	لماذا يرفض الشيوخ والفقهاء <u>العلمانية</u>؟
Secularism calls <u>marriage with minors</u> by its true name: <u>pedophilia</u> Secularism calls <u>forcing a wife to perform sexual intercourse</u> by its true name: <u>rape</u> Secularism calls <u>the capture of women in raids</u> by its true name: <u>war crime</u> Secularism calls <u>the spoils of war</u> by its true name: <u>theft</u> Secularism calls <u>the breast feeding of adults</u> by its true name: <u>sex in the workplace</u> Secularism calls <u>the Islamic system of courtesans/concubines</u> by its true name: <u>slavery</u> Secularism calls <u>temporary marriage</u> by its true name: <u>prostitution</u> Secularism calls <u>jihad for forcing beliefs</u> by its true name: <u>terrorism</u>	العلمانية تسمي زواج القاصرات باسمه الحقيقي: <u>بيدوفيل</u> العلمانية تسمي اجبار الزوجة على الجماع باسمه الحقيقي: <u>اغتصاب</u> العلمانية تسمي سبي النساء في الغزوات باسمه الحقيقي: <u>جريمة حرب</u> العلمانية تسمي الغنائم باسمه الحقيقي: <u>سرقة</u> العلمانية تسمي رضاعة الكبير باسمه الحقيقي: <u>جنس بمقر العمل</u> العلمانية تسمي نظام الجواري والإماء باسمه الحقيقي: <u>عبودية</u> العلمانية تسمي زواج المتعة، المسيار، المناكحة باسمه الحقيقي: <u>دعارة</u> العلمانية تسمي الجهاد لفرض معتقدك بالقوة باسمه الحقيقي: إرهاب
WAKE UP In short, secularism <u>exposes them</u>; for that reason, they reject it	WAKE UP باختصار العلمانية <u>تفضحهم</u> لذلك يرفضونها..

Reply to @observer_2012, August 30, 2018

Without secularism, there is no meaning or value in democracy. The two are identical; one is no good without the other	و بدون العلمانية لا قيمة و لا معنى للديمقراطية فهما متلازمتان حذو القذة بالقذة و لا يصلح احدهما بدون الاخر . . .

The author of the repair argues that because civil societies abhor and ban the listed practices (pedophilia, rape, slavery, terrorism, sex with coworkers,[11] prostitution during travel) while Islam condones them, religious authorities thus reject Muslim social reform. Stripping away the euphemisms invites questioning (and second-level repair) of key Islamic practices, ultimately making a case for the secularism that would help ban them. This suggestion for secularism is supported by a follower of the tweeting account, who argues that secularism and democracy must go together, which repairs what the account follower sees as a key misunderstanding among Arabs that religion and politics can remain intertwined. This example of multiscale repair operates at various levels—from repairing terms, to repairing practices, to repairing ideologies, and in turn, to repairing the Islamic Arabic culture.

Cultural Discourse Repair

Example 5 presents a multiscale repair of cultural discourses (Carbaugh 2007) that are authoritative and exhibit misunderstandings popularly held by Muslims. This tweet was widely liked, especially by a Twitter account that critiques Islam, probably due to its nonreligious nature and focus on a cultural belief. The liking action by the channel is what brought the tweet to my attention and led to further circulation.

According to Twitter posts I have analyzed and observations from my own ethnographic research, many Muslims in the Arabian Gulf where I reside believe that Darwin's evolution theory proposes that humans originated from apes. In the example below, to repair this cultural misunderstanding and subsequent rejection of science, a key figure in the Islamic reform movement facetiously tweets a fabricated statement by Charles Darwin himself that directly refutes the claim that humans originated from apes. As with the earlier examples, the trouble source (i.e., Muslims' misunderstandings of the theory of evolution) is missing but is indirectly referenced.

Example 5: Cultural discourse repair

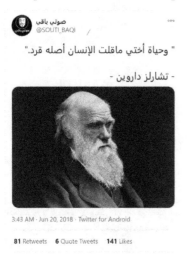

Tweet from @Souti_Baki, liked by Critique of Islam Channel

"By the life of all that I hold dear, I never said that the origin of humans is the apes" – Charles Darwin –	"وحياة أختي ماقلت الإنسان أصله قرد." -تشارلز داروين-

The tweet's author is @Souti_Baki (translation: My Voice Remains), whose avatar is a mask of the historic revolutionary figure Guy Fawkes, allowing him to maintain his anonymity and signal his revolutionary status in the community. Notably, rather than classical Arabic, the tweet draws on multimodality and an Egyptian colloquial idiom uttered in informal vowing situations, thus creating humor (among Arabs, Egyptians are known for their humor, and their dialect and idioms are often drawn upon in jokes). An official photo of a stern-faced Charles Darwin accompanies the tweet, accentuating the constructed monologue that refutes the misunderstanding in a tone that is somber but a verbal construction that is funny. The juxtaposition of the verbal joke with the serious image of Darwin and serious topic invites a light context in which followers discuss the evolution theory. Thus, this mediated action and repair indirectly desynchronize discourse on evolution by asking Muslims to learn about the theory of evolution instead of clinging to erroneous constructions and, in turn, to consider alternatives to creationism. In this manner, the repair of an erroneous cultural belief also works to discredit belief in creationism. These repairs are aimed at changing the larger Islamic society's attitude toward science.

The Goals of Arabic Repair on Twitter

Example 6 presents a Twitter interaction between two key figures of the Islamic re-form movement: @Rony_313131, a young Arab man living in Germany who self-identifies as a feminist, and @nbaa21, an account that @Rony_313131 follows. As in example 1, the retweet (@nbaa21) and comment (@Rony_313131) form a pair; however, in this case, both elements identify problematic texts and repair them by replacing them with twenty-first century humanistic actions. Accordingly, the sec-ond part of the pair complements and strengthens the first part. Similarly to previous examples, the authors again intertextually reference but do not explicitly state the well-known authoritative texts from the Quran and hadith that, according to the Ex-Muslim community, oppose the twenty-first century human rights of individuality and choice.

Example 6: Goals of repair

← Tweet

قلم لدعم نضال المرأة
@Rony_313131

"#النسوية
كنتم خير جماعة ارسلت لمجتمعاتنا الرجعية
تأمرون بالنسوية لاقامة العدل الاجتماعي
وتنهون عن الذكورية لازالة التسلط
ولتفرد بالسلطة"

صدق العقل العظيم

Translate Tweet

Alanoud Altamimi @nbaa2t
(من رأت منكن ذكورية، فلتغيرها بيدها، فإن لم تستطع
فبلسانها، فإن لم تستطع فبقلبها) /twitter.com
GhadeerAhmed_/...

4:41 PM · 07 Sep 18

Retweet from @Rony_313131

| "#feminism [authoritative text from Quran] You are the best group, whom I have sent to our backward (or reactionary) societies to command feminism and to abolish machismo for the establishment of social justice and the ending of (male) dominance and the monopoly of power"

 Mind the almighty has spoken truth | #النسوية
كنتم خير جماعة أرسلت لمجتمعاتنا الرجعية
تأمرون بالنسوية لاقامة العدل الاجتماعي
وتنهون عن الذكورية لازالة التسلط
و التفرد بالسلطة"

صدق العقل العظيم |

Original tweet from @nbaa21, September 7, 2018

| [authoritative text from Hadith] (Whoever amongst you sees machismo (male chauvinism, misogyny), she is to change it with her hand; but, if she cannot do it, then with her tongue; and, if she cannot do that, then in her heart) | (من رأت منكن ذكورية، فلتغيرها
بيدها، فإن لم تستطع
فبلسانها، فإن لم تستطع فبقلبها) |

Although not cited in the example, the original referenced Quranic source text reads: "You are the best of peoples, whom I have sent to mankind to enjoin good and forbid evil." The original referenced hadith reads, "Whoever amongst you sees evil (sin), he is to change it with his hand; but, if he cannot do it, then with his tongue; and, if he cannot do that, then in his heart, and that is the lowest form of faith ([right action])." Both texts urge Muslims to physically ("with his hand"), verbally ("with his tongue"), or mentally ("in his heart") change what they perceive, albeit subjectively, as opposing the teachings of Islam ("evil").

Multiscale repair is evident in the example in the following ways: "evil" is repaired with machismo, male chauvinism, misogyny, male dominance (linguistic repair). The pronoun "he" is replaced with "she" (linguistic repair). Forcibly imposing one's beliefs and subjective perceptions onto others and society at large is replaced with twenty-first-century ideologies, including feminism, social justice, and ending misogyny and tyranny (ideological repair). "Allah the almighty has spoken truth" (the common end phrase uttered after all readings of the Quran) is repaired with "Mind the almighty has spoken truth" (linguistic and ideological repair). These creative repair actions call out the Islamic practices that oppose individual choice (e.g., the choice to drink or dress as one pleases), ultimately initiating the reshaping of the tenets of Arabic and Islamic collective societies that are built on patriarchy.

Repair as Activism

I have used the term "multiscale repair" to describe the activities outlined in this chapter because it operates concomitantly on multiple trouble sources: the first level "corrects" a specific perceived production or linguistic error found in an authoritative text, thus repairing the originating authoritative text in the process and indirectly inviting others to examine the text, triggering second-level repair. At the second level, the holy status of the referenced texts is threatened, triggering desynchronization processes by which the constituents of such texts and their histories are examined. In turn, the authoritative texts are transformed into internally persuasive texts, ideally (for the reformers) giving way to third-level repair of the culture (the main goal of first-level repair actions). Thus, repair at the three scales—linguistic (grammatical, semantic, epistemic), textual, and cultural—interact as interconnected threads that together draw heavily on deep knowledge of authoritative texts and discourses and actions. Thus, multiscale repair is inherently an action undertaken and understood by those who are involved in debating the specific aspect of reform or repair. As a multimodal action that often takes the form of a meme, repairs of Islamic texts in this study are often asynchronic or uninteractive; when shared, they lead to discussions in the comment sections, prompting retweeting and further repairs and debates.

Whereas the traditional conceptions of repair embraced by conversational analysts limit this activity to production errors at the linguistic level and problems in hearing or understanding, this paper builds on research that takes a more expansive approach (e.g., Goodwin 1983; Gordon 2019) and extends such work to theorize repair as a resource for both repairing language and the meaning or the tenets of Islam. In turn, the function of repair extends beyond connection, disconnection, or creation of community to accomplish activism in discourse. I theorize repair in the context of Twitter as activism because the repair action (1) is mediated by various means and semiotic resources (e.g., intertextuality, photos, humor, emoji, sarcasm, contrast); (2) involves desynchronizing activities grounded in a nexus of larger discourses and their interconnections; and (3) is strategically employed to incite a revolution in the Arab world.[12]

Although the features and mechanisms of multiscale repair bear some similarity to repair as the term is traditionally used in discourse analysis, it also has its differences. As a type of aggravated repair (Goodwin 1983), multiscale repair is unmitigated, often face threatening, and intentionally thought provoking because its larger aim is global change. It further draws upon replacement (of the problematic text with something more palatable) as the main strategy for accomplishing the repair. Although the mechanism of multiscale repair also incorporates clarification, this is sometimes provided by commentators, making the repair a collaborative action that authors of tweets or retweets and their followers accomplish together. Unlike modulated and aggravated repair, whose main goal is to construct and maintain intersubjectivity, multiscale repair within Arabic political activism disrupts intersubjectivity, as it questions Islamic traditional understandings of texts and practices, thereby unleashing a process of cultural reflexivity key to creating new lines of intersubjectivity and religious discourse more aligned with twenty-first century humanistic values. As the strategy is built on an open invitation to desynchronize texts long held as unrepairable, multiscale repair presents a disruption of intersubjectivity, or the understanding and belief, as well as communication, around Islam. It constructs typical understandings of culture as problematic and attempts to fix them instead of preserving them. This disruption requires a new process of intersubjectivity rather than a return to normal business. In other words, new terms and ideas are required for a new type of Islam fit with the modern world.

Accordingly, whereas repair in typical conversations deals with breakdowns in communication or larger societal norms and accepted institutional superstructures (a strategy that defends intersubjectivity, according to Schegloff [1992]), repair in the aggravated digital Arabic activism context *challenges* norms and institutional super-structures by locating, addressing, and calling for change to problematic but accepted texts (an offensive action). Thus, in response to Schegloff's (1992) warning that social order is at risk when repair of intersubjectivity is lacking, multiscale repair deliber-ately confronts societal norms to shatter existing conventions and digitally negotiate new forms of intersubjectivity. By posting a synchronized tweet that draws upon an interplay of actions and discourses, reformers indirectly reveal the invisible connec-tions between texts and behaviors that reflect centuries-old beliefs and actions while also anticipating future ones, thus creating disconnection among cultural texts and Twitter users as well as sparking social change.

A word is in order on the methodology used to conduct the analysis. I adopted a mediated discourse approach following the tenets of mediated discourse analysis (Scollon 2001) and nexus analysis (Scollon and Scollon 2004), which theorize all actions as mediated and grounded. It was only through connecting the linguistic texts to the larger actions of Muslims and to prominent Islamic discourses that I was able to identify the multidimensionality of the linguistic strategy of repair. Had I not opened up the lens of analysis to survey other actions and actors, I would have missed the power and the function of multiscale repair. I would have also missed the historic actions Muslim Arabs are trying to address on Twitter and their effects on the society in general. MDNA gives credence to linguistic research: not only do we have access to large amount of data that was inaccessible before the internet (KhosraviNik 2016), but the internet has also helped create new social formations as previously argued by Blommaert (2018a) and Al Zidjaly (2019a, 2019b), such as the Arabic Ex-Muslim community and the Chinese *baifumei* identity (Kunming and Blommaert 2017). A mediated-action approach provides the opportunity to test and fully theorize terms and concepts in this case, allowing me to linguistically identify a new type of repair, new types of identities, and new types of actions with larger, yet-to-be-realized effects (for more on the cultural revolution, see Al Zidjaly 2019c). In this way, my analysis not only contributes to sociolinguistics and social media research, but also to research on Arab identity and sociolinguistic theory and method. The repair actions I have examined open various possibilities and in-vite ongoing desynchronization processes. Through such practices, Ex-Muslims, although not permitted in Muslim societies, create legitimacy on Twitter and ignite cultural revolution.

Acknowledgments
I am eternally indebted to David Wilmsen's assistance in providing careful transla-tions of the Arabic for this paper and the wider project of which it is a part. I am additionally indebted to Cynthia Gordon for her insightful editorial comments on various drafts of this chapter.

Notes

1   Huang (2011), who has explored the role of both Facebook and Twitter in the Arab Spring, is an exception.
2   My use of "scale" in this context is different from Lemke's (2000) and Norris's (2004) use in the sense that I do not distinguish between high-level and low-level (scales of) actions. The type of multiscale repair I identify is motivated by actions and discourses outside the immediate linguistic context; however, whether they are higher- or lower-level actions is irrelevant. What is relevant is that a multiscale repair at the linguistic level immediately repairs the text from which it is extracted and concomitantly the Islamic culture in which it is used.
3   For a detailed introduction to intertextuality, see Gordon (2006, 2009) and Tannen ([1989] 2007).
4   Yang (2009) provides an interesting analysis of repair in the Chinese digital context.
5   Refer to Al Zidjaly (2019a) for a detailed description of MDNA.
6   The project, funded by Sultan Qaboos University, is entitled "The impact of social media on Omani youth: A multimodal project (SR/ARTS/ENGL/15/01), 2015–20."
7   For more on the Arabic Reform Project, see Al Zidjaly (2019a).
8   Though it is not the focus of the chapter, it is worth noting that the action of repair on social media also provides Arab reformers legitimacy and digital inclusion through demonstrating the need to reform Islamic texts and culture.
9   I purposely used an example featuring a debatable error rather than an "actual" error to avoid engaging in the act of debasing the Quran.
10 I thank Francesco Sinatora for his insights into this example.
11 This questionable action originated as a solution to gender segregation. As Muslim women are not allowed to be in the presence of males who are not their relatives, some religious texts suggested that this problem be remedied by women nursing their male adult coworkers, thus metaphorically making these men their children (their relatives), so the men and women could work together.
12 My conceptualization of multiscale repair seems to have some connection with the idea that frames are laminated, and especially "embedded," in discourse (Gordon 2009), but this requires further exploration.

References

@Adab_a51a8. 2017. "أنا مسلم و الإسلام دين كامل." Twitter, October 10. https://twitter.com/k_moathra/status/917632673455230977.
Allan, Keith and Kate Burridge. 2006. *Forbidden words: Taboo and the censoring of language.* Cambridge: Cambridge University Press.
Al Zidjaly, Najma. 2010. Intertextuality and constructing Islamic identities online. In Rotimi Taiwo (ed.), *Handbook of research on discourse behavior and digital communication: Language structures and social interaction.* New York: IGI Global. 191–204.
———. 2012. What has happened to Arabs? Identity and face management online. *Multilingua* 31 (4): 413–39.
———. 2014. WhatsApp Omani teachers? Social media and the question of social change. *Multimodal Communication* 6 (1): 15–45.
———. 2017a. Memes as reasonably hostile laments: A discourse analysis of political dissent in Oman. *Discourse & Society* 28 (6): 573–94.
———. 2017b. Mental health and religion on Islamweb.net. *Linguistik Online.* http://dx.doi.org/10.13092/lo.87.4178.
———. 2019a. Digital activism as nexus analysis: A sociolinguistic example from Arabic Twitter. Tilburg Papers in Culture Studies, Paper 221.
———. 2019b. Introduction. *Multilingua* (Special issue: Society in digital contexts: New modes of identity and community construction) 38 (4): 357–75.
———. 2019c. Divine impoliteness: How Arabs negotiate Islamic moral order on Twitter. *Russian Journal of Linguistics* (Special issue: Politeness and impoliteness research in global contexts) 23 (4): 1039–64.

Al Zidjaly, Najma and Cynthia Gordon. 2012. Mobile phones as cultural tools: An Arabian example. *Intercultural Management Quarterly* 13 (2): 14–17.

Austin, John L. 1962. *How to do things with words*. Cambridge, MA: Harvard University Press.

Bakhtin, Mikhail. 1981. *The dialogic imagination*. Austin: University of Texas Press.

Becker, A. L. 1994. Repetition and otherness: An essay. In Barbara Johnstone (ed.), Repetition in discourse: Interdisciplinary perspectives (vol. II). Norwood, NJ: Ablex. 162–75.

Blommaert, Jan. 2005. *Discourse: A critical introduction*. Cambridge: Cambridge University Press.

———. 2018a. *Durkheim and the Internet: Sociolinguistics and the sociological imagination*. London: Bloomsbury.

———. 2018b. Formatting online actions: #Justsaying on Twitter. Tilburg Papers in Culture Studies, Paper 209.

Brown, Penelope and Stephen C. Levinson. (1978) 1987. *Politeness: Some universals in language usage*. Cambridge: Cambridge University Press.

Carbaugh, Donal. 2007. Cultural discourse analysis: Communication practices and intercultural encounters. *Journal of Intercultural Communication Research* 36 (3): 167–82.

Collister, Lauren Brittney. 2011. *-repair in online discourse. *Journal of Pragmatics* 43: 918–21.

Fairclough, Norman. 1999. *Discourse in late modernity: Rethinking critical discourse analysis*. Edinburgh: Edinburgh University Press.

@Genuineagnostik. 2018. "واعبدوا الله ولا تشركوا به شيئاً." Twitter, September 4.

Georgakopoulou, Alexandra. 2017. 'Whose context collapse?' Ethical clashes in the study of language and social media in context. *Applied Linguistics Review* 8 (2–3): 1–32.

Goodwin, Marjorie Harness. 1983. Aggravated correction and disagreement in children's conversations. *Journal of Pragmatics* 7: 657–77.

———. 1990. Retellings, pretellings and hypothetical stories. *Research on Language and Social Interaction* 14: 263–76.

Gordon, Cynthia. 2006. Reshaping prior text, reshaping identities. *Text & Talk* 26 (4/5): 545–71.

———. 2009. *Making meanings, creating family: Intertextuality and framing in family interaction*. Oxford: Oxford University Press.

———. 2015. "I would suggest you tell this ^^^ to your doctor": Online narrative problem-solving regarding face-to-face doctor-patient interaction about body weight. In Franziska Gygax and Miriam A. Locher (eds.), *Narrative matters in medical contexts across disciplines*. Amsterdam: John Benjamins. 117–40.

———. 2019. "You might want to look up the definition of 'continental breakfast'": Other-initiated repair and community-building in health and weight loss blogs. *Multilingua* (Special issue: Society in digital contexts: New modes of identity and community construction) 38 (4): 401–26.

Hamilton, Heidi E. 1996. Intratextuality, intertextuality, and the construction of identity as patient in Alzheimer's disease. *Text* 16 (1): 61–90.

Hodsdon-Champeon, Connie. 2010. Conversations within conversations: Intertextuality in racially antagonistic online discourse. *Language@Internet* 7, Article 10.

Huang, Carol. 2011. Facebook and Twitter key to Arab Spring uprisings: Report. *The National* 6: 2–3

Jefferson, Gail. 1974. Error correction as an interactional resource. *Language in Society* 3 (2): 181–99.

Khondker, Habibul Haque. 2011. Role of the new media in the Arab Spring. *Globalizations* 8 (5): 675–79.

KhosraviNik, Majid. 2016. Social media critical discourse studies (SM-CDS). In John Flowerdew and John E. Richardson (eds.), *The Routledge handbook of critical discourse studies*. London: Routledge. 582–96.

Kress, Gunther and Theo van Leeuwen. (1996) 2006. *Reading images: The grammar of visual design*. New York: Routledge.

Kristeva, Julia. (1967) 1980. Word, dialogue and novel. In Leon S. Roudiez (ed.), *Desire in language: A semiotic approach to literature and art* (trans: Thomas Gora, Alice A. Jardine and Leon S. Roudiez). New York: Columbia University Press. 64–91.

Kunming, Li and Jan Blommaert. 2017. The care of the selfie: Ludic chronotopes of *baifumei* in online China. Tilburg Papers in Culture Studies, Paper 197. https://www.tilburguniversity.edu/upload/9e59d9c2-fe63-4ed0-9e80-16148f872229_TPCS_197_Li-Blommaert.pdf.

Lemke, Jay L. 2000. Across the scales of time: Artifacts, activities, and meanings in ecosocial systems. *Mind, Culture and Activity* 7 (4): 273–290.

Lewinski, Marcin and Dima Mohammed. 2012. Deliberate design or unintended consequences: The argumentative uses of Facebook during the Arab Spring. *Journal of Public Deliberation* 8 (1): Article 11.

@Life__Check. 2017. "رجل دين"أمرهم وألوا قوم يفلح لن." Twitter, July 24. https://twitter.com/Life__Check/status/889691674435362816.

@MadhatAdib. 2017. "أمرهم"رجل دين", Reply to @Life__Check, "تجار الدين أخطر من تجار الهيروين", Twitter, July 25. لن يفلح قوم ولُوا." https://twitter.com/MadhatAdib/status/889881052138921984.

Meredith, Joanne and Elizabeth Stokoe. 2014. Repair: Comparing Facebook "chat" with spoken interaction. *Discourse & Communication* 8 (2): 181–207.

Mitra, Ananda. 1999. Characteristics of WWW text: Tracing discursive strategies. *Journal of Computer-Mediated Communication* 5 (1).

@nbaa21. 2018. "(من رأت منكن ذكورية، فلتغيرها بيدها، فإن لم تستطع فبلسانها، فإن لم تستطع فبقلبها)." Twitter, September 7. Reply to @Rony_313131, "#النسوية. كنتم خير جماعة ارسلت لمجتمعاتنا الرجعية."

@NeverknowOb. 2018. "تعديل طفيف", Twitter, May 26. Retweet of @Adab_a51a8, " و أنا مسلم و الإسلام دين كامل ." https://twitter.com/NeverknowOb/status/1000187539062435840.

Nishida, Kitarō. 1958. *Intelligibility and the philosophy of nothingness.* Tokyo: Maruzen.

Norris, Sigrid. 2004. *Analyzing multimodal interaction: A methodological framework.* London: Routledge.

Norris, Sigrid and Rodney Jones. 2005. *Mediated discourse analysis.* London: Routledge.

@observer_2012. 2018. "بعض الإسلاميين المتأسلمين يربطون العلمانية بانظمة طاغية مستبدة،" Twitter, August 30. https://twitter.com/observer_2012/status/1035085161480810497.

———. 2018. "و بدون العلمانية لا قيمة و لا معنى للديموقراطية" Twitter, August 30. Anonymous reply to @observer_2012, "بعض الإسلاميين المتأسلمين يربطون العلمانية بانظمة طاغية مستبدة،" https://twitter.com/observer_2012/status/1035086126103625728.

Radcliffe, Damian and Payton Bruni. 2019. *State of social media, Middle East: 2018.* Eugene: University of Oregon.

Reusch, James and Gregory Bateson. 1968. *Communication: The social matrix of psychiatry.* New York: W. W. Norton.

@Rony_313131. "#النسوية. كنتم خير جماعة ارسلت لمجتمعاتنا الرجعية." Twitter, n.d.

Sacks, Harvey, Emanuel A. Schegloff and Gail Jefferson. 1974. A simplest systematics for the organization of turn-taking in conversation. *Language* 50 (4): 696–735.

Schegloff, Emanuel A. 1992. Repair after next turn: The last structurally provided defense of intersubjectivity in conversation. *American Journal of Sociology* 97 (5): 1295–345.

———. 2013. Ten operations in self-initiated, same turn repair. In Makoto Hayashi, Geoffrey Raymond and Jack Sidnell (eds.), *Conversational repair and human understanding.* Cambridge: Cambridge University Press.

Schegloff, Emanuel A., Gail Jefferson and Harvey Sacks. 1977. The preference for self-correction in the organization of repair in conversation. *Language* 53 (2): 361–82.

Schiffrin, Deborah. 2000. Mother/daughter discourse in a Holocaust oral history: "Because then you admit that you're guilty." *Narrative Inquiry* 10 (1): 1–44.

Schönfeldt, Juliane and Andrea Golato. 2003. Repair in chats: A conversation analytic approach. *Research on Language and Social Interaction* 36 (3): 241–84.

Scollon, Ron. 2001. *Mediated discourse: The nexus of practice.* London: Routledge.

———. 2007. *Analysing public discourse: Discourse analysis in the making of public policy.* London: Routledge.

Scollon, Ron and Suzie Wong Scollon. 2004. *Nexus analysis: Discourse and the emerging internet.* London: Routledge.

Sinatora, Francesco. 2019a. Chronotopes, entextualization and Syrian political activism on Facebook. *Multilingua* (Special issue: Society in digital contexts: New modes of identity and community construction) 38 (4): 427–58.

———. 2019b. *Language, identity, and Syrian political activism on social media.* London: Routledge.

@Souti_Baki. "وحياة أختي ماقلت الإنسان أصله قرد." Twitter, n.d.

Tannen, Deborah. 2005. Interactional sociolinguistics as a resource for intercultural communication. *Intercultural Pragmatics* 2 (2): 205–8.

——. (1989) 2007. *Talking voices: Repetition, dialogue, and imagery in conversational discourse* (2nd ed.). Cambridge: Cambridge University Press.

Tovares, Alla V. 2012. Watching out loud: A television quiz show as a resource in family interaction. In Ruth Ayaß and Cornelia Gerhardt (eds.), *The appropriation of media in everyday life*. Amsterdam: John Benjamins. 107–30.

Yang, Robin Ruowei. 2009. Other-repair in Chinese conversation: A case of web-based academic discussion. *Intercultural Pragmatics* 6 (3): 315–43.

Zappavigna, Michele. 2011. Ambient affiliation: A linguistic perspective on Twitter. *New Media & Society* 13 (5): 788–806.

10

Online Political Trolling as Bakhtin's Carnival: Putin's "Discrowning" by Pro-Ukrainian Commenters

ALLA V. TOVARES

THE INTERACTIVE AFFORDANCES OF Web 2.0 have transformed internet users from consumers into both producers and consumers of online content. The participatory culture of digital media platforms (as described, e.g., by Burgess and Green 2009; Jenkins 2009) has led to emergent discursive phenomena (Herring 2013), including trolling. Despite being a frequently referenced, and debated, online activity, trolling remains underexplored and its definition, fluid. This chapter analyzes a particular type of trolling, political trolling, to demonstrate how Bakhtin's theorizing on carnival elucidates the complexity of this type of provocative online behavior. To do so, it deploys the analytical lens of stance (Du Bois 2007; Ochs 1996) and situates the analysis in the context of Russian-Ukrainian geopolitical conflict. Specifically, this study zeroes in on comments posted in reaction to an article posted on the website of a Ukrainian bilingual (Ukrainian-Russian) online newspaper, *KorrespondenT*, about the availability of a limited edition of an ultraexpensive version of the iPhone 7 commemorating Russian president Putin's birthday.

For Bakhtin (1984a, 1984b), carnival is a time when people subvert existing sociopolitical norms and hierarchies by being rebellious, satirical, and playful, and my analysis of the online comments—labeled by one commenter as "good [anti-Putin] trolling"—corroborates their offensive, provocative, and playful nature. This chapter demonstrates that in their collective stances, pro-Ukrainian trolls mobilize strategies that Bakhtin identifies as carnivalesque to "discrown" Putin and call out his supporters: wearing various masks, using curses and profanities, generating ambivalent laughter, producing strings of abusive language, and creating intentionally absurd word combinations, or *coq-à-l'âne* (which literally means "from rooster to ass"). Additionally, this work shows that while in English-language contexts trolling is primarily understood as a subcultural trend and individual antisocial activity (Barney 2016; Buckels et al. 2014; Dynel 2016; Hardaker 2010, 2013), in the context of Russia and Ukraine, as well as other post-Soviet states (Zelenkauskaite and

Niezgoda 2017), it is an ideologically charged political phenomenon and a collective online performance.

In what follows, I first address key ongoing discussions and debates that surround Bakhtin's work and then follow with an exploration of how Bakhtin's theorizing on carnival is recontextualized against the backdrop of contemporary politics and online communication. After a brief overview of online trolling, especially in the context of Russia and Ukraine, I introduce the dataset and analytical methods. I then offer an analysis of representative examples in which I explore the linkages between Bakhtin's features of carnival and the linguistic and multimodal strategies used by pro-Ukrainian trolls. In the conclusion, I summarize the findings and suggest that Bakhtin's work, and his notion of carnival in particular, can be productively used as a heuristic to approach online discourse.

Bakhtin's Work in the Second Decade of the Twenty-First Century

Bakhtin's theorizing on the notions of dialogue, polyphony, chronotope, and carnival, among others, has been widely discussed in a number of disciplines, including sociolinguistics and discourse analysis. While Bakhtin's ideas continue to inspire researchers worldwide, we have entered what Bakhtinian scholar Emerson (2016) terms a "post-boom" period of his scholarship when fascination with his work is replaced by critique. Whereas there are those who are quick to suggest that Bakhtin's ideas are passé, Russian philosopher Makhlin (2010) argues that labeling Bakhtin's or any work of literature, art, and philosophy as old fashioned is absurd and supports his assertion by referencing German philosopher Gadamer (1994, 40), who believed that "the word 'fashion' sounds so terribly bad in connection with science [*Wissenschaft*]," or systematic research. Makhlin goes on to suggest that any theory (and I add researchers) should always avoid the fashionable and instead thoughtfully engage with, using Bakhtin's (1981, 341) articulation, "the words of others." In this regard, Emerson suggests a careful (re)examination of Bakhtin's legacy, including productively engaging with the work of scholars who take critical positions toward Bakhtin's work, such as Russian scholars Mikhail Gasparov and Lydia Ginzburg. Similarly, but in a more critical tone, Zholkovsky (2017, 17) proposes "to move the author [Bakhtin] from the iconostasis, the 'icon shelf,' back onto the bookshelf proper." It is worth noting that Bakhtin himself observed that canonization "kills" any cultural phenomenon, which can survive only in "the atmosphere of freedom and free contest, competition …criticism" (Duvakin 1996, 77; my translation). In this regard, Emerson calls on Bakhtinian researchers to apply his "technical terms," including that of carnival, "with some discipline. If Bakhtin generalizes with flamboyance we, his students, should do so more cautiously" (Emerson 2016, 66).

Bakhtin, in his own words, was "more a philosopher than a philologist […], a thinker" (Duvakin 1996, 42; my translation). It is noteworthy that his ardent critic philologist M. Gasparov (2004, n.p.; see also Emerson 2016, 47) believes that unlike philology, which "systematizes and normalizes," philosophy—as a creative field—complicates "the picture of the world, introducing new values"; he confirms Bakhtin's self-identification by stating, "Bakhtin was a philosopher. […] and should be highly praised as a creator" [my translation]. Even Korovashko (2017, 5) who mockingly describes Bakhtin's popularity as "cult-like" in his biography of the Russian scholar, views Bakhtin's work as "a reliable source of energy that feeds 'the engine' of philological thought" (Yefremova 2017; my translation). Moreover, as Russian philologist Alpatov (2005, 63) indicates, even though Bakhtin viewed his ideas primarily through the lens of philosophy, this does not mean that they are extraneous to literature or linguistics. In sum, those interested in and inspired by Bakhtin's work should neither practice uncritical reverence nor succumb to sweeping criticism, but instead (re)visit and (re)contextualize Bakhtin's ideas in a genuine scholarly dialogue that involves Bakhtin's *own* words. This is one of my goals here.

Bakhtin's Carnival, from Literature to Politics

Bakhtin (1984a, 1984b) developed his notion of carnival through the lens of literary works of Rabelais and Dostoevsky. Yet for Bakhtin, the main interest was not literature per se, but the unofficial (centrifugal, marginal) folk culture, with its festive-grotesque manifestations (Pan'kov 2009). Bakhtin's carnival is the suspension, subversion, and inversion of the established hierarchies of power and official (centripetal) culture. It is the emancipation from the prevailing beliefs and norms—sociopolitical and linguistic—accompanied by ambivalent laughter: laughter that is directed at everyone and everything, including oneself and one's own fears. For Bakhtin (1984a), laughter cannot become a means of oppression because it is a weapon in the hands of the ordinary folk (1984a, 94). However, as Averintsev (1992) correctly points out, laughter could also be a weapon of power and terror, thus indicating its polysemous and ambiguous nature, an argument similar to that of Tannen (1994, 24) in the context of linguistics: "power and solidarity are bought with the same currency: the same linguistic means can be used to create either or both." Thus both laughter and language have to be examined, and understood, in context. The carnivalesque language, often dubbed as the language of the marketplace, is typically informal, often vulgar, but also creative and playful. As Bakhtin (1984a, 17) notes, "familiar language of the marketplace became a reservoir in which various speech patterns excluded from official intercourse could freely accumulate." The transgressive language and laughter of carnival are part of a "discrowning," or symbolic dethroning, that mocks the seriousness and self-importance of the officialdom. Discrowning, contend Morson and Emerson (1990, 443), "also symbolically points to the unstable and temporary nature of any hierarchy."

Bakhtin goes beyond academic theorizing and "humanizes" carnival (Gratchev and Gyulamiryan 2014) by extending the ideas he developed in his analysis of literature to provide discussions of people and actions. For instance, in an interview he describes Russian Futurist poet Khlebnikov as "a deeply carnivalesque person" whose carnival was not just an external mask, but his core, the inner state of his being, his thinking and creativity. Khlebnikov, Bakhtin continues, "could not fit anywhere, could not accept any existent conventions," but at the same time he was able to capture the infinite wholeness and interconnectedness of the world (Duvakin 1996, 124–25; my translation). By recontextualizing carnival, Bakhtin shows that for him it was a complex humanistic notion that goes beyond literature and festivities that is anchored in time and space while at the same time transcending them. Thus, it is not surprising that the notion of carnival is often used to describe actions that challenge and mock existent power structures, especially in suppressive and authoritarian contexts.

For instance, Volkova (2012) suggests that in Bakhtin's homeland, Russia, the 2012 anti-Putin political protests were the contemporary "incarnation" of Bakhtin's ideas of carnival. Namely, the protests—with their creative, provocative, and offensive slogans—were a carnivalesque response to the state-sponsored "theater" of Putin's Russia, where the main "actor" is portrayed as the only safeguard against (often self-manufactured) external and internal threats. With laughter as their weapon, the protestors—as Volkova observes—created a space, a new carnivalesque square, where all hierarchies were suspended and people were united in their anti-Putin and anti-corruption messages, "an ideal and at the same time real type of communication, impossible in ordinary life" (Bakhtin 1984a, 16). Since 2012, with the crackdown on political opposition, fewer independent media outlets, and tightly controlled state media, political carnival in Russia, with its humor and satire, increasingly found a home online (Miazhevich 2015).

Furthermore, Russia's 2014 annexation of Crimea (a Ukrainian territory) and ongoing geopolitical conflict in Eastern Ukraine in which Russia supports the separatist forces, intensified pro-Russian and pro-Putin propaganda that now permeates both mass media and new digital media, including social media, thus drowning out dissident voices. In this context, trolling—political trolling in particular—has acquired a new significance and urgency.

Online Trolling

The interactive affordances of Web 2.0 and participatory culture of digital media platforms (as discussed, e.g., by Burgess and Green 2009; Jenkins 2009) have led to what Herring (2013) defines as "emergent" discursive phenomena. One such emergent phenomenon is trolling. As a dynamic, and debated, online activity, trolling has been of interest to a number of researchers who have approached it from different perspectives. Dynel (2016), for example, views trolling through the lens of deception; Crystal (2001) and Turner et al. (2006) focus on how unsuspecting targets are duped into reacting to the off-topic and/or rude messages; and McCosker (2014) and Jane (2015) understand trolling as aggressive provocation. In this chapter, I draw on Jane's (2015, 66) understanding of online trolling, which she defines as "posting of deliberately inflammatory or off-topic material with the aim of provoking textual responses and/or emotional reaction."

The notions of trolls and trolling are not only polysemous, but constantly evolving. The stereotype of a troll as a basement-dwelling loner has been challenged and expanded to include practically anybody (Birkbak 2018; Cheng et al. 2017; Lindow 2014), and trolling has become a widespread and somewhat normalized practice, especially in the context of politics. As Hannan (2018, 221) observes, "politicians now routinely troll each other online" and "media commentators now distinguish better from worse trolling." Fichman and Sanfilippo (2016, 14) suggest that some types of trolling are ideologically motivated and should be understood as part of political activism and include "the perspective of trolls themselves." From being denounced as senseless meanness (Barney 2016; Buckels et al. 2014) to being regarded as part of digital citizenship (McCosker 2014), community building (Hopkinson 2013), and grassroots activism (Fichman and Sanfilippo 2016), trolling is thus ambiguous and polysemous and requires study and interpretation in context. In this regard, anti-Putin trolling messages posted by pro-Ukrainian trolls need to be understood against the deteriorated political relationship between Russia and Ukraine.

Trolling in the Context of Russia and Ukraine

After the 1991 collapse of the Soviet Union, its two former republics Ukraine and Russia—who share not only borders but also cultural, ethnic, and linguistic ties—embarked on divergent trajectories. While Russia preserved many Soviet symbols, traditions, and attitudes and transformed them into Russian national values (Ryazanova-Clarke 2016), Ukraine moved closer to the Western system of beliefs and abandoned its Soviet past. During the 2013 Ukrainian revolution, also known as Maidan, Ukrainians rejected the pro-Russian course and ousted pro-Russian president Viktor Yanukovitch. Russia's subsequent annexation of Crimea (a Ukrainian territory) and its meddling with and support of pro-Russian separatist forces in Eastern Ukraine further caused the relationship between the two countries to deteriorate. Thus, it is not surprising that the countries, and their citizens, engage in conflict talk marked by what Tracy (2008, 170) identifies as "reasonable hostility" or producing "emotionally marked criticism of the past and future actions" of the counterpart. While both countries engage in information warfare, Russia, as a more powerful country that is skilled in media manipulation (Abrams 2016; Giles 2016; Saran 2016), overpowers Ukraine. The war of words between the two countries goes beyond traditional mass media and is widely present online, including on a number of social media platforms (*VKontakte* [InContact], *Odnoklassniki* [Classmates], Facebook, and Twitter) where trolling tends to be more prominent. Zelenkauskaite and Niezgoda (2017), in their study of "Kremlin trolls," indicate that in "ideological trolling," or politically marked provocative messages, it is almost impossible to differentiate between paid trolls and individuals with politically divergent opinions. The allegedly government-sponsored contributors of pro-Russian, pro-Putin messages on social media are generally referred to as "an army of trolls" (Aro 2016; Chen 2015; Garmazhapova 2013). While Ukraine reportedly has its own trolls who post provocative anti-Putin comments (Sindelar 2014), their influence pales in comparison to the magnitude of Russia's propaganda machine (Giles 2016). At the same time, Ukrainian trolls inject counter discourse into online space and in so doing offer a contrasting—negative—portrayal of the Russian president, his politics, and supporters. As Birkbak (2018, n.p.) suggests, the "radical otherness of trolls may be used as a resource for an alternative kind of democratic politics that does not assume that a rational consensus is achievable." In this regard, Bakhtin's carnival, with its subversive language, laughter, and discrowning offers a productive heuristic to analyze anti-Putin trolling messages against the backdrop of a geopolitical conflict between Russia and Ukraine.

Data and Method

Data for this analysis is composed of a thread of comments that were posted in reaction to an article in the Ukrainian bilingual (Ukrainian-Russian) online newspaper *KorrespondenT*. The article profiles an ultraexpensive, limited edition of the iPhone 7 made to commemorate the sixty-fourth birthday of Russian president Vladimir Putin. The phone features Putin's picture and comes in a white- or yellow-gold finish. The price of this iPhone—207,000 to 232,000 rubles (roughly $3,250–$3,640)—at the time when it was released and when the article was published (October 2016) was roughly the equivalent of half the annual salary of the average Russian worker. Accordingly, most Russian citizens could not afford the commemorative version of the phone; for many even the price of a "regular" iPhone 7 (65,000–75,000 rubles, or $1,020–$1,177) was prohibitive. Not surprisingly, many commenters indicated that only corrupt pro-Putin bureaucrats could afford such "new toys" and pay for them with money stolen from the state budget.

My dataset can be described as sampling by theme (Herring 2004) because it includes all 104 publicly available comments to a single article. I examined all the comments posted anonymously, eliminating (for privacy concerns) the 33 that were linked to media platforms that require posters' names (like Facebook). Out of 104 comments, 7 comments are pro-Putin messages and appear to be a reaction to the anti-Putin comments in the thread. These comments, while interesting, are not considered. The analysis focuses on the remaining 97 comments, all of which can be classified as anti-Putin trolling. In addition to the comments, I also consider the commenters' avatars and usernames because many of them are rather provocative and thus can be viewed as an integral part of the trolling messages.

Prior to selecting the above thread for analysis—to contextualize the study and to ensure that the comments are representative of a larger trend—I conducted a three-month (September–December 2016) netnography (Nissenbaum and Shifman 2017). Specifically, I reviewed and cataloged the observed patterns of the online comments posted below any *KorrespondenT* article in which Putin was featured; I also perused social media platforms popular in Russia and Ukraine (*Odnoklassniki* [Classmates], Instagram, and Facebook), paying particular attention to the multimodal memes about Russians, Ukrainians, and the Russian president. I chose this particular thread because it contains provocative—trolling—comments of the type that typically appear below articles in which Putin is mentioned. Additionally, and confirming my observations, one commenter, raising no objection from other posters, metalinguistically labeled the comments in the thread as "good trolling" that would be appreciated by everyone except for "вата" (literally means "cotton," now a popular meme among Ukrainians that refers to Russians who blindly support Putin's regime).

I use the concept of stance (Du Bois 2007; Ochs 1996) as an analytical lens. As defined by Du Bois (2007, 163), stance is "a public act by a social actor, achieved dialogically through overt communicative means, of simultaneously evaluating objects, positioning subjects (self and others), and aligning with other subjects, with respect to any salient dimension of the sociocultural field." For Du Bois (2007, 159), when a stance object is shared, stance-takers engage in a dialogic construction of intersubjectivity. Through positioning and alignment, stance-takers may collaboratively create a shared collective stance toward the stance object. Elsewhere (Tovares 2019), I demonstrate that not only shared positive stances—as prior studies have shown (Chun 2013; Chun and Walters 2011; Zappavigna 2014)—but also shared negative stances (such as trolling) can serve as affinity-building strategies. In what follows, I demonstrate how pro-Ukrainian trolls align together in a shared negative stance to collectively ridicule Putin and his supporters and in so doing rely on carnivalesque tactics that link trolling to folk culture.

Before I turn to the analysis, I summarize the language in the data. Out of all anti-Putin messages, 89 are in Russian, 6 are in Ukrainian, 3 mix Russian and Ukrainian words, and 2 are also mixed-code (Russian/Ukrainian) but written using the Latin alphabet. Finally, in line with Bakhtin's description of the carnivalesque language, many comments contain offensive language, but—for the purposes of the analysis— are reproduced in their original form without any modifications.

Political Trolling as Carnival: "Discrowning" of Putin and Calling Out His Supporters

Putin's "discrowning" is accomplished through uses of usernames and avatars as carnivalesque masks, of laughter, and of strings of abusive words. While these strategies often appear together in posts, and indeed are intersecting, in this section, I illustrate each in turn.

Usernames and Avatars as Carvinalesque Masks

One of the key elements of Bakhtin's carnival is the mask. "The mask is related to transition, metamorphosis, the violation of natural boundaries, to mockery and familiar nicknames. It contains the playful element of life" (Bakhtin 1984a, 39–40). Online usernames and avatars can be compared to carnivalesque masks because they create a shield of anonymity for their owners (Kiernan 2017). In this section, I suggest that usernames and avatars, as carnivalesque masks, not only provide anonymity but also serve as multimodal semiotic resources that allow commenters to project identities and index ideologies. In the thread under analysis, most of the usernames and avatars are provocative, adversarial, and/or playful and serve as generic framing devices (Bauman 2004) of the trolling messages. For instance, some usernames index commenters' pro-Ukrainian patriotic stances. In this regard, the username Крым-Донбасс-Украина (Crimea-Donbass-Ukraine) shows that the commenter views Crimea (a Ukrainian territory annexed by Russia in 2014) and Donbass (a contested territory in Eastern Ukraine embroiled in armed conflict fueled by Russia) as integral parts of Ukraine, not Russia. Another username, Слава Україні (Glory to Ukraine), deploys a patriotic Ukrainian slogan that gained wide prominence during the 2014 revolution and is used to indicate Ukraine's resistance to outside, especially Russian, influence. Both usernames, Crimea-Donbass-Ukraine and Glory to Ukraine, display positive stances toward Ukraine and simultaneously challenge and reject Russia's geopolitical actions and agenda.

As Bakhtin (1984a, 5) observes, carnivalesque language lies outside the "official" norms and includes such traditional folk features as curses and profanities, as do some of the usernames. Such usernames reproduce either familiar Ukrainian curses like Щоб у наших ворогів у горлі пір'ям поросло (May feathers grow in the throats of our enemies) or widely used offensive terms for Putin, such as путин-ХУЙЛО (putin-DICKHEAD). Other commenters ironically mobilize popular memes that refer to Russians' illicit online activities in Ukraine and elsewhere, like кремлебот из Ольгино (kremlinbot from Ol'gino). Ol'gino is a St. Petersburg suburb known as the headquarters of Russian trolling activities and popularly dubbed the "Russian troll factory" (Garmazhapova 2013). By deploying curses, offensive referring terms, and irony in their usernames, pro-Ukrainian trolls create a counter discourse that delegitimizes Putin and his supporters, including the Russian "army of trolls."

Another carnivalesque strategy that the commenters utilize is coq-à-l'âne, or absurd word combinations. As Bakhtin (1984a, 423) puts it, this refers to when "common sequences of terms […] had been released from the shackles of sense, to enjoy a play period of complete freedom and establish unusual relationships among themselves." For instance, one commenter's username is Хамон Пармезанович Бульдозер (Jamon Parmesanovitch Bulldozer), which structurally resembles a typical three-part Russian name that consists of the first name "Jamon" (i.e., a type of ham) followed by a patronymic "Parmesanovitch" (built on the word "Parmesan," meaning the cheese), and the last name "Bulldozer." The name, of course, is completely absurd: two food items followed by a piece of machinery. This coq-à-l'âne indexes and mocks the absurd situation of Putin's Russia (and questions the wisdom of its leader), where Western imported foods, such as jamon and Parmesan, are literally and publicly bulldozed into the ground in retaliation for the sanctions that the West imposed on Russia after its annexation of Crimea.

As with their usernames, commenters draw on similar strategies and display similar stances in their avatars. For instance, some show their patriotism by using as their avatars the Ukrainian coat of arms; other patriotic avatars include pictures of the Ukrainian Cossacks (a celebrated military fraternity of the thirteenth to eighteenth centuries known for its independence and self-governance), of famous Ukrainian patriots, and even of the late US senator John McCain, an ardent supporter of Ukraine's struggle for independence and democracy. Other avatars, and such are the majority, are playful, ironic, and sarcastic. For example, several avatars feature funny or eccentric characters from global and local popular culture, from Homer Simpson (a US cartoon character) and Doctor House (a cranky US TV series physician) to Captain Vrungel (a Soviet cartoon character known for his tall tales). Critical stances and biting satire underlie two avatars, one that pictures Putin as Hitler (with a superimposed mustache) and the other Putin with Hitler, thus drawing a parallel between the two. It is noteworthy that in avatars, usernames, and comments, Putin is compared to other past and present dictators, including Gaddafi, Hussein, and Kim Jong-un, thus undermining his publicly cultivated image of a democratic leader. One avatar features a Colorado beetle (a popular meme that refers to pro-Putin Russians); the beetle is on its back and appears to be dead—a rather powerful, but playful, statement. In other words, from serious to ridiculous to ridiculing, commenters' avatars collectively contribute to the overarching goal of the trolling messages: they challenge Russia's—and its leader's—image and politics, especially toward Ukraine.

Also contributing to the trolling messages are ten avatars that are pictures of various animals, from goats to squirrels to cloned sheep. Some commenters have both their avatar (e.g., a cat) and their username (e.g., *Kot Zloi*, or Angry Cat) as animals. In a different study (Tovares 2019), in which I draw on the same dataset as I do in this chapter, I note that in their comments, pro-Ukrainian political trolls mock Putin and his supporters by referring to them as animals, such as скоты (cattle), *стадо* (herd), and свиньи (pigs). Such "transformation of the human element into an animal one; the combination of human and animal traits," Bakhtin (1984a, 316) argues, is part of carnival's tradition of creating and ridiculing the grotesque. The fact that pro-Ukrainian trolls choose animals as their usernames and avatars points to the playfulness of carnival and the ambivalent nature of carnivalesque laughter, which can be simultaneously self- and other-directed. In other words, in the carnival of trolling, both trolls and the trolled wear animal masks.

Carnivalesque Laughter

Laughter, like carnivalesque masks, is an integral part of carnival. It is a "discrowning" strategy used to challenge those in power and to function as a bonding mechanism, uniting those who share laughter. Prior studies on trolling (Fichman and Sanfilippo 2016; Kiernan 2017) indicate that playfulness, humor, and symbolic "put-downs"— all laughter-provoking mechanisms—are part of trolling. In the thread under analysis, the commenters make fun of Putin's height, Russian prime minister Medvedev's obsession with imported electronic gadgets, and the morbid seriousness of Foreign Minister Lavrov, dubbed "a somber horse" (in line with the point about animal masks made in the previous section). Even more, they aligned together in putting down typical Putin supporters by suggesting that they treat their leader with religious-like fervor and adoration. For instance, several commenters ironically observe that Putin supporters will replace religious icons with Putin-adorned iPhones and pray before them. One commenter mockingly remarks that such phones will be an addition to the existent Putin memorabilia in the homes of his supporters:

Example 1

Теперь пацретики путена будут не только дома в цапоподобных стоять, но и в карманах лежать, зорко наблюдая не уплетает ли владелец, например хамон или пармезан запрещённый))

Now putin's portraits will be not only in the homes of (ka)tsaplike [a derogatory term for Russians] but also in their pockets, keenly watching whether the owner, for instance wolfs down the forbidden jamon or parmesan))

In example 1, the commenter derides the hypocrisy of Putin's supporters who overtly display their loyalty (having portraits and phones with Putin's image) but who secretly may eat Western foods that Putin's administration has banned.

Furthermore, the commenter hints at the surveillance and control of Russian citizens by jokingly suggesting that the phone can be used as a spying device, also signaling Putin's former career as a KGB officer. The mocking and joking key of the comment in example 1 is indexed and emphasized by a laughter emoticon (represented by two parentheses at the end of the comment). Overall, the comments under analysis have twenty-five instances of laughter emoticons. Similar to findings of prior work in the context of Russia and Ukraine (Christiansen et al. 2017; Klimanova and Dembovskaya 2013), most of the "smiley" or "laughter" emoticons in the comments under analysis do not have a colon, or "eyes"; instead they have only one or several parentheses. This is explained by the keyboard layout of the Cyrillic alphabet, which makes accessing the colon uncomfortable. It is worth noting that twenty-one emoticons have two or more parentheses clustered together. A Ukrainian-Russian bilingual I asked about this noted that multiple parentheses typically indicate joking and/or "dissing." Thus, it can be suggested that the multiple parentheses in the next example indicate a "dissing" stance that is intended to mock, and provoke, Putin's supporters. In this way, multiple parentheses also serve as what Gumperz (1982) calls a contextualization cue.

In the next example, the commenter suggests having the Russian anthem as the only ring tone for the iPhone. In so doing, the commenter uses laughter to highlight not only the ridiculousness of that suggestion, but also to bring into sharper focus Putin supporters' overt, often over-the-top, patriotism and loyalty:

Example 2

И зашить единственную мелодию без возможности изменения - ГИМН))))))))))

And install a single melody [ring tone] without the possibility of changing—ANTHEM))))))))))

By using ten parentheses—indicating the intensity and duration of laughter and serving as what Tannen (2013) identifies as an "enthusiasm marker"—the commenter appears to be inviting others to join in the laughter and shared "fun" activity of trolling. Thus, laughter is used both to call out Putin's supporters and to create affinity among fellow trolls. I suggest that, for pro-Ukrainian trolls, laughter is both the means and the ends of the carnivalesque behavior.

The notions of laughter and fun are also deployed to stress the "us" (anti-Putin) vs. "them" (pro-Putin) distinction. While pro-Ukrainian political trolls tell jokes, laugh, use subversive language and images, and entertain one another with all sorts of carnivalesque witticisms, Putin supporters are portrayed as gloomy, narrow-minded, and miserable. For instance, in example 3 a commenter demonstrates mock pity for Russians who do not know joy, fun, laughter, or happiness:

Example 3

Все же жалко негодных рашиков. За что им такое наказание из поколения в поколение? Когда человек психически больной, это понятно. Но даже больной радуется время от времени. А путинозависимые, какая у них радость? Всю свою жалкую, обездоленную и бесправную жизнь прожить во злобе, ненависти, фанатизме...

Still [I feel] sorry for the worthless rushiks [a derogatory term for Russians]. Why do they endure such punishment from generation to generation? When a person is mentally ill, this is understandable. But even a sick person is happy from time to time. And the putin-dependent, what is their joy? To live all their miserable, destitute and deprived lives in anger, hatred, fanaticism ...

Bakhtin (1984a, 165) labels people "who do not know how to laugh" as *agelasts*. *Agelasts*, according to Bakhtin, "are too serious and do not appreciate or understand laughter, jokes, and trickery" (Duvakin 1996, 115; my translation). Bakhtin links perpetual seriousness with hypocrisy and fanaticism and suggests that the ambivalent laughter of carnival completes seriousness and purifies it "from dogmatism, from the intolerant and the petrified; it liberates from fanaticism and pedantry, from fear and intimidation, from didacticism, naiveté and illusion, from single meaning, the single level, from sentimentality" (1984a, 123). In other words, Bakhtin sees laughter as restorative from the ills of society. In a similar vein, the commenter in example 3 draws on medical discourse to compare support for Putin to a chronic medical condition ("mentally ill" and "putin-dependent"), with anger, hatred, and fanaticism as its symptoms. Thus, without the purifying carnivalesque laughter, Putin supporters are doomed to live miserable, unhealthy, and unhappy lives.

Strings of Abusive Words

As Bakhtin (1984a, 421) points out, on the carnivalesque public square polite words "are discarded and are replaced either by terms of abuse or by words created according to this abusive pattern." Moreover, abusive words can be clustered together, creating a string of abuse. While the relatively short strings of abusive words in the comments under analysis cannot compete with the twenty-eight-word string of abuse that Bakhtin identified in Rabelais's work, they are nevertheless complex and lexically dense, allowing the commenters to display critical stances toward Putin and his supporters, as the following example shows:

Example 4

Интересно сколько сот песен будет написано и исполнено о Путине ко дню рождения карлика? Сколько имен получат младенцы, Владимир и Владимира (ударение на последнем слоге), Сколько календариков, плакатов, билбордов, книг, фильмов, сказок и прочей разной не нужной хрени будет заполнена Расея? Срочно пора и массово ставить памятники «Сортиромоченный Денегнет Коленоневставший Владимир Путин»

I wonder how many hundred songs will be written and performed about Putin on the birthday of the dwarf? How many babies will receive the names of Vladimir and Vladimira (emphasis on the last syllable), how many calendars, posters, billboards, books, movies, fairy tales and other miscellaneous crap will fill Raseya [a derogatory term for Russia]? Urgently it's time to erect a lot of monuments "Whackedintheouthouse Thereisnomoney Risenfromtheknees Vladimir Putin"

The example above includes several strings of words that demonstrate different levels of abuse, from irony to merciless sarcasm. The commenter uses the first two strings to ironically hypothesize, and mock, how Putin's birthday will be celebrated. These strings list actions (*"songs will be <u>written</u> and <u>performed</u>"* and *"babies will <u>receive</u> the* *names of Vladimir and Vladimira*") and various birthday-related memorabilia (*"calendars, posters, billboards, books, movies, fairy tales and other miscellaneous crap"*), all used to create a scenario of a cult-like adoration that includes an over-the-top nationwide birthday celebration of the Russian president. The last string contains adjectival compounds (*"Whackedintheouthouse," "Thereisnomoney," "Risenfromtheknees"*) that satirically describe Putin's main "achievements" to be inscribed on his monument. The compounds refer to the phrases that have become widely circulated memes, with numerous spin-offs. *"Whackedintheouthouse"* insinuates *"в сортире их замочим"* (*"[we] will whack [them] in the outhouse,"* a rather crude expression Putin used during a press conference when he was describing his determination to find and punish terrorists. While for Putin's supporters this saying indexes his resolve and strength, for his opponents it reveals the criminal politics in Putin's Russia (the expression resembles criminal argot). *"Thereisnomoney"* is a fusion of a phase attributed to Putin's "second in command" Dmitry Medvedev, who in response to a complaint about a small pension told the pensioner that *"денег нет"* (*"there is no money"*) but suggested *"но вы держитесь"* (*"but you hold on"*). The "there is no money" expression is widely referenced, on- and off-line, to index the hypocrisy of Russian leaders who suggest to the ordinary people that they "tighten their belts" and "hold on," while they themselves continue to enjoy luxury goods. The final word in the string, *"Risenfromtheknees,"* goes back to 1990s, when then prime minister Putin, reacting to Russia's post-Soviet socioeconomic and geopolitical turmoil, suggested that "Россия может подняться с колен и как следует огреть" ("Russia can rise from its knees and throw a hard punch"). With time, this expression was shortened to "rise from its knees"; it typically is used to indicate Russia's post-Soviet efforts to (re)gain its place among the world powers. It is worth pointing out that in the comment all three words are lexicalized phrases, with each behaving "like a word, an indivisible unit" (Tannen 2007, 97): they are double voiced in the Bakhtinian sense; that is, they are parodically (re)produced with a deliberate orientation toward prior uses.

By using a string of abusive words that are recognizable lexicalized phrases, the commenter, with surgical precision, identifies the "true nature" of Putin and his associates, who rely on threats, fear, and intimidation; disregard the plight of ordinary people while lining their own pockets; and promote aggressive geopolitics as a way of getting ahead. This allows me to suggest that political trolling is a form of active engagement with political discourse: through playful carnivalesque strategies, it reveals to the public the proverbial Achilles heel of those in power by exposing their hypocrisies and hidden weaknesses and agendas. Such desacralization of power contributes to "discrowning," or the carnivalesque downward movement of the powerful to the level of the powerless.

Conclusion

This study has explored how Bakhtin's theorizing on carnival can be adapted and applied to an analysis of the relatively new and evolving phenomenon of online trolling, and political trolling in particular. My analysis of comments posted by pro-Ukrainian trolls demonstrated how they draw on the multimodal and linguistic resources that

Bakhtin identified as carnivalesque: the mask, ambivalent laughter, parody, irony, coq-à-l'âne, and strings of abusive words. Bakhtin (1984a, 380) warns that when separated from its context, the carnivalesque language would appear "vulgar and dirty." Similarly, many trolling messages in isolation would come across as crass and rude, but in the context of Russian-Ukrainian geopolitical conflict, the negative collective stances taken up by pro-Ukrainian trolls can be understood as "reasonable hostility" (Tracy 2008) directed at the more powerful and aggressive adversary. While in Western contexts trolling tends to be associated with individual actions by members of subcultures, this study, building on prior research in post-Soviet countries (Zelenkauskaite and Niezgoda 2017), suggests that against the backdrop of the progressively deteriorating relations between Ukraine and Russia, trolling is an ideological phenomenon that often involves collective actions.

Bakhtin (1984a, 33) dubbed carnival the "second life" because it offers people a chance to subvert, albeit temporarily, their ordinary lives and to challenge the status quo. New media, with its anonymity, interactivity, fluidity of rules, and time/space compression, can be viewed as a modern version of Bakhtin's carnival square where political trolls—armed with ambivalent laughter—"discrown" the powerful and their supporters by mercilessly ridiculing their hypocrisy, weaknesses, and actions. In other words, serious criticism is delivered in a humorous and sarcastic way. Thus, trolling is a carnivalesque madness that makes people "look at the world with different eyes, not dimmed by 'normal,' that is by commonplace ideas and judgments" (Bakhtin 1984a, 39). I showed how anti-Putin trolls invite others to view Putin's inner circle and supporters as hypocrites whose adulation of the Russian president and his policies is motivated by nothing more than greed and self-interest.

This analysis has also demonstrated that Bakhtin's work remains relevant for contemporary humanistic research, as it not only continues to raise important and complex questions, but also facilitates observation and exploration of links between long-recognized and emergent phenomena, such as carnival and political trolling. All this allows me to suggest that for those who seek definitive answers, Bakhtin's work would likely be frustratingly unfinalized and unfinalizable, but for those who view his philosophical theorizing as guiding questions, Bakhtin offers a fitting lens through which to approach the inherently imprecise, ambiguous and polysemous, and evolving nature of human interaction.

Acknowledgments

I am grateful to Cynthia Gordon for her insightful comments and helpful suggestions on an earlier draft of this chapter. I am also indebted to Raúl Tovares for his unwavering support of my research activities.

References

Abrams, Steve. 2016. Beyond propaganda: Soviet active measures in Putin's Russia. *Connections: The Quarterly Journal* 15 (1): 5–31.

Alpatov, Vladimir. 2005. Волошинов, Бахтин и лингвистика. Moscow: Языки славянских культур.

Aro, Jessikka. 2016. The cyberspace war: Propaganda and trolling as warfare tools. *European View* 15 (1): 121–32.

Averintsev, Sergey. 1992. М.М. Бахтин как философ. Moscow: Наука.

Bakhtin, Mikhail. 1981. *The dialogic imagination.* Austin: University of Texas Press.

———. 1984a. *Rabelais and his world.* Bloomington: Indiana University Press.

———. 1984b. *Problems of Dostoevsky's poetics.* Minneapolis: University of Minnesota Press.

Barney, Rachel. 2016. [Aristotle], On trolling. *Journal of the American Philosophical Association* 2 (2): 193–95.

Bauman, Richard. 2004. *A world of others' words: Cross-cultural perspectives on intertextuality.* Oxford: Blackwell.

Birkbak, Andreas. 2018. Into the wild online: Learning from Internet trolls. *First Monday* 23 (5). https://doi.org/10.5210/fm.v22i5.8297.

Buckels, Erin E., Paul D. Trapnell and Delroy L. Paulhus. 2014. Trolls just want to have fun. *Personality and Individual Differences* 67: 97–102.

Burgess, Jean and Joshua Green. 2009. *YouTube: Online video and participatory culture.* Malden, MA: Polity Press.

Chen, Adrian. 2015. The agency. *New York Times Magazine,* June 2. http://www.nytimes.com/2015/06/07/magazine/the-agency.html?_r=0.

Cheng, Justin, Michael Bernstein, Christian Danescu-Niculescu-Mizil and Jure Leskovec. 2017. Anyone can become a troll: Causes of trolling behavior in online discussions. *Proceedings of the Conference on Computer-Supported Cooperative Work and Social Computing.* doi: 10.1145/2998181.2998213.

Christiansen, M. Sidury, Shikun Li and Melissa R. Bailey. 2017. The role of texting and digital multiliteracies in the EFL classroom. *MEXTESOL Journal* 41 (3). http://www.mextesol.net/journal/index.php?page=journal&id_article=2515.

Chun, Elaine. 2013. Ironic Blackness as masculine cool: Asian American language and authenticity on YouTube. *Applied Linguistics* 34 (5): 592–612.

Chun, Elaine and Keith Walters. 2011. Orienting to Arab Orientalisms: Language, race, and humor in a YouTube video. In Crispin Thurlow and Kristine Mroczek (eds.), *Digital discourse: Language in the new media.* Oxford: Oxford University Press. 251–73.

Crystal, David. 2001. *Language and the Internet.* New York: Cambridge University Press.

Du Bois, John. 2007. The stance triangle. In Robert Englebretson (ed.), *Stancetaking in discourse: Subjectivity, evaluation, interaction.* Amsterdam: John Benjamins. 139–82.

Duvakin, Victor. 1996. Беседы В.Д. Дувакина с М.М. Бахтиным. Moscow: Прогресс.

Dynel, Marta. 2016. "Trolling is not stupid": Internet trolling as the art of deception serving entertainment. *Intercultural Pragmatics* 13 (3): 353–81.

Emerson, Caryl. 2016. Creative ways of not liking Bakhtin: Lydia Ginzburg and Mikhail Gasparov. *Bakhtiniana* 11 (1): 39–69.

Fichman, Pnina and Madelyn R. Sanfilippo. 2016. *Online trolling and its perpetrators: Under the cyberbridge.* Lanham, MD: Rowman & Littlefield.

Gadamer, Hans-Georg. 1994. What is truth? In Brice R. Wachterhauser (ed.), *Hermeneutics and truth.* Evanston, IL: Northwestern University Press. 33–46.

Garmazhapova, Alexandra. 2013. Где живут тролли. И кто их кормит. *Novaya Gazeta,* September 7. https://www.novayagazeta.ru/articles/2013/09/07/56253-gde-zhivut-trolli-i-kto-ih-kormit.

Gasparov, Mikhail. 2004. История литературы как творчество и исследование: Случай Бахтина. Вестник Гуманитарной Науки 6 (78). http://vestnik.rsuh.ru/article.html?id=54924.

Giles, Keir. 2016. *Russia's 'new' tools for confronting the West: Continuity and innovation in Moscow's exercise of power.* London: Chatham House. https://www.chathamhouse.org/2016/03/russias-new-tools-confronting-west-continuity-and-innovation-moscows-exercise-power.

Gratchev, Slav N. and Tatevik Gyulamiryan. 2014. Duvakin's oral history and Bakhtin in his own voice. *CLCWeb: Comparative Literature and Culture* 16 (1). https://doi.org/10.7771/1481-4374.2288.

Gumperz, John. 1982. *Discourse strategies.* Cambridge: Cambridge University Press.

Hannan, Jason. 2018. Trolling ourselves to death? Social media and post-truth politics. *European Journal of Communication* 33 (2): 214–26.

Hardaker, Claire. 2010. Trolling in asynchronous computer-mediated communication: From user discussions to academic definitions. *Journal of Politeness Research* 6 (2): 215–42.

———. 2013. "'Uh.… not to be nitpicky,,,,but…the past tense of drag is dragged, not drug.': An overview of trolling strategies." *Journal of Language Aggression and Conflict* 1 (1): 58–86.

Herring, Susan. 2004. Computer-mediated discourse analysis: An approach to researching online behavior. In Sasha A. Barab, Rob Kling and James H. Gray (eds.), *Designing for virtual communities in the service of learning*. New York: Cambridge University Press. 338–76.

———. 2013. Discourse in Web 2.0: Familiar, reconfigured, and emergent. In Deborah Tannen and Anna Marie Tester (eds.), *Discourse 2.0: Language and new media*. Washington, DC: Georgetown University Press. 1–25.

Hopkinson, Christopher. 2013. Trolling in online discussions: From provocation to community-building. *Brno Studies in English* 39 (1): 5–25.

Jane, Emma. 2015. Flaming? What flaming? The pitfalls and potentials of researching online hostility. *Ethics and Information Technology* 17 (1): 65–87.

Jenkins, Henry. 2009. *Confronting the challenges of participatory culture: Media education for the 21st century*. Cambridge, MA: MIT Press.

Kiernan, Patrick. 2017. *Language, identity and cycling in the new media age: Exploring interpersonal semiotics in multimodal media and online texts*. London: Palgrave Macmillan.

Klimanova, Liudmila and Svetlana Dembovskaya. 2013. L2 identity, discourse, and social networking in Russian. *Language Learning & Technology* 17 (1): 69–88.

Korovashko, Aleksei. 2017. Михаил Бахтин. Серия: Жизнь замечательных людей. Moscow: Молодая Гвардия.

Lindow, John. 2014. *Trolls: An unnatural history*. London: Reaktion Books.

Makhlin, Vitaly. 2010. Теория и ее "другие." Институт гуманитарных историко-теоретических исследований имени А. В. Полетаева (ИГИТИ). https://igiti.hse.ru/Meetings/Conferences/Makhlin.

McCosker, Anthony. 2014. Trolling as provocation: YouTube's agonistic publics. *Convergence: The International Journal of Research into New Media Technologies* 20 (2): 201–17.

Miazhevich, Galina. 2015. Sites of subversion: Online political satire in two post-Soviet states. *Media, Culture & Society* 37 (3): 422–39.

Morson, Gary Saul and Caryl Emerson. 1990. *Mikhail Bakhtin: Creation of prosaics*. Stanford: Stanford University Press.

Nissenbaum, Asaf and Limor Shifman. 2017. Internet memes as contested cultural capital: The case of 4chan's /b/board. *New Media & Society* 19 (4): 483–501.

Ochs, Elinor. 1996. Linguistic resources for socializing humanity. In John Gumperz and Stephen Levinson (eds.), *Rethinking linguistic relativity*. Cambridge: Cambridge University Press. 407–37.

Pan'kov, Nikolai A. 2009. Вопросы биографии научного творчества М. М. Бахтина. Moscow: Издательство МГУ.

Ryazanova-Clarke, Lara. 2016. Linguistic mnemonics: The Communist language variety in contemporary Russian public discourse. In Petre Petrov and Lara Ryazanova-Clarke (eds.), *The vernacular of communism: Language, ideology and power in the Soviet Union and Eastern Europe*. New York: Routledge. 169–95.

Saran, Vladislav. 2016. Media manipulations and psychological war in Ukraine and the republic of Moldova. CES Working Papers 8 (4): 738–52.

Sindelar, Daisy. 2014. The Kremlin's troll army: Moscow is financing legions of pro-Russia Internet commenters. But how much do they matter? *The Atlantic*, August 12. https://www.theatlantic.com/international/archive/2014/08/the-kremlins-troll-army/375932/.

Tannen, Deborah. 1994. *Gender and discourse*. New York: Oxford University Press.

———. 2007. *Talking voices: Repetition, dialogue and imagery in conversational discourse* (2nd ed.). Cambridge: Cambridge University Press.

———. 2013. The medium is the metamessage: Conversational style in new media interaction. In Deborah Tannen and Anna Marie Tester (eds.), *Discourse 2.0: Language and new media*. Washington, DC: Georgetown University Press. 99–117.

Tovares, Alla. 2019. Trolling as creative insurgency: The carnivalesque delegitimization of Putin and his supporters in online newspaper commentary. In Andrew Ross and Damian Rivers (eds.), *Discourses of (de)legitimization: Participatory culture in digital contexts.* New York: Routledge. 228–47.

Tracy, Karen. 2008. "Reasonable hostility": Situation-appropriate face-attack. *Journal of Politeness Research* 4 (2): 169–91.

Turner, Tammara C., Marc A. Smith, Danyel Fisher and Howard T. Welser. 2006. Picturing usenet: Mapping computer-mediated collective action. *Journal of Computer-Mediated Communication* 10 (4). doi: 10(4) 10.1111/j.1083-6101.2005.tb00270.x.

Volkova, Elena. 2012. Карнавал–это серьезно: М.М. Бахтин и С.С. Аверинцев как теоретики протестного движения. Ежедневный Журнал. February 7. http://www.ej.ru/?a=note&id=11922.

Yefremova, Daria. 2017. *Алексей Коровашко: "Бахтин был вызывающе неточным." Культура.* December 7. https://portal-kultura.ru/articles/country/164824-/.

Zappavigna, Michele. 2014. CoffeeTweets: Bonding around the bean on Twitter. In Philip Seargeant and Caroline Tagg (eds.), *The language of social media: Identity and community on the Internet.* Basingstoke, UK: Palgrave Macmillan. 139–160.

Zelenkauskaite, Asta and Brandon Niezgoda. 2017. "Stop Kremlin trolls:" Ideological trolling as calling out, rebuttal, and reactions on online news portal commenting. *First Monday* 22 (5). https://doi. org/10.5210/fm.v22i5.7795.

Zholkovsky, Alexander. 2017. Between Groys and Gasparov. *Dialogic Pedagogy: An International Online Journal* 5: 16–22.

11

From Post-Truth to Post-Shame: Analyzing Far-Right Populist Rhetoric

RUTH WODAK

ALTHOUGH MANY POLITICAL SCIENTISTS, historians, anthropologists, sociologists, and discourse analysts have studied the electoral success of the Jean Marie Le Pen's *Front National* (FN), Jörg Haider's *Austrian Freedom Party* (FPÖ), and Silvio Berlusconi's *Forza Italia* since the 1980s in much detail, the Brexit referendum in June 2016 and Donald Trump's election as US president in November 2016 have reinvigorated existing research traditions in respect to far-right populist parties and movements and have also generated new (interdisciplinary) approaches (Bevelander and Wodak 2019; Wodak 2021).

Far-right populist actors, parties, and movements, across Europe and beyond, draw on and combine different *political imaginaries* and different traditions; evoke (and construct) different nationalist pasts in the form of *identity narratives*; and emphasize a range of different issues in everyday politics. Some parties gain support via flaunting an ambivalent relationship with *fascist* and *Nazi* pasts (e.g., in Austria, Hungary, Italy, Romania, and France); some parties focus primarily on one or two issues, such as the *perceived threat from Islam* (e.g., in the Netherlands, Denmark, Austria, Germany, Poland, Sweden, and Switzerland); some parties primarily stress a *perceived danger to their national identities* from ethnic minorities (e.g., in Hungary, Greece, Italy, and the United Kingdom); and some parties primarily endorse a *traditional Christian (fundamentalist) conservative-reactionary agenda* (e.g., in the United States, Poland, and Russia). In their free-for-all rush for votes, most far-right parties evidently pursue several such strategies at once, depending on the specific audience and context; thus, the aforementioned distinctions are primarily of an analytic nature. Left-wing populist parties, such as *Syriza* in Greece and *Podemos* in Spain, have also succeeded in winning in national elections due to the severe economic recession since 2008, the negative impact of austerity politics in Greece and Spain, and the eurozone crisis. While both far-right and left-wing populist parties regard the European Union (EU) as part of the élite, the latter do so using social rather than nationalist-nativist arguments (Stavrakakis and Katsambekis 2014; Zakaria 2016, 9).

It is important to emphasize that fundamental conceptualizations of populism as a political phenomenon differ not only in terms of definition but also of evaluation. Thus, the Laclauan approach sees it as the essence of politics and an emancipatory force (Laclau 2005), the popular agency approach views populism as a positive force for the mobilization of the people (Goodwyn 1976), and the socioeconomic approach regards it as irresponsible economics (Dornbusch and Edwards 1992). More recent approaches in the political sciences launched by Mudde and Kaltwasser (2017), Müller (2016), and Moffitt (2016) focus mostly on the ideological, strategic, and performative aspects of populism, while emphasizing the overall negative discriminatory policies of the far right (e.g., see the comprehensive internet platform Centre for Analysis of the Radical Right [CARR] for continuous updates).[1]

Moreover, in studying populist rhetoric and its relation to discourse, (critical) discourse analysts have drawn on diverse types of data, employed various methods, and analyzed a range of linguistic features pertaining to the core traits of populism: i.e., dividing society into "the people" and "the élite" while also moralizing this dichotomy, claiming to exclusively represent the "will of the people," creating crises scenarios, breaking taboos, endorsing charismatic leadership, and resorting to mediatization (Wodak 2015, 2017, 2019a, 2019b; 2021; Wodak, KhosraviNik and Mral 2013; Wodak and Krzyżanowski 2017; Wodak and Rheindorf 2019). Crisis narratives and scenarios of danger and threat dominate the media and construct a sense of dystopia and immediate and pending catastrophe (although all economic and sociopolitical facts speak to the contrary).

Indeed, as illustrated by the study *Fear not Values* conducted by the Bertelsmann Stiftung (2016) in eight EU member states, in which a representative sample was interviewed about their fears and hopes, over 50% of voters for far-right parties viewed *globalization* as *the* major threat.[2] Moreover, 53% of those who fear globalization perceive *migration* as *the* major global challenge, 55% have no contact with foreigners, and 54% display anti-foreigner sentiments. This is in contrast to interviewees who perceive globalization as an opportunity: in this case, 42% believe migration to be a major challenge, 43% have no contact with foreigners, and 36% display anti-foreigner sentiments. The authors of the study emphasize that other major global challenges, such as economic crisis, poverty, war, terror, crime, and climate change, seem to cause only minor differences between these two groups. In a similar vein, political scientist Ivan Krastev concludes in his widely acknowledged essay *Europadämmerung* (2017, 48–49) that the "refugee crisis" of 2015, which triggered a moral panic, i.e., fears that Western culture and the model of the liberal welfare state would be destroyed by "barbaric invaders," and fear of a genuine loss of control, might eventually lead to the destruction of the EU.

At this point, the necessity of integrating research from the perspective of *critical discourse studies, rhetoric,* and *argumentation theory* becomes apparent: Uitz (2015, 293ff.) provides sufficient evidence of the impossibility of drawing on the traditional agreed conventions of *dialoguing, negotiating,* and *compromising* if one of the two partners in these interactions does *not* want to comply with the established rules of such language games (e.g., Wodak 2019a). As Uitz states, there is *no* "productive dialogue" (2015, 294). The Hungarian and Polish governments seem to believe that these conventions do not apply to them; they are driven "by the urge to establish exceptions, in the spirit of constitutional parochialism" (2015, 296). In other words, context-dependent discursive strategies of blame avoidance, distraction, denial, Manichean (dualistic) division, victim-perpetrator reversal, and eristic (destructive) argumentation dominate official communication, resulting in ever-more nationalism, chauvinism, and nativism.

This is why I claim that this kind of rejection of dialogue relates to a *post-shame era* rather than, as many scholars believe, merely to a *post-truth era* (e.g., Hahl, Kim and Zuckerman Sivan 2018; Scheff 2000): anti-élitist and anti-pluralist/exclusionary rhetoric, symbolic politics (such as focusing on the headscarves of Muslim women while neglecting complex socioeconomic issues associated with migration and integration), digital demagogy, bad manners, and anti-politics support the noncomplying behaviors of powerful politicians, which frequently resonate as "authentic" with the respective core followers of these politicians, their parties, or governments. Instead of discussing and providing solutions for major sociopolitical problems, such as globally rising inequality and youth unemployment, and the consequences of climate change for migration politics, refugees and migrants serve as *the* scapegoat and simplistic explanation for all woes. Against this background, *anti-politics* is defined as a specific attitude and related discourse that systematically undermine democratic institutions (Diehl 2017, 28–29). The entire political system is challenged, as in reality TV: shamelessness, humiliation of other participants, defamation, lies, and ad hominem attacks dominate. Indeed, such shameless behavior could be observed, for example, in several TV debates during the presidential election campaign in Austria in 2016, when it was employed by Norbert Hofer, the far-right populist candidate of the FPÖ (e.g., Wodak 2017). Mastropaolo (2000, 36) mentions similar patterns of scandalization, "*politicotainment*," and the decay of democratic procedures in Italian politics in the 1990s.

Before elaborating on far-right populist rhetoric and the manifold stages of transforming liberal pluralistic democracies into illiberal and even (neo-)authoritarian regimes, it is important to briefly clarify the various concepts used ("Defining Concepts" section; e.g., Wodak 2019a, 2019b). Of course, a comprehensive discussion of all these concepts would certainly exceed the scope of this paper. Thus, I restrict myself to a few considerations on the concepts of populism/right-wing populism/ far-right/populism/right-wing extremism, authoritarianism/neo-authoritarianism, and illiberal democracy. I then proceed to summarize the discourse-historical approach (DHA) employed in these analyses and illustrate some important discursive strategies used by far-right populist politicians in their front-stage and backstage performances ("Analyzing Far-Right Text and Talk" section).[3] The "Conclusions: Shameless Normalization" section points to what I propose to label a process of *normalization*: normalization of far-right ideologies, both in content and form, heavily supported by the tabloid media and catering to the rich and powerful élites, as part of the post-shame era.

Defining Concepts

Obviously, there is no consensus on whether far-right populism/populist right-wing extremism is an ideology (Kriesi and Pappas 2015, 5); a philosophy (Priester 2007, 9); a specific media phenomenon (Pajnik and Sauer 2017); a strategic option for right-wing extremists, like the strategies used by the Nazi Party in the 1930s and 1940s (Salzborn 2018); or a specific political style (Brubaker 2017, 3; Moffitt 2016) that manifests itself mainly in performance and communication. As a discourse analyst, however, and unlike Brubaker and Moffit, I believe it is important to stress that far-right populism/populist right-wing extremism should be seen *not only* as a rhetorical style or as a *purely* media performance phenomenon (although the significance of [media] staging should, of course, never be underestimated), and that the ideological contents that are expressed remain crucial. Indeed, following Pels (2012, 32), it would be wrong to think that there is no substance behind this populist style, and that it is precisely the *dynamic mixing of content and form* that has led to the success of far-right populist politics with voters in today's media democracies.

"Populism"

While defining far-right populist ideologies and practices (Wodak 2021, 6–15, 32–39), four dimensions seem crucial to me:

- *Nationalism/nativism/anti-pluralism.* Far-right populist parties stipulate a seemingly *homogenous ethnos*, a *populum* (community, *Volk*), which can be arbitrarily defined—often in nativist (blood-related) terms. Such parties value the *homeland* or *Heimat* (or *heartland*, if an internal distinction within the nation is sought), which seems to require protection from dangerous invaders. In this way, *threat scenarios* are constructed—the homeland or the "we" is threatened by "others."

- *Anti-élitism.* Such parties share an anti-élitist and anti-intellectual attitude (the *"arrogance of ignorance"*), which is related to strong EU skepticism. According to these parties, democracy should essentially be reduced to the majoritarian principle, i.e., the rule of the (arbitrarily defined) "people."

- *Authoritarianism.* A *savior*, a *charismatic leader*, is worshipped, alternating between the roles of Robin Hood (protecting the welfare state, supporting the "simple folks") and the "strict father" (Lakoff 2004). Such charismatic leaders require a hierarchically structured party and *authoritarian structures* to guarantee "law and order" and "security."

- *Conservativism/historical revisionism.* Far-right populist parties represent *traditional, conservative values* (for example, traditional gender roles and family values) and insist on preserving the status quo or the return to former, "better" times. The aim of protecting the homeland also builds on the *shared narrative of the past*, in which *"we"* are either heroes or victims of evil (of a conspiracy, of enemies of the *fatherland*, etc.). This transforms past suffering or defeat into stories of the success of the people or into stories of betrayal and treachery by others. Social welfare, in the resulting *welfare chauvinism*, should be given only to the so-called "true" members of the *ethnos*.

Although not all far-right populist parties endorse all of the above contents, they—realized in specific combination—can be generalized as typical ideologies of the populist far-right. In all cases, such parties will advocate for *change*, for moving away from an allegedly highly dangerous path that would lead straight to an apocalyptic end.

Illiberal Democracy

Since its official use in 2014 by Hungarian prime minister Victor Orbán, leader of the far-right/national-conservative party Fidesz, "illiberal democracy" has entered into everyday discourse and has been adopted as a positive model to be followed by some politicians, and as a political system to be vehemently rejected by others. In his speech on July 30, 2014, Orbán maintained that "the new state that we are constructing in Hungary is an illiberal state, a non-liberal state. It does not reject the fundamental principles of liberalism such as freedom, and I could list a few more, but it does not make this ideology the central element of state organization, but instead includes a different, special, national approach."[4] Here, Orbán defined his form of illiberal democracy as rejecting toleration of minorities, while supporting strong forms of majoritarianism. He strongly emphasized his beliefs in nationalism (i.e., Hungary's uniqueness vis-à-vis the EU and the other, then twenty-seven, EU member states) and separatism. The Hungarian Constitution, which was revised and accepted by the Hungarian Parliament on April 25, 2011, reflects Fidesz's illiberal values, which have been implemented by, for example, cutting the freedom of the press, reforming the electoral system in unfair ways, changing checks and balances by challenging and undermining the independence of the judiciary, and so forth (Uitz 2015, 285–88). In Poland, developments similar to the Hungarian trajectory are taking place under the national-conservative government of the PiS party and its leader, Jarosław Kaczyński (Kerski 2018; Sutowski 2018, 17–18).

(Neo)-Authoritarianism

Mudde (2007, 22) points to Juan Linz's influential work and his definition of authoritarianism as a *form of government* characterized by strong central power and limited individual freedoms. Following Linz (1964), four dimensions are emphasized as salient elements for an authoritarian government: first, *limited political pluralism*; hence, there are constraints on political parties, interest groups, and nongovernmental organizations (NGOs). Second, *legitimacy* is hugely dependent on *emotions*, on identification with the regime; third, *suppression* of the *opposition*; and finally, *vague and nontransparent definition* of the *powers of the executive*. Obviously, these criteria overlap with the definitions of illiberal democracy mentioned above. Furthermore, Levitsky and Way (2002, 53) point to another relevant concept which, the authors argue, could be applied to Putin's Russia: competitive authoritarianism. Here "Elections are regularly held and are generally free of massive fraud, but nevertheless incumbents routinely abuse state resources, deny the opposition adequate media coverage, harass opposition candidates and their supporters, and in some cases, manipulate electoral results. Journalists, opposition politicians, and other government critics may be spied on, threatened, harassed, or arrested. Members of the opposition may be jailed, exiled, or—less frequently—even assaulted or murdered. Regimes characterized by such abuses cannot be called democratic."

In sum: it becomes apparent that we are confronted with an abundance of labels for, and definitions of, illiberal democracy, authoritarianism, and populism, which sometimes overlap, sometimes substitute for or complement each other, and sometimes exclude each other. Therefore, context-dependent detailed, interdisciplinary research is of utmost importance to trace and understand specific sociopolitical developments, discursive shifts, and structural changes—without worrying too much about terminology.

Analyzing Far-Right Text and Talk

In this section I am concerned with the *micropolitics* of far-right political parties—*how they produce and reproduce their ideologies and exclusionary politics in everyday politics, in the media, when campaigning, on posters, in slogans and in speeches* while employing the framework of the DHA approach (see Wodak 2015, 2021). Below, I list a few widely used discursive strategies and performative elements of the far right, which are characteristic for genres such as party programs, political speeches, campaign rallies and events, posters and slogans, websites, social-media posts and tweets, and television and radio interviews as well as TV debates.

The Discourse-Historical Approach

The DHA allows for relating the macro-level of contextualization to the micro-level analyses of texts. Such analyses consist primarily of two levels: the so-called (macro-level) entry-level analysis, focusing on the thematic dimension of texts, and the (micro-level) in-depth analysis, which scrutinizes coherence and cohesion of texts in detail. The general aim of the entry-level thematic analysis is to map out the contents of analyzed texts and thus to assign them to particular discourses (or structures of knowledge). The key analytical categories of thematic analyses are discourse topics, which, "conceptually, summarize the text, and specify its most important information" (van Dijk 1991, 113).

The in-depth analysis, on the other hand, is informed by the research questions. The in-depth analysis consists of the analysis of the genre (e.g., TV interview, policy paper, election poster, political speech, or home page), the macrostructure of the respective text, and strategies of identity construction, and argumentation schemes, as well as of other means of linguistic realization. Most importantly, the DHA focuses on texts—be they audio, spoken, visual, and/or written—as they relate to discourses and are realized in specific genres, and which must be viewed in terms of their situatedness. That is, many texts cannot be fully understood without considering different layers of context. Here, I follow a four-level model of context that includes the historical development of the respective political party (the sociopolitical/historical context), discussions that dominate a specific debate/event (the current context), a specific text (text-internal co-text), and intertextual and interdiscursive relations (Reisigl and Wodak 2001, 40–41). The sociopolitical/historical context and the current context are of significance, as they allow for deconstructing intertextual and interdiscursive relations, presuppositions, implicatures, and insinuations in the texts as arguments, topics, and opinions as recontextualized from other genres or public spheres. The terminological pair interdiscursivity/intertextuality denotes the linkage between discourses and texts across time and space—established via explicit or implicit references. If text elements are taken out of their original context (decontextualization) and inserted into another (recontextualization), a similar process occurs, forcing the element in question to (partly) acquire new meaning(s).

Second, the DHA views discourse as a set of "context-dependent semiotic practices," as well as "socially constituted and socially constitutive," "related to a macro-topic," and "pluri-perspective," that is linked to argumentation (Reisigl and Wodak 2009, 89). Third, positive self- and negative other-presentation are realized via discursive strategies (Reisigl and Wodak 2001, 45–90). Here, I primarily focus on nomination (how events/objects/persons are referred to) and predication (what characteristics are attributed to them). The strategy of perspectivization realizes the author's involvement, for example, via deïxis, quotation marks, metaphors, etc.

The DHA also draws on the concept of topos, apart from employing and elaborating Toulmin's model (2003) when appropriate.[5] Kienpointner (2011, 265) defines topoi as "search formulas which tell you how and where to look for arguments. At the same time, topoi are warrants which guarantee the transition from argument to conclusion." At this point, it is important to emphasize that topoi are not necessarily fallacious. Many examples below manifest flawed logic, but in particular contexts,

Table 11.1. Selected List of Content-Related Topoi in Far-Right Populist Discourses

Topoi	Warrant
Topos of advantage or usefulness	If an action from a specific relevant point of view will be useful, then one should perform it.
Topos of the people	If the people want/do not want a specific action/policy, then this action has to be implemented/rejected.
Topos of uselessness or disadvantage	If one can anticipate that the prognosticated consequences of a decision will not occur, then the decision has to be rejected.
Topos of threat or danger	If there are specific dangers or threats, one should do something to counter them.
Topos of humanitarianism	If a political action or decision does or does not conform to human rights or humanitarian convictions and values, then one should or should not make it.
Topos of finance	If a specific situation or action costs too much money or causes a loss of revenue, one should perform actions that diminish those costs or help to avoid/mitigate the loss.
Topos of reality	Because reality is as it is, a specific action/decision should be taken/made.
Topos of numbers	If the numbers substantiate/do not substantiate a specific standpoint, a specific action should be taken/not carried out.

arguments using a specific topos could be right: topoi are thus—neutrally speaking—a useful shortcut appealing to existing knowledge. The use of topoi in specific ways and contexts (which are often very complex), and what they ignore or sidestep, can be fallacious and manipulative (e.g., Wodak 2021, 74–76).

In summary, the DHA focuses on ways in which power-dependent semiotic means are used to construct positive self- and negative other-presentations (us and them, the good people and the scapegoats, the pro and contra of the crisis or any other topic/event). This also captures the ability to select specific events in the flow of a narrative as well as increased opportunities to convey messages through opening space for "*calculated ambivalence*" (Engel and Wodak 2013). The latter is defined as the phenomenon that one utterance carries at least two more-or-less contradictory meanings, oriented toward at least two different audiences. This not only increases the scope of the audience to, for example, the Austrian people and international audiences, but also enables the speaker/writer to deny any responsibility: after all, "it wasn't meant that way." Finally, the power of discourse creates regimes of quasi "normality," i.e., what is deemed "normal" about the political messages circulating during the financial crisis and the heated debates related to it.

"Us" and "Them": The "people," "the élites," and "the others"

Far-right political rhetoric relies on the construction of a distinct dichotomy that aims to divide the people living in a country into two quasi-homogenous blocs: *the people* are juxtaposed with *the élites* within a specific narrative of threat and betrayal, accusing the "establishment" of having intentionally or subconsciously neglected the "people," having instead pursued only their own interests, thus failing to protect the people and to voice their interests, and having ignored the obvious anxieties of the people. Indeed, this narrative arbitrarily constructs two groups via texts and images in manifold ways. Such a Manichean opposition portrays these two groups as vehemently opposed to each other: two epistemic communities, one defined as powerless, the other as powerful; the former described as good, innocent, and hard working, the latter as bad, corrupt, criminal, lazy, and unjustly privileged, and so forth. For far-right populists, immigration constitutes a threat to the presumed (constructed) identity of the people and their traditional values. The definition of *the other* varies pursuant to nationally specific conditions. In Hungary, the targets include Roma and Jewish minorities, while the Tea Party and Trump focus on Muslims, Mexicans, and other immigrants from Latin America.

Accordingly, the mechanism of *scapegoating* constitutes an important feature of such parties' discourse. Sometimes, the scapegoats are Jews, sometimes Muslims, sometimes Roma or other minorities, sometimes capitalists, socialists, career women, NGOs, the EU, the United Nations, the governing parties, the élites, the media, and so forth. "They" are foreigners, defined by "race," religion, or language. "They" are élites, not only within the respective country but also on the European stage ("Brussels") or at the global level ("Financial Capital"). Important fissures and divides within a society, such as class, caste, religion, gender, and so forth, may be neglected in focusing on such internal or external "others" when expedient, and are interpreted as the result of "élitist *conspiracies*." Following an aggressive campaign mode implies the use of *ad hominem arguments* as well as other fallacies, such as the *straw-man fallacy* or the *hasty generalization fallacy* (a fallacy implies an intentionally deceptive argument). Politicians tend to deny and justify even obvious failures (euphemistically labeled as mistakes) and quickly find somebody else to blame; under much pressure, *ambiguous, evasive,* and *insincere apologies* may be made, or no apologies given at all (see figure 11.1, which maps "us" and "them" in the populist mindset). "Bad manners" (Moffitt 2016, 61–63; Montgomery 2017, 632; Wodak 2017, 559–60) also play a much bigger role, as do deliberate impoliteness, lies, insults, destructive (*eristic*) argumentation and intentional breaches of taboos (Wodak, Culpeper and Semino 2020). Norms of *political correctness* are not merely violated without apology, but explicitly challenged as restricting free speech; this offers identification with anti-élitist behavior (Scheff 2000).

   Some far-right populist parties have become more and more explicitly racist (anti-Muslim, antisemitic, and anti-Ziganist). These parties tend to emphasize the violence of immigrants while also vindicating violence against immigrants (the German far-right populist party *Alternative für Deutschland* (*AfD*) is an example). They deny the discrimination to which immigrants are subjected and maintain that the native population is discriminated against (Fennema 2004). Moreover, Fennema (2004, 9) argues that if a party defines the criminality of immigrants or the number of asylum-seekers as the one and only agenda, then this party may be labeled racist, even if their public statements regarded in isolation are not explicitly racist. In distinguishing far-right populist parties from the extreme right and even neo-Nazis (such as the *Golden Dawn*, the *Nationaldemokratische Partei Deutschlands*, the *British National Party*, and *Jobbik*), Fennema (2004, 15) concludes that in the former, "front-stage" activities are conscientiously screened, while "backstage," explicitly racist activities are usually hidden from public view (e.g., Rheindorf and Wodak 2019; see figure 11.1).

   Two brief examples serve illustrating such exclusionary rhetoric in respect to the *racialization of space* (Wodak 2020). The discriminatory practices employed by the FPÖ in the aftermath of the refugee movement of 2015 draw on traditional nativist discourses: their slogans, which appeared in the media and on posters in 2018 in Vienna appeal to, and recontextualize, antisemitic and racist proposals and slogans of the 1930s, which served to exclude Jews from council housing and other apartments, schools, and professions: "The slogan must be: no more Muslim migrants allowed in council housing in Döbling [the nineteenth district in Vienna, a wealthy area]."[6] Such explicit anti-Muslim racism implies grave danger for any pluralist and liberal democracy, because it is hugely divisive, excludes specific people because of their religion, and is instrumentalized by nativist movements. Extensive historical research illustrates that such proposals and appeals have not been seen or heard in Vienna and Austria since Nazi times (SOS Mitmensch 2019, 4).[7] Racialization in this instance began with the forced relocation of a group of persons distinguished as (morally) different and identified by a particular ethnic feature—their religion—to a physical space that was isolated from other areas of the city. In such rhetoric, migrants are dehumanized and their number is exaggerated, implying an invasion by another dangerous culture that would subsequently destroy the "pure" Christian Austrians,

decent, honest, good,
industrious, dutiful, charismatic,
honorable, noble, brave,
trustworthy, incorruptible

amoral, deceitful, lazy,
without conscience,
evil, bad, cowardly

The good
The true
The upright
The victims

WE

The "good" fight

THE OTHERS

The bad
The fake
The liars
The perps

"The people,"
represented by the
populists

*"The others" are a threat
to us!*
We must fear "the others"!
*We have the right to
defend ourselves against
"the others"!*

Enemy stereotypes
Those up there
The elites, politicians,
upper classes,
the East Coast,
fake media
Those out there
Asylum seekers,
economic refugees,
welfare tourists
Those down there
Spongers, parasites,
the work-shy

Figure 11.1. The mind-map of far-right populism

a threat scenario that subsequently legitimizes the *moralization* of borders and walls (Rheindorf and Wodak 2018).

The second example refers to Donald Trump's manifold proposals to *build a wall at the border with Mexico*. As Demata (2019, 276ff.) argues while analyzing several speeches by Trump where this topic is addressed, Trump is merely resurrecting the divisive politics of nativism that has a long historical precedent in American politics (2019, 291). Indeed, it is obvious that Trump would rather spend money building the wall than combating climate change. He intentionally triggers and substantiates *fear*, which draws on the historically recurring theme of criminal foreigners who attempt to invade the country to take jobs away from law-abiding citizens and that evokes the image of Mexicans as illegal aliens, rapists, and criminals.[8]

In the following extract, I summarize some salient argumentative moves distilled from four of Trump's speeches (from New York, November 21, 2015; Birmingham, December 8, 2015; Iowa, June 16, 2016; and Las Vegas, July 11, 2016):

1. "We have illegal immigrants who are being taken care of better than our incredible veterans." "People flow through like water."
2. "When Mexico sends its people, they're not sending their best.... They're sending us not the right people"; "They're sending people they don't want." "When Mexico sends its people, ...they're sending people that have lots of problems"; "[they] take our jobs, and then we pay them interest"; "It's going to get worse and worse."

3. "ISIS authorizes such atrocities as murders against nonbelievers; beheadings
    and unthinkable acts that pose great harm to Americans, especially women";
    "They want to kill us." "These are people [who] don't want our system. They
    don't want our system and lead a normal life."

First, Trump depicts a dangerous situation in which, he claims, the United
States presently finds itself: he employs the almost universally used metaphor of
migrants as floods, which implies that there is no way to defend oneself against such
a natural catastrophe. Americans, thus, have to be defined as victims. Moreover,
he appeals to resentment by employing the *topos of comparison*, setting veterans
against "illegal immigrants," who, he claims, receive more support than veterans, a
highly respected group in the United States. His second move then depicts Mexi-
can migrants as criminals and enemies, unworthy to enter the United States. They
threaten the "true and pure" Americans as they would, he further claims, take their
jobs away. Finally, in these first moves, he mentions ISIS (which is of course not
connected to Mexico); this serves as enforcing the danger created by strangers.
Maybe, via analogy, listeners might see similarities between radical fundamentalist
ISIS warriors who kill, rape, and murder innocent people, and "illegal immigrants"
from Mexico.

After all these claims, Trump continues with the "data," the evidence for the
alleged danger:

1. "We're out of control. We have no idea if they love us or hate us. We have no
    idea if they want to bomb us"; "And it's got to stop and it's got to stop fast."
2. "We have to be vigilant"; "We have tremendous eyes and ears"; "We have
    millions and millions and millions of eyes and ears"; "Database is OK and
    watching them is OK and surveillance is OK"; "I want to know who they are."
3. "To make the country strong, we have to stop the border"; "We have to es-
    tablish borders and we have to build a wall"; "We have to and we will."
4. "You can't be great if you don't have a border."

Here, Trump claims that the government is out of control and has to win back
control in order to protect the United States and its people. Trump does not provide any evidence for his claims. However, this move is reinforced by the topos of
urgency, as otherwise crisis and catastrophe are to be expected. Urgency implies
that decisions have to be made quickly. And, as is presupposed throughout this argumentation scheme, only he as leader of the American people would be able to
make these decisions and promise to implement more security. In this way, the discursive construction of fear and resentment is linked to the promise of hope, of a
savior protecting the American people. Law and order, Trump argues, would have
to be strengthened via more surveillance and, finally, borders would then be better
controlled—specifically if a wall is built. Only then, he concludes, will America be
great again!

A simple argumentation scheme (e.g., Toulmin 2003) is employed here: crisis
and dystopia are presented as immediate dangers that can only be prevented if a wall
is built that would keep the "illegal immigrants" out—who are claimed to be the cause

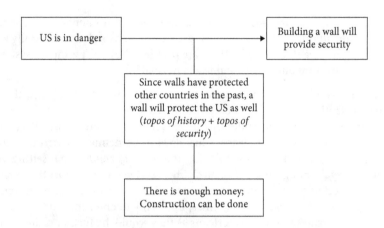

Figure 11.2. Simple Toulmin argumentation scheme: "If the US is in danger, a wall will provide security"

of all social and economic problems in the United States. This is a typical scapegoating strategy, coupled with the evocation of fear and—in a second step—hope, with the promise of a savior—Trump—who will urgently implement all necessary steps to make all problems disappear and guarantee safety and wealth, i.e., will "make America great again" (see figure 11.2).

Claiming Victimhood and Conspiracy Theories

Constructing conspiracies necessitates *unreal scenarios* where some perpetrators (lobbies, parties, bankers, and the "other") are allegedly pulling the strings; these are frequently dramatized and exaggerated. Lies and rumors are spread that denounce, trivialize, and demonize "others," following the slogan of "Anything goes." Rheindorf (2019) maintains that while "Donald Trump may be credited with popularizing the term 'fake news' for this goal [i.e., disseminating conspiracy theories], he was certainly not the first populist to pursue it." Of course, online media and social media—due to their globalized outreach—have been instrumental in constructing conspiracy theories because such media construct the kind of immediacy between populist actors and "the people" that enables strong identification (Fuchs 2018; Moffitt 2016, 88–94). *Conspiracy theories* draw on the traditional antisemitic world-conspiracy stereotype that also characterized Nazi and fascist ideologies. For example, Hungarian prime minister Victor Orbán published a list of two hundred so-called Soros mercenaries[9] (including scholars, journalists, intellectuals, and NGOs that allegedly support the Hungarian-American philanthropist, who is Jewish) who are trying to help refugees in Hungary. Indeed, Soros has been demonized via traditional antisemitic conspiracy stereotypes and subsequently by all Visegrad countries in Europe (i.e., the Czech Republic, Slovakia, Hungary, and Poland) and even further afield (Wodak 2018b, 2021, 139-41).

To quote just one of many examples, this one related to Italian interior minister Matteo Salvini (from the extreme-right Italian party Lega): on June 13, 2018,

Salvini presented NGO rescue boats like the *Aquarius* as tools of sinister conspiracies (launched by Soros) against the Italian people (e.g., European Stability Initiative 2018, 5): "It is not possible that some private NGOs paid by nobody-knows-whom decide the speed and times of immigration. I love every kind of generosity and voluntarism, I am a blood and organ donor myself, but when I read that behind certain initiatives there is the Open Society Foundation[s] of George Soros, I start having doubts about how spontaneous this kind of generosity is."[10]

Moreover, recent research observes that far-right populists endorse a sense of *looming crises* that are threatening "the people" (Mazzoleni 2008; Rheindorf and Wodak 2018, 2019; Triandafyllidou, Wodak and Krzyżanowski 2009). Conspiracy theories lend themselves to supporting such apocalyptic scenarios, i.e., a continuous state of siege of the "homeland" (Müller 2016, 43). Ultimately, such constructions of crisis advertise strong leadership as a method for overcoming the crisis while creating hope and promising change, and thus these populists recontextualize the political agenda into a simplistic common-sense choice of either-or (ibid.).

The Use of Euphemisms

Euphemisms are frequently used in media reporting with the aim of making restrictive new migration policies acceptable: in January 2019, for example, the suggestion by the Austrian minister of interior affairs, Herbert Kickl (FPÖ), to change the term "reception center" for asylum seekers and refugees (*Aufnahmezentrum*) to "departure center" (*Ausreisezentrum*) scandalized the Austrian public.[11] This label implies that the safe haven, the space where refugees would finally not have to fear for their lives, is not a place to stay but—by definition—a place from where one should leave. This might seem quite absurd at first; however, in the context of ever-more restrictive migration policies and explicit racist rhetoric of exclusion against so-called illegal migrants, this label indicates that asylum seekers are *not* welcome at all; indeed, that they should immediately leave again. They are not wanted in Austria. Obviously, this is a cleverly chosen indirect euphemism, carrying the meaning of "deportation center" via an intermediate stage of insinuating the concept *Abschiebezentrum* (deportation center), which would have probably been unacceptable. "Departure center," then, one could argue, actually represents a euphemism for "deportation center." And it would be possible to speculate even further that such labels are intertextually related to the many euphemisms listed by Victor Klemperer (2018) when describing the neologisms and euphemisms created in Nazi Germany in the 1930s and 1940s.

Far-right rhetoric is full of such euphemisms. Minister Kickl also suggested—after a state employee had been killed by a migrant who had already committed several criminal acts and should have left Austria—that potentially dangerous migrants and asylum seekers should be *preventively* incarcerated; which criteria would be used to determine potentially dangerous people, however, has remained completely unclear and vague. Another euphemism was launched: *Sicherungshaft* (preventive detention). Legal experts and the political opposition are, of course, vehemently opposing such a measure, which contradicts the Austrian Constitution and all principles of equality and freedom.[12] Moreover, in the Austrian context, such a measure and its name evoke many negative associations with the Gestapo of the Nazi regime.

Indeed, the Nazi term *Schutzhaft* implied that: "Opponents of the regime and other 'unpopular' persons were arbitrarily detained without a time limit. This was initially carried out mainly by members of National Socialist organizations such as the SA and the SS, later by the Gestapo, also comprised of SS members. The prisoners were detained and mistreated in detention centers controlled by the National Socialist party, the so-called concentration camps. It was not possible for courts to question imprisonment in a concentration camp."[13]

When confronted by the opposition that held such rhetoric to be unacceptable, and—moreover—illegal, Kickl stated that he did not really care if something was legal or not, or if implementing his proposal would violate any laws or even the constitution "because I am simply sick and tired of being slowed down/deterred by legal regulations." Kickl even repeated and reinforced this statement in a TV interview by declaring that "I still believe that the principle applies that the law has to follow politics and not politics the law."[14] In other words, he believes that legislation should follow the will of the government. The law that he refers to, by the way, is the Declaration of Human Rights (proclaimed by the United Nations on December 10, 1948). One could legitimately raise the question of which historical period Kickl is actually referring to.[15]

Conclusions: Shameless Normalization

Most of the breaches of constitutional order, such as freedom of opinion, freedom of assembly, freedom of press, and the independence of the legal system in illiberal democracies (Poland and Hungary) are not announced explicitly; they are made in small—seemingly unimportant—steps, like the intervention into the Supreme Court in Poland, where replacing irremovable judges was implemented through a small, banal paragraph about the retirement age of judges, although the constitution sets a fixed term for Supreme Court judges.[16] In this case, some of the Supreme Court judges resisted, and thus this incident made international headlines.[17] As Grabbe and Lehner (2017, 3) argue, these changes imply "mind-closing narratives," which are obviously "gaining force as formerly liberal politicians run after populists."

Such a dynamic corresponds to what I have labeled elsewhere *shameless normalization* (e.g., Wodak 2018a; 2021), which can be observed not only in Central and Eastern Europe but also in the United States, Austria, the United Kingdom, and Italy. The noncompliance with human rights and internationally agreed-upon treaties and conventions, and the yearning for exceptionalism, vehemently challenge the European project; the rejection of all dialogue, agreed-upon norms, and established conventions seems to render negotiations impossible and to pave the way for illiberalism and neo-authoritarianism.

Acknowledgments

I am very grateful to Cynthia Gordon for her constructive comments and for inviting me to the GURT conference. Of course, I am solely responsible for the finalized version.

Notes

1 See https://www.radicalrightanalysis.com for more information.
2 To be more specific: 78% of AfD voters, 76% of FN voters, 69% of FPÖ voters, 66% of Lega Nord voters, 57% of PVV voters, 58% of PiS voters, 61% of Fidesz and 50% of Jobbik voters, and 50% of UKIP voters.
3 In this chapter I focus primarily on the manifold ways of realizing the Manichean division between "us" and "them" in our globalized societies, on the use of euphemisms in order to breach taboos, and on argumentation schemes. Due to space restrictions, I have to refer readers to, *inter alia*, Wodak (2015, 2017, 2019a, 2019b, 2019c, 2021) and Wodak and Rheindorf (2019) for the many other discursive strategies and the manifold performances and the performativity of far-right populist parties and their leaders.
4 See http://hungarianspectrum.org/2014/07/31/viktor-orbans-speech-at-the-xxv-balvanyos-free-summer-university-and-youth-camp-july-26-2014-baile-tusnad-tusnadfurdo/.
5 Which kind of persuasive and rhetorical means can be used depends on topic, genre and audience orientation as well as intention; these factors thus also determine which argumentation schemes seem most adequate and appropriate. In the concrete analysis, therefore, it will sometimes be Toulmin's model ([1958] 2003), sometimes Walton's practical reasoning, and sometimes van Eemeren's Pragma-dialectics; see Walton (1996).
6 See *„Die Devise muss lauten: Keine weiteren muslimischen Migranten in Döblings Gemeindebauten!"* The translation necessarily neglects the rhyme in this slogan (SOS Mitmensch 2019, 34).
7 http://www.islamiq.de/2019/01/24/antimuslimischer-rassismus-hat-in-politik-fuss-gefasst/
8 It is impossible to cover and present the entire debate about walls that has taken place during Trump's presidency in detail in this chapter; moreover, the debate is still ongoing at the time of this writing in the winter of 2018–19, and a range of conflicts between the Democratic-led Congress (since the midterm elections in November 2018) and the White House dominate the US media and public sphere. In this chapter I primarily deconstruct the macro-argument and will therefore refer readers to other detailed studies of Trump's rhetoric and speeches (e.g., Demata 2019; Lakoff 2017; Montgomery 2017; Wodak 2020).
9 https://www.dw.com/en/hungarys-viktor-orban-targets-critics-with-soros-mercenaries-blacklist/a-43381963
10 Italian Senate. 2018. *Informativa del Ministro dell'interno sulla vicenda della nave Aquarius e conseguente discussion*, June 13.
11 https://derstandard.at/2000098647513/Warum-Kickl-aus-Aufnahmestellen-Ausreisezentren-macht
12 https://derstandard.at/2000098766875/Die-Opposition-ist-sich-nun-einig-Keine-praeventive-Sicherungshaft?ti=KshtqNsFDgjhNmIsK01RJXWuS9JjeyrAzVgA6vlo1KcO2w4QPCi7C2NhtdQiDZxhn-L8G4eKF1gBZtm_08aWJAVxup4WijztAaGmeI0JJax-
13 In the original German: *„Regimegegner und andere „missliebige" Personen willkürlich inhaftiert, ohne dass dies einer zeitlichen Begrenzung unterlag. Dieses geschah anfänglich überwiegend durch Mitglieder nationalsozialistischer Organisationen wie der SA und der SS, später durch die auch aus SS-Angehörigen bestehende Gestapo. Die Gefangenen wurden in—der nationalsozialistischen Partei unterstehenden—Haftstätten, den sogenannten Konzentrationslagern, festgehalten und misshandelt. Es war Gerichten nicht möglich, eine Inhaftierung in ein Konzentrationslager in Frage zu stellen."* (https://educalingo.com/de/dic-de/schutzhaft)
14 https://www.profil.at/oesterreich/video-kickl-orf-report-10610601
15 See Huemer (2019), *Eine gefährliche Drohung? Kleine Zeitung* for an extensive discussion (https://www.neue.at/tribuene/2019/01/24/eine-gefaehrliche-drohung-2.neue).
16 I am very grateful to Jan Grzymski for pointing me to this case, as it provides more evidence for my overall argument.
17 https://orf.at/stories/2328900/2328903/

References

Bertelsmann Stiftung. 2016. Fear not values: Public opinion and populist vote in Europe. *Eupinions* 26 (3).

Bevelander, Pieter and Ruth Wodak (eds.). 2019. *Europe at the crossroads: Contesting the populist challenge.* Göteborg, Sweden: Nordicum.

Brubaker, Rogers. 2017. Why populism? *Theory and Society.* https://doi.org/10.1007/s11186-017-9301-7

Demata, Massimiliano. 2019. "A great and beautiful wall": Donald Trump's populist discourse on immigration. In Andreas Musolff (ed.), *Public debates on immigration.* Amsterdam: John Benjamins. 274–94.

Diehl, Paula. 2017. Antipolitik und postmoderne Ringkampf-Unterhaltung. *APuZ* 67 (44–45): 25–30.

Dornbusch, Rudiger and Sebastian Edwards. 1992. *The macroeconomics of populism in Latin America.* Chicago: University of Chicago Press.

Engel, Jakob and Ruth Wodak. 2013. "Calculated ambivalence" and Holocaust denial in Austria. In Ruth Wodak and John E. Richardson (eds.), *Analysing fascist discourse: European fascism in talk and text.* London: Routledge. 73–96.

European Stability Initiative. 2018. *ESI Newsletter* 7/2018. Berlin: European Stability Initiative.

Fennema, Meindert. 2004. Populist parties of the right. *ASSR Working Paper* 04/01. Amsterdam: Amsterdam School for Social Science Research.

Fuchs, Christian. 2018. *Digital demagogue: Authoritarian capitalism in the age of Trump and Twitter.* London: Pluto Press.

Goodwyn, Lawrence. 1976. *Democratic promise: The populist moment in America.* New York: Oxford University Press.

Grabbe, Heather and Stefan Lehner. 2017. *The closing of the European mind—and how to reopen it.* Brussels: Carnegie Europe.

Hahl, Oliver, Minjae Kim and Ezra W. Zuckerman Sivan. 2018. The authentic appeal of the lying demagogue: Proclaiming the deeper truth about political illegitimacy. *American Sociological Review* 83 (1): 1–33.

Huemer, Peter. 2019. Eine gefährliche Drohung? *Neue Vorarlberger Tageszeitung,* 25 January. www.neue.at/tribuene/2019/01/24/eine-gefaehrliche-drohung-2.neue.

Kerski, Basil. 2018. Was uns trennt, verbindet uns. *APuZ* 68 (1011): 4–8.

Kienpointner, Manfred. 2011. Rhetoric. In Jan Ostman and Jef Verschueren (eds.), *Pragmatics in practice.* Amsterdam: John Benjamins. 264–27.

Klemperer, Viktor. 2018. *LTI.* London: Routledge.

Krastev, Ivan. 2017. *Europadämmerung: Ein Essay.* Frankfurt: Suhrkamp.

Kriesi, Hanspeter and Takis S. Pappas (eds.). 2015. *European populism in the shadow of the great recession.* Colchester, UK: ECPR Press.

Laclau, Ernesto. 2005. *On populist reason.* London: Verso.

Lakoff, George. 2004. *Don't think of an elephant: Know your values and frame the debate.* White River Junction, VT: Chelsea Green.

Lakoff, Robin T. 2017. The hollow man: Donald Trump, populism, and post-truth politics. *Journal of Language and Politics* 16 (4): 595–606.

Levitsky, Steven and Lucan A. Way. 2002. The rise of competitive authoritarianism. *Journal of Democracy* 13 (2): 51–65.

Linz, Juan. 1964. An authoritarian regime: The case of Spain. In Robert A. Dahl (ed.), *Regimes and oppositions.* New Haven: Yale University Press. 171–259.

Mastropaolo, Alfio. 2000. *Antipolitica: all'origine della crisi italiana.* Naples: Ancora.

Mazzoleni, Gianpietro. 2008. Populism and the media. In Daniele Albertazzi and Duncan McDonnell (eds.), *Twenty-first century populism.* London: Palgrave Macmillan. 49–64.

Moffitt, Benjamin. 2016. *The global rise of populism. Performance, political style, and representation.* Stanford: Stanford University Press.

Montgomery, Martin. 2017. Post-truth politics? Authenticity, populism and the electoral discourses of Donald Trump. *Journal of Language and Politics* 16 (4): 619–39.

Mudde, Cas. 2007. *The populist radical right parties in Europe*. Cambridge: Cambridge University Press.

Mudde, Cas and Cristobal R. Kaltwasser. 2017. *Populism*. Oxford: Oxford University Press.

Müller, Jan-Werner. 2016. *What is populism?* Philadelphia: University of Pennsylvania Press.

Pels, Dick. 2012. The new national individualism—populism is here to stay. In Eric Meijers (ed.), *Populism in Europe*. Linz: Planet. 25–46.

Priester, Karin. 2007. *Populismus. Historische und aktuelle Erscheinungsformen*. Frankfurt/Main: Campus.

Reisigl, Martin and Ruth Wodak. 2001. *Discourse and discrimination: Rhetorics of racism and antisemitism*. London: Routledge.

———. 2009. The discourse-historical approach (DHA). In Ruth Wodak and Michael Meyer (eds.), *Methods of critical discourse analysis*. London: Sage. 87–121.

Rheindorf, Markus. 2019. Disciplining the unwilling: Normalization of (demands for) punitive measures against immigrants in Austrian populist discourse. In Michael Kranert and Geraldine Horan, (eds.), *'Doing politics': Discursivity, performativity and mediation in political discourse*. Amsterdam: John Benjamins. 179–208.

Rheindorf, Markus and Ruth Wodak. 2018. Borders, fences and limits: Protecting Austria from refugees. Metadiscursive negotiation of meaning in the current refugee crisis. *Journal of Immigrant and Refugee Studies* 16 (1). doi: 10.1080/15562948.2017.1302032

———. 2019. "Austria First" revisited: A diachronic cross-sectional analysis of the gender and body politics of the extreme right. *Patterns of Prejudice* 53(3): 302–20.

Salzborn, Samuel. 2018. Right-wing populism as a strategy of the radical right. Centre for Analysis of the Radical Right. https://www.radicalrightanalysis.com/2018/05/21/right-wing-populism-as-a-strategy-of-the-radical-right/.

Scheff, Thomas. 2000. Shame and the social bond: A sociological theory. *Sociological Theory* 18 (1): 84–99.

SOS Mitmensch. 2019. Antimuslimischer Rassismus hat in Spitzenpolitik Fuß gefasst. www2.sosmitmensch.at/antimuslimischer-rassismus-in-der-spitzenpolitik.

Stavrakakis, Yannis and Giorgos Katsambekis. 2014. Left-wing populism in the European periphery: The case of SYRIZA. *Journal of Political Ideologies* 19 (2): 119–42.

Sutowski, Michał. 2018. "Guter Wandel" zum "Neuen Autoritarismus"—und wie weiter? *APuZ* 68 (10–11): 15–18.

Triandafyllidou, Anna, Ruth Wodak and Michał Krzyżanowski (eds.). 2009. *The European public sphere and the media: Europe in crisis*. Basingstoke, UK: Palgrave Macmillan.

Toulmin, Stephen. (1958) 2003. *The uses of argument*. Cambridge: Cambridge University Press.

Uitz, Renata. 2015. Can you tell when an illiberal democracy is in the making? An appeal to comparative constitutional scholarship from Hungary. *International Journal of Constitutional Law* 13 (1): 279–300.

van Dijk, Teun A. 1991. *News as discourse*. New York: Erlbaum.

Walton, Douglas. 1996. *Argumentation schemes for presumptive reasoning*. Mahwah, NJ: Erlbaum.

Wodak, Ruth. 2015. *The politics of fear: What right-wing populist discourses mean*. London: Sage.

———. 2017. The "establishment," the "élites," and the "people": Who's who? *Journal of Language and Politics* 16 (4): 551–65.

———. 2018a. Vom Rand in die Mitte—„Schamlose Normalisierung." *Politische Vierteljahres Zeitschrift* 75. doi: 10.1007/s11615-018-0079-7

———. 2018b. The revival of numbers and lists in radical right politics. Centre for Analysis of the Radical Right. https://www.radicalrightanalysis.com/2018/06/30/the-revival-of-numbers-and-lists-in-radical-right-politics/.

———. 2018c. Antisemitism and the radical right. In Jens Rydgren (ed.), *Handbook of the Radical Right*. Oxford: Oxford University Press. 61–85.

———. 2019a. Entering the "post-shame era"—the rise of illiberal democracy, populism and neo-authoritarianism in EU-rope: The case of the turquoise-blue government in Austria 2017/2018. In Russell Foster and Jan Grzymski (eds.), *The limits of EU-rope*. *Global Discourse*, Special issue. https://doi.org/10.1332/204378919X15470487645420.

———. 2019b. Analysing the micropolitics of the populist far right in the "post-shame era." In Pieter Bevelander and Ruth Wodak (eds.) *Europe at the crossroads. Contesting the populist challenge*. Göteborg, Sweden: Nordic Academic Press. 63–92.

———. 2019c. Austria's smoking gun: Strache, "Ibiza-gate" and "Saint" Sebastian. www.socialeurope.eu/austria-strache-ibiza-gate.

———. 2020. The language of walls—Inclusion, exclusion, and the racialization of space. In John Solomos (ed.), *Routledge international handbook of contemporary racisms*, London: Routledge. 160–77.

———. 2021. *The Politics of fear. The shameless normalization of far-right discourse.* (2nd revised and extended edition). London: Sage.

Wodak, Ruth, Majid KhosraviNik, and Brigitte Mral (eds.). 2013. *Rightwing populism in Europe: Politics and discourse.* London: Bloomsbury.

Wodak, Ruth and Michał Krzyżanowski. (eds.). 2017. Right-wing Populism in Europe & USA. Special Issue. *Journal of Language and Politics* 16(4).

Wodak, Ruth and Markus Rheindorf. 2019. The Austrian Freedom Party. In Alan Waring (ed.), *The new authoritarianism: A risk analysis of the alt-right phenomenon.* New York: Ibidem.171–97.

Wodak, Ruth, Jonathan Culpeper and Elena Semino. 2020. Shameless normalisation of impoliteness: Berlusconi's and Trump's press conferences. *Discourse & Society* doi.org/10.1177/0957926520977217.

Zakaria, Fareed. 2016. Populism on the march. *Foreign Affairs* 85 (11–12): 9–15.

Contributors

Najma Al Zidjaly is Associate Professor in the Department of English Language and Literature at Sultan Qaboos University (Oman). She is the author of *Disability, Discourse and Technology: Agency and Inclusion in (Inter)action* (Palgrave Macmillan, 2015) and the editor of the special issue "Society in Digital Contexts: New Modes of Identity and Community Construction" (*Multilingua*, 2019). Al Zidjaly has published articles in journals such as *Language in Society*; *Discourse and Society*; *Discourse, Context & Media;* and *Visual Communication*. Her research focuses on social media and Arab (Omani) identity. Al Zidjaly serves on the editorial board of the *Journal of Multimodal Communication*, is an Associate Editor (for the Arab World) of the *IPrA Bibliography of Pragmatics Online*, and is a founding member of PanMeMic: Researching social interaction during the COVID-19 pandemic and beyond.

Donal Carbaugh is Professor of Communication at the University of Massachusetts Amherst. His interests are in developing a communication theory of culture and nature, known as cultural discourse analysis, with special attention to Amskapi Piikuni (Blackfeet), popular American, and Finnish views of social interaction. His recent books include *Reporting Cultures on 60 Minutes* (with Michael Berry) and *Communication in Cross-cultural Perspective* (both available from Routledge). He has enjoyed colleagues' works in this volume and also lecturing around the world.

Susan Ehrlich is Professor of Linguistics in the Department of Languages, Literatures, and Linguistics at York University, Toronto, Canada. She has written extensively on language, sexual violence, and the law and is currently working on a project that investigates intertextual practices in the legal system, demonstrating how such an investigation can shed light on broader patterns of social inequalities. Books include *Representing Rape* (Routledge, 2001), *"Why Do You Ask?": The Function of Questions in Institutional Discourse*, co-edited with Alice Freed (Oxford, 2009), *The Handbook of Language, Gender, and Sexuality*, co-edited with Miriam Meyerhoff and Janet Holmes (Wiley Blackwell, 2014), and *Discursive Constructions of Consent in the Legal Process*, co-edited with Diana Eades and Janet Ainsworth (Oxford, 2016).

Cynthia Gordon uses theories and methods of discourse analysis to examine everyday social interactions in family, educational, and digital contexts. The author of *Making Meanings, Creating Family*, she was a 2012–13 fellow at the Center for Advanced Study in the Behavioral Sciences at Stanford University. She is a coeditor of *Family Talk* and *Identity and Ideology in Digital Food Discourse*.

Eean Grimshaw is a doctoral candidate in Communication at the University of Massachusetts Amherst with a concentration in language and social interaction, cultural discourse analysis, and intercultural communication. Currently, Eean studies communication of the Blackfeet (Amskapi Piikuni) within the Native America Speaks Program in Glacier National Park, the longest-running Indigenous Speaker Series in the National Park Service. Using and developing ethnographic studies of communication, Eean specializes in the integration of communication and culture.

John Heritage is Distinguished Research Professor of Sociology at UCLA. His primary research field is conversation analysis, together with its applications in the fields of mass communication and medicine. He is the author of *Garfinkel and Ethnomethodology* (1984) and, with Steven Clayman, *The News Interview* (2002) and *Talk in Action* (2010). He is the editor of *Structures of Social Action* (1984, with Max Atkinson), *Talk at Work* (1992, with Paul Drew), and *Communication in Medical Care* (2006, with Douglas Maynard), among other works. He has published over 150 papers on communication and interaction, of which around sixty are focused on primary care. He is currently working on a range of topics in physician-patient interaction, and on US presidential press conferences.

Michal Marmorstein is Lecturer in the Department of Linguistics at the Hebrew University of Jerusalem. Her areas of research are discourse analysis and interactional linguistics and she works primarily in Arabic and Hebrew. She is the author of *Tense and Text: A Discourse-oriented Study of the Tense System in Classical Arabic* (2016), and coeditor of the special issue "Adapted and emergent practices in text-based digital discourse" in *Discourse, Context & Media* (forthcoming). She is currently conducting a large research project on the distribution and use of discourse markers in spoken and written Egyptian Arabic and across sociolinguistic systems, specifically in the context of Arabic-Hebrew language contact.

Susan U. Philips is Professor Emerita of Anthropology at the University of Arizona. She is the coeditor of *Language, Gender and Sex in Comparative Perspective* (1987) and author of *The Invisible Culture: Communication in Classroom and Community on the Warm Springs Indian Reservation* (1983) and *Ideology in the Language of Judges: How Judges Practice Law, Politics and Courtroom Control* (1998). More recently she has published a number of papers from a study of language and law in the Polynesian Kingdom of Tonga, including a series on Tongan lexical honorifics. Currently she is interested in the lives of women in US retirement communities.

Diana de Souza Pinto is Associate Professor at the Social Memory Graduate Program at Federal University of the State of Rio de Janeiro (UNIRIO/Brazil). Pinto has an MA in Applied Linguistics and a PhD in Mental Health from the Federal University of Rio de Janeiro (UFRJ/Brazil). She has been a co-investigator on a NIMH-supported interdisciplinary Project on Sexuality, Mental Health and AIDS (PRISSMA). Her research activities and publications focus on the development of an interdisciplinary approach to the study of inmates' discourse in institutional contexts. She is interested in how participants perform cultural identities in light of narratives told in research interviews as well as in ethnographic field work. Other themes of interest include criminality, violence, and trauma.

Branca Telles Ribeiro is Distinguished Professor at Lesley University (Cambridge, MA), and Senior Researcher at the Institute of Psychiatry, Federal University (Rio de Janeiro, Brazil). She has developed research in language and health communication; language, health, and immigration; mediated intercultural communication; and language, communication, and gender. Her most recent publications are "Positioning self and other: how psychiatric patients, psychiatric inmates, and mental health care professionals construct discursively their relationship to total institutions" (coauthored with D. Pinto); "Face, conflict and adaptability in mediated intercultural invitations" (coauthored with L. Bunning and L. Cabral Bastos) and "Sexual harassment as reported Contributors by the Brazilian press" (coauthored with L. Cabral Bastos). She has organized or contributed to several publications on interactional sociolinguistics and narrative analysis in Brazil.

Jürgen Streeck (PhD FU Berlin) is Professor of Communication Studies, Anthropology, and Germanic Studies at the University of Texas at Austin. His work is devoted to the microethnographic study of talk and embodied interaction in everyday life, and he investigates embodied interaction from the perspective of body-mind unity. In 2002 he organized the founding conference of the International Society of Gesture Studies and subsequently served as its inaugural president. Among his books are *Social Order in Child Communication* (1981); *Gesturecraft – The Manu-facture of Meaning* (2009); *Embodied Interaction: Language and the Body in the Material World* (coedited with C. Goodwin & C.D. LeBaron); *Self-Making Man: A Day of Action, Life, and Language* (2017); *Intercorporeality. Emerging Socialities in Interaction* (2017, co-edited with C. Meyer and J.S. Jordan); and *Time in Embodied Interaction* (2018, co-edited with A. Deppermann).

Deborah Tannen is University Professor and Professor of Linguistics at Georgetown University. Her 26 books (13 authored, 13 edited or co-edited) and over 100 articles address such topics as conversational interaction, cross-cultural communication, frames theory, conversational vs. literary discourse, gender and language, and social media discourse. Her books include *Conversational Style* (Oxford), *That's Not What I Meant!* (Harper), *Talking Voices* (Cambridge), *Gender and Discourse* (Oxford), *Talking from 9 to 5* (Harper) and *Finding My Father* (Ballantine). She has been McGraw Distinguished Lecturer at Princeton University and is the recipient of five honorary doctorates.

Alla V. Tovares is Associate Professor in the Department of English at Howard University in Washington, DC. Her main research interests include Bakhtin's theory of dialogue and carnival, language ideologies, and online communication, especially digital food discourse. She is the coauthor (together with Raúl Tovares) of *How to Write about the Media Today* (ABC-CLIO, 2010) and coeditor (together with Cynthia Gordon) of *Identity and Ideology in Digital Food Discourse: Social Media Interactions Across Cultural Contexts* (Bloomsbury, 2020); her articles have appeared in *Discourse, Context & Media*; *Text & Talk*; *World Englishes*; *Narrative Analysis*; *Discourse & Society*; and *Multilingua*.

Ruth Wodak is Emerita Distinguished Professor of Discourse Studies at Lancaster University, UK. She was awarded the Wittgenstein Prize for Elite Researchers in 1996, an Honorary Doctorate from the University of Örebro in Sweden in 2010, and an Honorary Doctorate from Warwick University in 2020. She is member of the British Academy of Social Sciences and member of the Academia Europaea. In March 2020, she became Honorary Member of the Senate of the University of Vienna. She is coeditor of the journals *Discourse and Society, Critical Discourse Studies*, and *Language and Politics*. Recent book publications include *The Politics of Fear: The Shameless Normalization of Far-Right Populist Discourses* (Sage, 2021); *Sociolinguistic Perspectives on Migration Control* (Multilingual Matters, 2020; with M. Rheindorf); *Europe at the Crossroads* (Nordicum, 2019; with P. Bevelander); and *The Routledge Handbook of Language and Politics* (Routledge, 2018; with B. Forchtner).

Index

CPSIA information can be obtained
at www.ICGtesting.com
Printed in the USA
BVHW081501130821
613575BV00003B/12

9 781647 121105